THE ROCKIES

RICHARD CANNINGS

THE ROCKIES

A Natural History

GREYSTONE BOOKS

Douglas & McIntyre Publishing Group

VANCOUVER/TORONTO/BERKELEY

Greystone Books
A division of Douglas & McIntyre Ltd.
2323 Quebec Street, Suite 201
Vancouver, British Columbia
Canada V5T 4S7
www.greystonebooks.com

David Suzuki Foundation
2211 West 4th Avenue, Suite 219
Vancouver, British Columbia
Canada V6K 4S2

Library and Archives Canada Cataloguing in Publication

Cannings, Richard J. (Richard James)
    The Rockies : a natural history / Richard Cannings.

Co-published by the David Suzuki Foundation.
Includes bibliographical references and index.

ISBN 13: 978-1-55365-114-7
ISBN 10: 1-55365-114-6

    1. Natural history—Rocky Mountains. 2. Natural history—
Rocky Mountains—Pictorial works. 3. Mountain ecology—
Rocky Mountains.
I. David Suzuki Foundation. II. Title.

QH104.5.R6C36 2005   508.7   C2005-903175-1
Library of Congress information is available upon request

Editing by Nancy Flight
Copyediting by Naomi Pauls
Jacket and text design by Ingrid Paulson and George Vaitkunas
Front jacket photograph by Douglas Leighton
Back jacket photograph by Gordon Court
Maps by Eric Leinberger
Typeset by Ingrid Paulson
Printed and bound in Canada by Friesens
Printed on acid-free paper
Distributed in the U.S. by Publishers Group West

We gratefully acknowledge the financial support of the Canada
Council for the Arts, the British Columbia Arts Council, and the
Government of Canada through the Book Publishing Industry
Development Program (BPIDP) for our publishing activities.

Contents

Advisory Board

DAVID ALT, Professor Emeritus, Geology
Missoula, Montana

DANIEL CASEY, Northern Rockies Bird Conservation
Region Coordinator
American Bird Conservancy
Kalispell, Montana

TREVOR GOWARD, Botanist
Clearwater, British Columbia

LARRY HALVERSON, Naturalist
Kootenay National Park, British Columbia

TERRY MCENEANEY, Ornithologist
Yellowstone National Park, Wyoming

JOANNE NELSON, Senior Project Geologist
B.C. Geological Survey
Victoria, British Columbia

DR. RONALD R. RYDER
Professor Emeritus, Wildlife Biology
Colorado State University
Fort Collins, Colorado

DR. JOHN G. WOODS, Biologist
Mount Revelstoke and Glacier National Parks
Revelstoke, British Columbia

peak in this range (3 954 meters / 12,972 feet), is a classic example. In sloping peaks, such as Mount Rundle, the shale layers are exposed, allowing them to erode and thus causing the carbonate layers above to collapse.

West of the Canadian Rockies in British Columbia, northern Idaho, and northwestern Montana is a group of smaller ranges. One of them, the Purcells, is geologically very similar to the adjacent Canadian Rockies, consisting of very old sedimentary strata. The other ranges—the Cariboo, Monashee, Selkirk, Cabinet, and Bitterroot mountains and a series of ranges along the Salmon River in central Idaho—are composed of granitic or metamorphic rocks. All these ranges, like the Canadian Rockies, trend north-south or northwest-southeast, the product of continental collisions along the Pacific coast.

In central Idaho and southern Montana, the Rockies balloon in width, going from a well-organized range about 150 kilometers (100 miles) wide to a jumble of ranges more than 500 kilometers (300 miles) across. From the Salmon River Mountains of Idaho to the Yellowstone Plateau and east to the Bighorns of Wyoming, the geological diversity is astounding. The eastern ranges of the Rocky Mountains in Montana are mostly sedimentary rock except for those around the Yellowstone Plateau. The Absaroka Range, in northwestern Wyoming, was created by vast lava flows 53 million years ago, and the Yellowstone Plateau itself is a much more recent volcanic structure.

East and south of the Yellowstone Plateau lie a myriad of small ranges, often widely separated from each other and aligned in random directions. The Tetons, in western Wyoming, are a huge fault block—rock lifted to the skies very recently in geological time. The Beartooth, Bighorn, Owl Creek, and Wind River ranges are edged by younger sedimentary rocks, but the bulk of their mountains are eroded to their ancient metamorphic and igneous cores. The Beartooths contain the oldest exposed rocks in the entire Rockies.

The Wyoming Basin brings fingers of the Great Plains through the mountains to touch the Great Basin at South Pass, northeast of Salt Lake City, Utah. This flat, arid plain of short-grass prairie cuts the Rocky Mountains in two. Many species—especially plants—do not cross this gap, making the ranges to the south biologically distinct from those to the north.

The Laramie Mountains rise out of the Wyoming Basin, and the nearby Medicine Bow Mountains trend southeast to link up with the core of the southern Rockies in Colorado. The Snowy Range sits on top of the northern Medicine Bows like the sails of some great ship, its quartzite cliffs sparkling white in summer as well as winter. The highest peaks in the Rocky Mountains are in its southern ranges—the Colorado Rockies have many mountains over 4 000 meters (13,000 feet) in elevation, whereas the Canadian Rockies have none. These mountains rise from plains that are themselves over 1 600 meters (5,200 feet) in elevation. Denver, the "Mile-High City," sits at an altitude of

Overleaf: A rainbow brightens a dark morning sky over Longs Peak, one of the highest mountains in Colorado's Front Range.

Preface

THE ROCKY MOUNTAINS are an immense subject, in both geographical size and biological diversity. Most natural history books about the Rockies are restricted by political or even park boundaries, but I felt it was worthwhile to cover the entire range in a single volume. In doing so, I could not make the book an exhaustive compendium of facts about the Rockies; nor would it be a species-by-species field guide to all the plants and animals. I instead aimed to provide an introduction to the ecosystems of the Rocky Mountains, hoping to entice readers into their own explorations by offering a few captivating stories about life in the mountains.

Covering both sides of the forty-ninth parallel has brought some stylistic challenges. I have presented measurements in both metric and imperial systems. Plant, animal, and even geographical names differ in spelling on either side of the border; I have generally used the official Canadian names but give common American names in parentheses as well. There are many unofficial names of living things, especially for plants. Readers can find the scientific names for any plant or animal mentioned in the text by looking up the common name in the index.

The first four chapters of the book present background information about the geology and climate of the Rocky Mountains and about the origin and distribution of their plants and animals. Although these chapters will enhance your understanding of the natural history of the Rockies, you may skip these chapters if you wish and go directly to the chapters on the individual ecosystems, beginning with chapter 5. Each chapter stands on its own, so you need not read the chapters in order. However, I have tried to write this book so you will want to read it from cover to cover.

Acknowledgments

I WOULD FIRST LIKE to thank Doug Leighton of Banff for his help and encouragement in writing this book. He has provided many fine photographs for the book, hours of thought-provoking discussion, and gracious hospitality when I have visited Banff or the Blaeberry Valley. Other photographs were provided by Steve Ogle, Al and Jude Grass, Gordon Court, Laure Neish, Robert Cannings, Dan Casey, Larry Halverson, and Parks Canada, and some come from the collection of my late father, Steve Cannings. Donald Gunn's wonderful illustrations add tremendous life to the text.

The eight members of the advisory board all provided excellent suggestions and corrections that improved early drafts of this book. I especially wish to thank David Alt for his patience with my struggles with the complex geological histories of the Rocky Mountains. My brothers, Robert and Sydney Cannings, gave constant advice and help throughout the writing process; I only wish they had been available as co-authors for the project. Several other colleagues offered advice about the text, including Robb Bennett, Jack Bowling, Don Gayton, Steve Gniadek, Geoff Hammerson, Robin Leech, Jeff Marks, Don McPhail, Eric Taylor, and John and Mary Theberge.

In my travels throughout the Rocky Mountains, I occasionally prevailed upon the hospitality of friends, including Doug and Myriam Leighton in Banff and the Blaeberry Valley, Dan and Susanna Casey on the shores of Flathead Lake, and Anne de Jager in Creston. My son, Russell, was a wonderful companion on two trips to either end of the range.

Finally, I thank my editors, Nancy Flight and Naomi Pauls, for their careful work in making this a much better book, and I also thank my wife, Margaret Holm, for her patience and sage advice throughout this long project.

1 The Shining Mountains

At length the Rocky Mountains came in sight like shining white clouds on the horizon, and as we proceeded they rose in height, their immense masses of snow appeared above the clouds and formed an impassible barrier, even to the Eagle.

—DAVID THOMPSON, NEAR CALGARY, 1787

The Shining Mountains

CHAPTER 1

LATE ONE SUMMER EVENING, I stood on top of Tonquin Ridge, an alpine knoll on the border of British Columbia and Alberta. My friends and I leaned into a warm west wind and looked into the sunset, drinking in the sweet air and admiring range upon range of peaks before us. Hundreds of feet below, the mighty Fraser River was a mere stream, starting its long journey to the Pacific. Behind us towered the Ramparts, one of the most spectacular collections of peaks in the Rockies—spires of rock frosted with snow and lit by the orange sun. White-tailed Ptarmigan cackled as they flew in to roost; a small herd of Caribou clattered across the scree. We could see no sign of human hand, no road, no logging scar, no building. For a breathless moment, we felt like the first people to see this landscape. We were awed by its grandeur and richness.

These are the Rocky Mountains. The wild West, the crown of the continent. A broad line of wilderness drawn through the center of a forever-altered landscape. Mountains that shape the climate of the continent just as they shaped the psyche of the people who settled there. Mountains that carry the Arctic tundra to the deserts of New Mexico.

The Rocky Mountains have always been a source of wonder. Who were the first humans to see these mountains? Perhaps they were a group of nomads looking for new hunting grounds along an ice-free corridor between the steppes of northern Yukon and the Great Plains, searching for mammoths as the numbers of great mammals dwindled. Perhaps people first came from the west after wandering down the Pacific coast, and the Rockies were only one more of a series of mountains to cross before they discovered the vast prairies and their herds of bison.

European explorers first saw the Rockies from the south or east, the mountains gradually rising from the plains like a bank of silver clouds, day by day growing larger, resolving into what seemed to be an insurmountable barrier to

further exploration. In 1540, Francisco Vásquez de Coronado set out from Guadalajara in search of the Seven Cities of Cíbola. He and his three hundred men did not find the legendary cities, but they did pass through the southern Rockies in New Mexico before giving up and turning around in the middle of the Great Plains. The Spanish explorers called the mountains simply Sierra. Almost two centuries later, the La Vérendrye brothers came from eastern Canada and reached the foothills of the Rockies in central Montana on New Year's Day in 1743. They and the many French fur traders who followed called the mountain barrier les Montaignes de Roche or simply les Rocheuses—the Rockies. Later accounts mention that indigenous guides called them the Mountains of Bright Stones, or the Shining Mountains.

Eastern slopes of the Canadian Rockies near Exshaw, Alberta

What Are the Rocky Mountains?

Western North America is filled with mountains. From southern Mexico to the Arctic Ocean and from the Great Plains to the Pacific Ocean, the North American cordillera covers the landscape with range upon range of high peaks. Which of these are the Rockies?

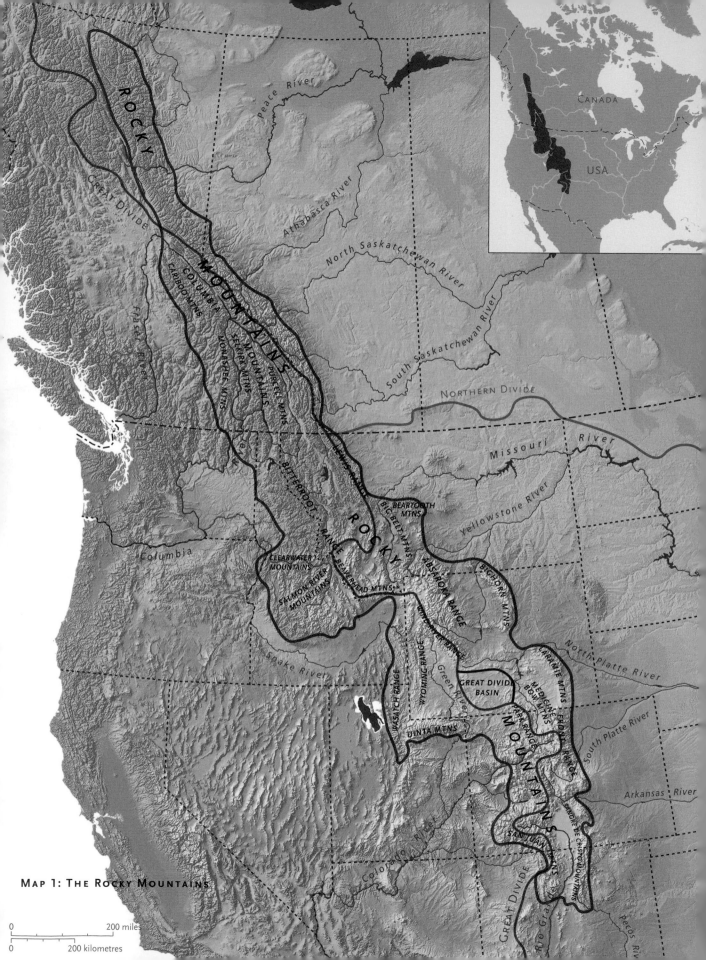

ROCKY

PEACE RIVER

GREAT DIVIDE

MOUNTAINS

CARIBOO MTNS

COLUMBIA

MOUNTAINS

MONASHEE MTNS

SELKIRK MTNS

PURCELL MTNS

Athabasca River

North Saskatchewan River

South Saskatchewan River

NORTHERN DIVIDE

Missouri River

Fraser River

BITTERROOT RANGE

Columbia

CLEARWATER MOUNTAINS

SALMON RIVER MOUNTAINS

BEAVERHEAD MTNS

ROCKY

BIG BELT MTNS

BEARTOOTH MTNS

ABSAROKA RANGE

Yellowstone River

BIGHORN MTNS

Snake River

WASATCH RANGE

WYOMING RANGE

WIND RIVER RANGE

Green River

GREAT DIVIDE BASIN

LARAMIE MTNS

MEDICINE BOW MTNS

PARK RANGE

FRONT RANGE

North Platte River

South Platte River

UINTA MTNS

M O U N T A I N S

Colorado River

SAN JUAN MTNS

SANGRE DE CRISTO MOUNTAINS

Arkansas River

GREAT DIVIDE

Rio Grande

Pecos River

CANADA

USA

MAP 1: THE ROCKY MOUNTAINS

0 — 200 miles

0 — 200 kilometres

To Canadians, the answer seems straightforward—the Rocky Mountains are the range between the prairies and the Rocky Mountain Trench. These mountains are a cohesive group of sedimentary rocks thrust up and broken into sheets, extending without a break from northern British Columbia to Montana. The Trench, a long, surprisingly straight valley, separates this range from the Columbia and Cariboo mountains to the west, mountains composed largely of granitic and metamorphic rocks.

In the United States, the issue is much more complex; the American Rockies have a diverse geology and consist of many individual ranges. The southern ranges merge into the red sandstones of the Colorado Plateau, and on the west the Rockies are separated from the Sierra Nevada and Cascade Mountains by the sagebrush deserts of the Great Basin and the Columbia Basin, respectively. The southern Wasatch Range of Utah and the Wallowa and Blue mountains of Oregon are often considered parts of the Rockies, but in most standard physiographic schemes they are grouped with the Colorado and Columbia plateaus, respectively, so are not included in this book. In Idaho and western Montana, a series of ranges considered part of the American Rocky Mountains merge northward into the Columbia Mountains of Canada. For this reason the Columbia Mountains are included in this treatment of the Rockies, as are the very similar Cariboo Mountains to the north.

THE RANGES OF THE ROCKIES

The Canadian Rockies are the largest range in the Rocky Mountains, stretching 1 450 kilometers (900 miles) from the Liard River in northern British Columbia to Helena, Montana. They are bounded on the west by the Rocky Mountain Trench, a long, linear valley. The Canadian Rockies consist of long thrust faults of sedimentary strata, the old continental shelf of North America that was broken up and pushed eastward starting about 100 million years ago. Many of the mountains show the characteristic form of thrust faults—long western slopes with sharply broken eastern faces. They also show a repeated sequence of hard, erosion-resistant carbonate rocks (such as limestone) on top of softer shales. The carbonate rocks form the stupendous rock walls in this range, whereas the shales form talus slopes that lead to the next carbonate layer. Many of the Canadian Rockies thus have a stepped appearance because of the cliff-talus-cliff-talus sequence. The valleys are also eroded out of the softer shale layers. Shale, or its metamorphic equivalent, slate, becomes predominant in the western parts of this range, since these rocks were formed in the deeper, muddier regions of the outer continental shelf.

Overleaf: Medicine Bow Peak in the Snowy Range of Wyoming is reflected in the still waters of Mirror Lake.

The highest part of the Canadian Rockies is in the central ranges, and the highest peaks are those with more or less horizontal strata; the hard carbonate layers on top protect the shale layers from erosion. Mount Robson, the highest

Explorers and fur traders in the 1700s were anxious to cross the Continental Divide and find the River Oregon, a fabled stream that, according to Native guides, would carry them from the Great Plains to the Pacific Ocean. The River Oregon was first mentioned by fur traders in the Great Lakes region who heard about the river from Cree trappers. The river was so much a part of the lore of early western explorers that the land west of the Rockies became known as the Oregon Territory. The river was never identified for certain, although after the mouth of the Columbia was discovered, explorers assumed that it was the River Oregon. Local indigenous people never mentioned the word, however.

In 1793, Alexander Mackenzie traveled through the Rocky Mountains along the Peace River and was guided to a major river called Tacoutche Tesse by the local people. Mackenzie thought it was the Columbia; we know it today as the Fraser. This river was well known to the indigenous people of western Canada; it was part of the Grease Trail, or Great Road, which was used by coastal Native people carrying Eulachon grease into the Interior for trading. Eulachons, or ooligans, as they are also known, are small, smeltlike fish that are caught in great numbers as they come up coastal rivers during their spring spawning runs. The oil rendered from the fish was one of the most valuable trading commodities in the West.

Scott Byram, an anthropologist from the University of Oregon, finally put the pieces of the puzzle together. Whereas aboriginals along the Pacific coast pronounce the word "ooligan," the western Cree, who do not pronounce the letter *l*, would say "oorigan." Hence, when they told the British and French fur traders of the River of the West, they called it the River Oorigan—the Fraser River. And so the name for a small but important fish became the name for the entire region west of the Rockies and, eventually, the name of a state far south of its namesake river.

The Fraser River flowing below Mount Robson

1 610 meters, 500 meters (1,640 feet) higher than its Canadian counterpart, Calgary. The entire continent is high here, gradually sloping eastward all the way to the Mississippi River. The Front Range rises like a wall behind the pine-covered hills west of Denver and Colorado Springs; behind them the Sawatch Mountains have the highest peaks in the Rocky Mountains, including Mount Elbert at 4 401 meters (14,440 feet). South of the Sawatch are the volcanic San Juan Mountains. The final range on the eastern edge of the Rockies is the Sangre de Cristo Mountains, extending south to Santa Fe, New Mexico. There the Rocky Mountains give way to the canyons and mesas of the Colorado Plateau.

The Great Divide

As the backbone of the continent, the Rocky Mountains are the source of most of its major rivers—the Missouri, the Mackenzie, the Fraser, the Columbia, and the Colorado. The boundaries of these watersheds lie along the spine of the mountains, the Great Divide. On one side the water flows to the Pacific Ocean or the Great Basin, and on the other side it flows to the Arctic Ocean, Hudson Bay, or the Gulf of Mexico. This divide has great ecological as well as cultural meaning, the western slopes of the range being wetter and milder than those on the east. The westward-flowing rivers were eagerly sought by early European explorers searching for an overland route to the Pacific coast.

The Great Divide is not always a line through the center of the Rockies. At the northern end of the Rocky Mountains, the Divide lies to the west—the entire width of the Rockies falls within the Liard and Peace river drainages, whose waters flow into the Arctic Ocean via the Mackenzie River. Just north of Prince George, where the Fraser River makes its big turn south, the Divide jogs sharply eastward to the Rockies and stays in them throughout their length. The huge Columbia Icefields in Jasper National Park are one of the so-called triple divides in the Rockies, sending water to the Pacific via the Columbia River, to the Arctic Ocean via the Athabasca and Mackenzie rivers, and to Hudson Bay via the Saskatchewan River. At Triple Divide Peak in Glacier National Park, Montana, water flows to the Columbia, Saskatchewan, and Missouri watersheds.

The Divide forms the state line in the southwestern corner of Montana, wiggling east across the Yellowstone Plateau just south of Old Faithful. It continues south through Wyoming along the Wind River Range, which sends its water to the Columbia, Missouri, and Colorado rivers. Southeast of the Wind Rivers, the Divide splits in two, tracing out the Great Divide Basin, where the waters flow to neither the east nor the west—they simply disappear into the dry soil or evaporate in the hot summer sun. At the southeast corner of the basin, the Divide continues south through the Park Range into Colorado, where it swings sharply east until it reaches the height of land in the Front Range, within sight of the Great Plains once again. From here it snakes around the north end of South Park, one of the large, mountain-rimmed valleys in the southern Rockies, then winds through the San Juan Mountains and into northern New Mexico.

The rain, snow, and ice of the Rocky Mountains are the water supply of North America. The Fraser and Columbia rivers irrigate the dry interiors of British Columbia, Washington, and Oregon. The Colorado gives all its water to the arid Southwest, its channels dry before they reach the sea. Even the ancient Rockies provide water today. As they eroded between 24 and 5 million years ago, their sands and gravels built and their meltwaters filled the Ogallala Aquifer, a huge underground water storage structure that stretches from South Dakota to Texas—the largest source of groundwater in North America. The aquifer is now replenished only through meager local rainfall, and its level is dropping about a half-meter (20 inches) per year.

PATTERNS OF LIFE
The Rockies are an archipelago of cool forest and cold tundra stretching southward from the great boreal forests of northern Canada, surrounded by a sea of warm valleys and high deserts. An ecosystem map of North America shows broad swaths of color in the east, but the western mountains are a kaleidoscope of multicolored stripes and dots, each representing a different ecosystem—cold peaks, warm lowlands, wet western slopes, and dry rain-shadowed valleys. This is a land of mind-boggling diversity, where the forest changes with every turn of the road, from juniper to pine to aspen to spruce to sagebrush, where you can drive from lower to upper tree line in a matter of minutes.

Naturalists who live in the mountains know by second nature the altitude of their home and can hazard a good guess at their altitude anywhere they travel nearby. I know when I leave my house—just west of the Rockies in the Okanagan Valley of British Columbia—at 450 meters (1,475 feet) elevation and hike uphill, I'll be walking among Ponderosa Pines until I reach the Douglas-fir forest at about 1 000 meters (3,300 feet); if I keep going I'll see my first spruce at about 1 500 meters (5,000 feet) elevation and Subalpine Fir at 1 700 meters (5,600 feet). If I took the easy route—downhill—I would quickly see sagebrush slopes as I came through the lower tree line at 400 meters (1,300 feet). In contrast, naturalists living in flat or gently rolling regions often have no idea what elevation they live at, simply because it is not especially useful knowledge in that countryside.

In the mountains, elevation is everything. It is the biggest single factor in determining what plants or animals you will see at any given site, although the

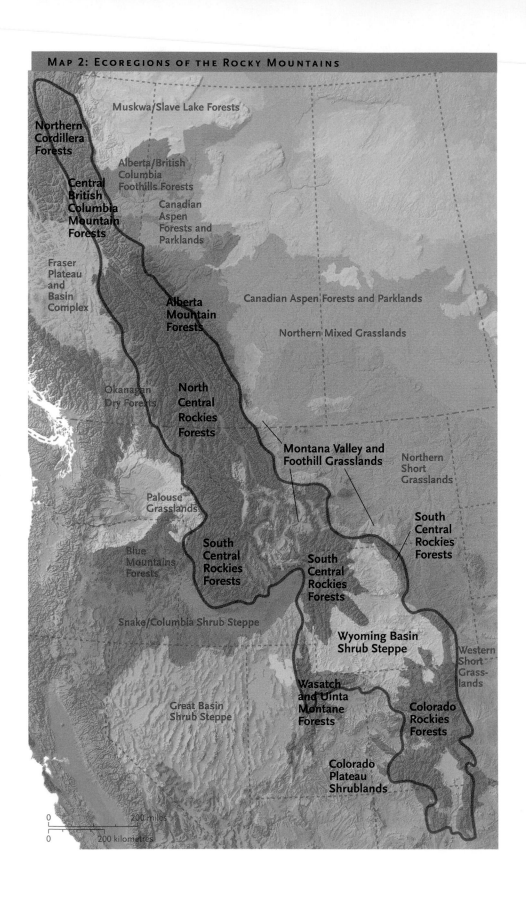

Muskwa/Slave Lake Forests

Northern Cordillera Forests

Alberta/British Columbia Foothills Forests

Central British Columbia Mountain Forests

Canadian Aspen Forests and Parklands

Fraser Plateau and Basin Complex

Alberta Mountain Forests

Canadian Aspen Forests and Parklands

Northern Mixed Grasslands

Okanagan Dry Forests

North Central Rockies Forests

Montana Valley and Foothill Grasslands

Northern Short Grasslands

Palouse Grasslands

South Central Rockies Forests

Blue Mountains Forests

South Central Rockies Forests

South Central Rockies Forests

Snake/Columbia Shrub Steppe

Wyoming Basin Shrub Steppe

Western Short Grass lands

Great Basin Shrub Steppe

Wasatch and Uinta Montane Forests

Colorado Rockies Forests

Colorado Plateau Shrublands

0   200 miles

0   200 kilometres

specific effects of elevation change with latitude. I must admit I get a bit confused hiking in Colorado, where Ponderosa Pines grow at an elevation of 2 000 meters (6,500 feet). At that altitude at home, I would be in alpine meadows.

Ever since the birth of ecology as a science in the last half of the 1800s, biologists have realized that plants and animals live together in recognizable communities. In 1889 C. Hart Merriam traveled to northern Arizona to study the patterns of plant and animal life across a wide range of elevations, from the bottom of the Grand Canyon to the top of the San Francisco Peaks. As a result of these studies, Merriam identified six broad zones, or "life zones," to describe the habitats throughout the mountains of western North America. These zones were the Arctic-Alpine zone, the tundra on the highest peaks; the Hudsonian zone, the spruce-fir forests in subalpine areas; the Canadian zone, the mixed conifer forests at mid-elevations; the Transition zone, the open forests dominated by Ponderosa Pine at the lower tree line; the Upper Sonoran zone, the grasslands and shrub-dominated habitats below the forests, and the Lower Sonoran zone, the warm deserts typical of lower elevations in Arizona. The Rocky Mountains have all but the last one of these zones. Merriam's system was too generalized to be of much local use but was very helpful for broad-scale comparisons of ecosystems across the West. It remained in common use among ecologists until the 1960s, when more detailed schemes were developed.

With the advent of highly complex computerized mapping techniques in the 1990s, ecosystem mapping has evolved into an indispensable tool for landscape management and conservation planning. Various classification schemes have arisen, but most have been developed at provincial or state levels and so cannot be used across the range of the Rocky Mountains. At that broad scale, the ecoregional approach is most appropriate. This approach starts by dividing the landscape into broad climatic areas. It then subdivides these into smaller areas based on physiographic units such as mountain ranges, plateaus, and plains.

A scheme developed by the World Wildlife Fund divides the Rocky Mountains into ten ecoregions. This scheme eliminates the complication of different bands of vegetation at different elevations, greatly simplifying the map. It is assumed that within each ecoregion, the vegetation at a given elevation will be roughly the same.

The northernmost of these ecoregions is the Northern Cordillera Forests, characterized by vast boreal forests of Subalpine Fir and White Spruce with Black Spruce in boggier areas. This is the land of the black fly and mosquito. The long, hot summer days and short, bitterly cold winter days promote subalpine ecosystems dominated by willow and dwarf birch; tree line lies at about 1 700 meters (5,000 feet) elevation.

The Central British Columbia Mountain Forests ecoregion is warmer and wetter than the Northern Cordillera Forests, and the North Central Rockies Forests are warmer still. The latter ecoregion is the mostly wet, western side of the Continental Divide in the Rockies; antique forests of redcedar and hemlock grow in moist valleys, festooned with tree lichens. This is also the snowiest part of the Rocky Mountains, with accumulated depths over 20 meters (65 feet) in some winters; tree line is at 2 100 meters (7,000 feet) elevation. The North Central Rockies Forest includes such parks as Mount Robson, Wells Gray, Mount Revelstoke, Glacier (British Columbia), Kootenay, Yoho, Waterton Lakes, Glacier (Montana), the Bob Marshall Wilderness, and the Selway-Bitterroot Wilderness.

On the eastern side of the Canadian Rockies is the Alberta Mountain Forests ecoregion, drier and cooler than the west side forests. Spruce, Lodgepole Pine, and Trembling Aspen cloak the lower mountain slopes, and Douglas-fir is common in the southern parts. Banff and Jasper national parks are the show-pieces of this ecoregion. To the south, the Montana Valley and Foothill Grasslands ecoregion is warmer and drier than the Alberta Mountain Forests, and grasslands predominate at lower elevations. This is chinook country, where regular warm spells punctuate cold winters. At the southwestern end of this ecoregion, the valley vegetation is predominantly shrub steppe, with Antelope-brush and Big Sagebrush flats reminiscent of the Columbia Basin to the west.

The South Central Rockies Forests ecoregion is otherwise known as the Greater Yellowstone Ecosystem, a high plateau surrounded by mountains. Most of the forests are Lodgepole Pine, a great many of them burned in the fires of 1988. The pine forests themselves were seral stands—forests regen-erating after fires burned climax forests of Engelmann Spruce, Subalpine Fir, and Douglas-fir. Whitebark Pine is an important species at tree line—about 3 000 meters (10,000 feet) elevation. This region includes Yellowstone and Grand Teton national parks as well as the Bighorn and Wind River ranges.

In central Wyoming, where the Rocky Mountains fragment into small, isolated ranges separated by arid grasslands and plains, is the Wyoming Basin Shrub Steppe ecoregion, similar in many ways to the Columbia Basin and Great Basin to the west but higher and cooler. It lies in the rain shadow of several ranges and receives much of its summer rain from storms moving north from the Gulf of Mexico. Two parts of the region—the Bighorn Basin and the Great Divide Basin—are sheltered from these storms as well and are the driest part of the Rocky Mountains.

South and west of the Wyoming Basin, the Wasatch and Uinta Montane Forests ecoregion is similarly arid. The dry climate promotes extensive areas of Gambel Oak, with conifers at higher elevations. Ranges to the east are in the Colorado Rockies Forests ecoregion. Bristlecone Pines appear on high, windswept ridges in the southern part of this region, a niche elsewhere filled by Whitebark and Limber pines. Tree line is about 3 500 meters (11,500 feet) elevation. In contrast to most parts of the eastern Rockies, Ponderosa Pine is the dominant tree at lower elevations here.

The southernmost edges of the Rocky Mountains merge into the Colorado Plateau Shrublands ecoregion, a high desert covered by Pinyon Pine, juniper, and sagebrush. The red-rock plateau is starkly different from the green mountains to the north and provides an obvious southern boundary to the Rockies.

What We Don't Know about the Rocky Mountains

This book presents a small fraction of what we know about the natural history of the Rocky Mountains. But there is also a lot that we don't know. Our ignorance is staggering.

Among the various animal groups, we know a disproportionate amount about birds. Every day, armies of amateur bird enthusiasts gather data about where birds occur and how their populations are faring. Compared to our knowledge of small mammals, frogs, and especially insects, this is a voluminous and incredibly detailed set of data. And yet we still know so little about birds.

One example is the Boreal Owl, a small owl about 25 centimeters (10 inches) in length, which lives in spruce-fir forests around the Northern Hemisphere. Being nocturnal, it is not often seen during the day, when it roosts against the trunks of trees in dense forests. But the males call continuously on spring nights, giving a musical series of whistled notes that can be heard for hundreds of meters.

In the 1960s, Boreal Owls were thought to be restricted to the forests of Alaska and northern Canada; there were records of nesting birds as far south as central Alberta. Then, in 1963, a family of newly fledged young was found at Deadman Lookout in Larimer County, Colorado, about 1 600 kilometers (1,000 miles) south of the known breeding range. The Colorado population was touted as a "Pleistocene relict," a remnant left over from the Ice Age.

Over the next three decades, however, biologists actively searched for these owls at night and found them nesting in almost every mountain range from southern British Columbia to New Mexico. After birding in southern British Columbia for thirty years, I went out with my father one night into the hills around our home and found Boreal Owls at the third place we stopped. We had never looked for them before. Instead of a small, isolated group, as previously supposed, the Rocky Mountain Boreal Owls were actually a large, intact population.

The Boreal Owl represents that huge part of the natural world we know nothing about. We can guess at some things—for example, that perhaps

The Boreal Owl is locally common in high-elevation forests, but its presence in the Rockies was largely unknown until the 1960s.

only one-third of the insect species of the Rockies have even been described. Ecologists are trying to restore forests and grasslands to their natural conditions after a century of abuse; yet they can only make educated guesses as to what those conditions were. Geologists are not even sure how the Rocky Mountains were formed. Despite a long history of exploration, despite millions of visits each year by dedicated naturalists and a large number of curious people living within the Rockies, our ignorance about these mountains and their natural history, like our ignorance of the world in general, greatly exceeds our knowledge.

About This Book

In a book about the natural history of mountains, the deep history, the geological story, needs to be told. The geological history of any mountain range has profound consequences for the plants and animals that live there—the height and direction of the range dictates the local climate, and different bedrocks produce different soils, which produce different plant communities. Thus, chapter 2 is a short description of the very complex geology of the Rocky Mountains, an attempt to make sense of processes that took place over unimaginable time scales and changed the face of a continent, processes that still puzzle geologists today. Chapter 3 covers a more recent event that shaped the Rockies—the glaciations of the Pleistocene. Chapter 4 looks at the climate of the Rocky Mountains, including how it might affect the plants and animals that live there and how the mountains themselves shape weather patterns locally and across the continent.

The remainder of the book is an examination of the major ecosystems that give the Rocky Mountains their great diversity. Chapter 5 starts at the top, exploring the essence of the mountains—the treeless tundra. Moving downhill, chapter 6 describes the cool, fragrant spruce and fir forests of the subalpine zone, filled with snow in winter, alive with bird song in summer. Chapter 7 looks at the wet interior forests of the western slopes, with their ancient trees and great diversity of tree species. The drier Douglas-fir and Ponderosas Pine forests, open and inviting with grass and flowers beneath, are the subject of chapter 8. In chapter 9, we come down through the lower tree line into the semidesert grasslands and shrub steppes of aromatic sage as well as the Pinyon Pine and juniper hillsides. And in chapter 10, we reach the valley bottoms, diving into the clear mountain waters of lakes and streams. Finally, the epilogue discusses the future of natural ecosystems in the Rocky Mountains and the importance of these mountains to conservation on a continental scale.

When I was a young park naturalist in the Canadian Rockies, one of my colleagues, Bob Sandford, had the same response to almost every mountain tale. Whether it was a narrow escape from a bear, an exciting roadkill find, or a misadventure in the local bar, Bob would always say, "You gotta be tough to live in the mountains." In a way, that is the unifying theme of this book. Whether it is the killing winds of the high ridges, the deep snow of the spruce forests, or the searing summer sun on the sagebrush, the Rocky Mountains challenge life in all its forms. These are the stories of the plants and animals that survive and even thrive in this, the most spectacular natural realm in North America.

2 Beginnings

. . . There it was too that David
Taught me to read the scroll of coral in limestone
And the beetle-seal in the shale of ghostly trilobites,
Letters delivered to man from the Cambrian waves.

—Earle Birney, *David*

Beginnings

CHAPTER 2

Geology is an obvious place to start when relating the natural history of such a spectacular range as the Rocky Mountains. Not only is the formation of the mountains a fascinating story in itself, but their structure influences everything else. The formation of the Rockies as a north-south trending range, perpendicular to the prevailing winds off the Pacific Ocean, created much of the tremendous diversity of life in them—rain forests on the west, semidesert grasslands on the east.

The type of bedrock affects the amount of water and type of soil available to plants. For example, sandstones retain water well, allowing trees to grow in dry areas; volcanic rocks tend to produce deep, rich soils; granitic rocks produce poorer, acidic soils; and limestones produce little soil at all, since the rock dissolves easily in water. At many places in Rocky Mountain tundra, you can see a classic soil boundary between limestone rocks and shale; the shale produces acidic soils typically covered by dwarf shrubs in the heather family, whereas tundra over limestone bedrock is dominated by sedges and grasses.

The origin of the Rocky Mountains has two parts, reflected in the words *Rocky* and *Mountains*. The rocks that form these mountains were created in many different ways over a period of more than three billion years, whereas the mountains themselves were created by a series of events that began about 180 million years ago and continue to this day. This creation story begins long before the mountains themselves—or even the continent they traverse—were born. A third part can be added to this story: the role of erosion through water, wind, and ice. For as immense as the Rocky Mountains are today, most of the rock that formed them has vanished, washed down raging rivers to the sea, blown away in dust clouds, or ground off valley floors by rivers of ice.

ROCK OF AGES

The oldest rocks in the Rockies are what geologists call the basement. As the name suggests, these rocks form the bulk of the continental crust. They develop below the surface of the earth, formed as older rocks melt under tremendous heat and pressure, then cool to their crystalline structure. They can be divided into two types—plutonic rocks (granites and their relatives), which form from large bodies of molten magma that crystallize below the surface of the earth, and metamorphic rocks (gneisses and schists), which began as sedimentary or volcanic rocks that recrystallized under high temperature, but did not melt. Basement rocks formed in Precambrian time— most more than 3 billion years ago, some as recently as 1 billion years ago. They are the most common type of rock on continents but are only locally seen at the surface, since many are buried by more recent geological formations. In most of the Canadian Rockies, they are about 9 kilometers (6 miles) below the surface, but blocks of the basement have been raised to the surface in many parts of the American Rockies.

The oldest sedimentary rocks in the region were laid down between 1,500 and 900 million years ago on a continent that predates North America or even Pangaea, the supercontinent from which North America sprang. This was

The rocks forming Height of the Rockies Provincial Park, British Columbia, as in most of the Canadian Rockies, were laid down between 200 and 750 million years ago along the western coast of what is now North America.

Millions of years ago	Geological event	Era	Period
3200	Formation of the rocks of the eastern Beartooth Plateau—the oldest in the Rocky Mountains.	PRECAMBRIAN	
2700	Formation of most basement rocks in Montana and Idaho.		
2300	Oldest rocks in Colorado form.		
1500	Belt Sedimentary Basin forms, accumulates mudstones and sandstones for 800 million years.		
	The ancient continent of Rodinia splits and western part drifts away. Sediments of the Windermere group begin to be deposited on new west coast.		
750	The diversification of complex life marks the beginning of the Paleozoic Era. Sea level rises early in the Cambrian, flooding inland. Sandstone beaches form in Montana; to the west is open ocean and to the east an inland seaway. Throughout the Paleozoic Era, marine sediments are deposited throughout much of the Rocky Mountains.	PALEOZOIC	Cambrian
570	The Burgess Shale fauna lives along the western shelf of North America. Fossils preserved near the town of Field, British Columbia.		
360	Sea floods Montana again; Madison limestone laid down over Montana, eastern Idaho, northern Wyoming, and Dakotas. World-continent Pangaea forms as smaller continents collide; Appalachian Mountains form as Africa collides with Uramerica; land vertebrates appear.		Mississippian
350	Antler mountain-building event in Nevada and Idaho.		
320	Land rises above sea level in Montana; Ancestral Rockies uplifted in Colorado.		Pennsylvanian
280	Continued erosion of Ancestral Rockies creates redbed sandstones.		Permian
276	Earliest dinosaurs.		
255	Inland sea invades Montana.		
245	Permian ends with mass extinction; Rocky Mountain region still fringe of partly submerged coastline of Pangaea; more red sandstones and mudstones; first birds appear.	MESOZOIC	Triassic
208	Atlantic Ocean begins to open; Pacific subduction zone forms.		
180	Quesnellia terrane collides with Pacific coast of North America.		Jurassic
115	Inland sea floods west over Wyoming and Montana.		
110	Desert plain east of early mountains.		
100	Seven Devils terrane docks to Pacific coast of North America.		Cretaceous
	Insular Superterrane collides with Pacific coast of North America; Rocky Mountain thrust faulting begins.		
90	Masses of granite begin to form in Idaho.		
70	Thrust faulting forms Overthrust Belt in Wyoming and Montana.		

Rodinia, a barren continent, since it existed before life on land, even before complex multicellular life in the lakes and oceans. For at least 600 million years, sediments washed off the mountains of Rodinia onto its continental shelf and into a shallow central basin. These sedimentary layers are often preserved in amazing detail, perhaps because there were no animals disturbing the mud, and include thin layers of algae that covered the shallow floor of the inland sea. The sedimentary rocks of Rodinia are visible in the Rocky Mountains

Millions of years ago	Geological event	Era	Period
65	Asteroid strikes Yucatan Peninsula, destroying almost all life on North America. Extinction of dinosaurs.		
60	Rockies uplifted from New Mexico to Montana.		
60–55	Tectonic pressure eases in British Columbia and Alberta, thrust faulting ends, and Rocky Mountain Trench opens up.		
55	Volcanic activity in central Idaho and western Montana.		
50	Eocene begins; climate generally wet. Foreland ranges come up, compressed from various directions; volcanic activity forms Absaroka Range in northwestern Wyoming, creates petrified forests.		Tertiary
37	Oligocene deposition begins; lasts until mid-Miocene.		
37	Large Cascade volcanoes start erupting, deposit thick layers of ash on American Rockies.		
35	Vulcanism begins in Colorado in San Juan and West Elk mountains.		
29	Second phase of vulcanism in Colorado.	CENOZOIC	
28	Uplift of Colorado, parts of Utah, Arizona, and New Mexico.		
25	Continued vulcanism causes basalt floods in San Juan Mountains of Colorado.		
24	Miocene begins; big Cascade volcanoes stop erupting.		
17	Increased precipitation and uplift combine to rejuvenate rivers in the American Rockies; erosion carves mountain ranges from the high plateaus; huge basalt flows on the western edge of the Rockies in the Pacific Northwest.		
5.3	Pliocene begins; uplift of American Rockies ends.		
2	Pleistocene begins; ice sheets cover all of Canada and much of the Rocky Mountains. Yellowstone volcano erupts; ash covers almost all of western North America; erupts again 1.2 and 0.6 million years ago.		
14,000 years ago	Ice sheets reach their maximum extent in western North America.		Quaternary
10,000 years ago	Pleistocene ends as ice melts from all lowland areas.		

today as the Belt or Purcell formations in western Montana, Idaho, and south-eastern British Columbia and as the Muskwa Formation in northern British Columbia. These formations are thickest at their western ends, where they abruptly disappear. This is not what you would find in a normal deposition pattern—each formation has clearly been cut in two.

Rodinia's high mountains were not fated to become the Rockies. About 750 million years ago, Rodinia began to split in two roughly along a line tracing the western edge of today's Rocky Mountains. The western part drifted away and is now part of eastern Australia or northeastern Asia. The eastern half of Rodinia is now the core of North America, and the western shoreline created by the split lasted for about 500 million years. Over that long period,

Penstemons bloom next to ripples on an ancient mudflat perfectly preserved in mudstone at Logan Pass, Montana. The rock is part of a Belt formation, more than 1 billion years old.

huge quantities of sediments were laid down off the coast. Rivers brought mud, sand, and gravel to great deltas, and these sediments gradually hardened into shale, sandstone, and conglomerate rock as they were buried. Marine organisms secreted calcium carbonate within their cells or as skeletons around their bodies; the carbonate settled to the seafloor and under pressure turned to limestone and dolomite.

Throughout the Precambrian era, life slowly evolved as unicellular organisms—bacteria and their close relatives the blue-green algae, or cyanobacteria. Most of these organisms left little trace behind in the rocks, though some cyanobacteria colonies are preserved as cabbagelike stromatolites. About 570 million years ago, this pattern changed—an evolutionary explosion occurred as organisms became much more complex; suddenly animals had skeletons

About 515 million years ago, where today the Rockies tower over the small community of Field, British Columbia, an underwater escarpment—the wall of a limestone reef—snaked along the ocean floor west of the continental shore. At the base of this wall, a thriving community of animals lived on, in, and above the muddy sediments that drifted down from above.

Periodic mudslides buried these animals in fine silts, which hardened over the millennia to form shale. These muds are now the Burgess Shale, the most remarkable fossil bed in the world. Few sites can boast such finely detailed fossils, and few preserve animals of this age. The Burgess fauna lived only geological moments after the Cambrian explosion, the great diversification of complex animal life, and the Burgess Shale provides the sharpest picture we have of that extraordinary period.

Perhaps the most amazing feature of the Burgess fauna is its diversity—not in numbers of species, for today's oceans are richer in species, but in the basic anatomical designs for life. Steven Jay Gould, in his book *Wonderful Life* (a fascinatingly thorough account of the Burgess Shale), uses the term *disparity* to describe this richness of body plans.

The disparity in the Burgess Shale fauna reaches across all levels of classification. At the upper level, at least seven anatomical designs occur that do not fit into any previously known phylum, the highest grouping in the Animal Kingdom. There are oddities such as *Opabinia,* a segmented creature with five eyes and a clawed, frontal nozzle, and *Anomalocaris,* a large (about 50 centimeters/ 20 inches long) swimmer with stalked eyes, a mouth that looks like a pineapple ring, and a series of lobed fins. At a lower level, within the phylum Arthropoda, at least twenty animals are not closely related to other major arthropod groups, living or extinct.

What does this disparity mean? It means that early in the evolution of multicellular animal life, there was a much greater variety in basic body plans than there is among modern animals. Life did not evolve as a cone of ever-increasing diversity; rather, there was a great flourishing of possibilities

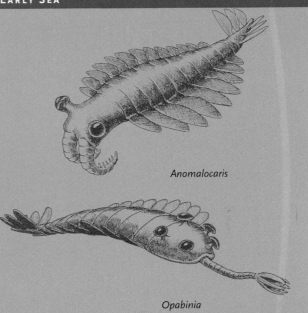

Anomalocaris

Opabinia

at the beginning, followed by great decimations. The loss of many anatomical possibilities has resulted in today's pattern; the vast majority of animal life is contained within a handful of phyla, each with a standard body plan—the arthropods, mollusks, echinoderms, annelid worms, roundworms, cnidarians, and chordates.

As to why this great decimation of animal possibilities occurred, the textbook answer would be that a few of the body plans were more efficient and successful than the others; they prevailed while others vanished. But if you compared the "failures" with their contemporaries, the early representatives of modern groups, you would find that there is no way to predict why one would survive and another disappear. Evolution at the phylum level might be more related to historical accidents than to evolutionary "fitness." As Gould puts it, if we rewound the tape of life and let it play again, we would get an entirely different world.

with a mind-boggling diversity of forms. These forms are well preserved in fossils and allow easy identification of fossil-bearing rocks to a detailed time sequence. This blossoming of multicellular evolution marks the end of the Precambrian era and the beginning of the Paleozoic era. For the next 350 million years, rich deposits of limestone and shale were laid down in the region, both on the shallow continental shelf to the west and in an inland sea to the east. These Paleozoic rocks form the bulk of the sedimentary strata in the Rocky Mountains today.

The red sandstones in these ridges in Roxborough State Park, Colorado, were laid down more than 250 million years ago as the Ancestral Rocky Mountains eroded. The sandstone beds were tilted as the modern Rockies rose about 60 million years ago.

Previous pages: The pale lower half of Mount Fitzwilliam in Mount Robson Provincial Park, British Columbia, is dolomite—carbonate rocks laid down in the Precambrian era. The darker rocks above are quartzites deposited during the Cambrian period. The sharp line between them thus represents one of geology's great boundaries—the Cambrian evolutionary explosion.

ANCESTRAL ROCKIES

All the world's continents coalesced to form Pangaea, the "world continent," about 350 million years ago. At that time, the major mountain spine of North America was the Appalachians, pushed up as Europe and Africa collided with eastern North America. The west coast of North America must have been pushed against the seafloor of the ancestral Pacific Ocean at that time, since a series of mountain-building events occurred along the coast in what is now Nevada, Idaho, and British Columbia. Almost all evidence of these mountains was obliterated by later mountain-building events. Another mountain range rose in Colorado and southern Wyoming about 300 million years ago. Dubbed the Ancestral Rockies, these mountains were subsequently eroded out of existence over the next 50 million years, but their granitic and metamorphic cores arose once again about 200 million years later to become the centerpiece of the modern Colorado Rockies. The later uplift also raised alluvial fans from

that period of erosion, beds that are now tilted to form the redbed sandstone formations along the eastern edge of the modern Rockies in central Colorado.

The Paleozoic era ended 245 million years ago with a catastrophic extinction event that eliminated almost all living species on earth, totally changing ecosystems on land and in the sea. The cause of this extinction is unknown but may be related to climate changes caused by massive volcanic activity in Asia, probably the Tungusska basalts of western Siberia. A new era began—the Mesozoic—and a new group of animals, the dinosaurs, quickly rose to prominence and continued to dominate life on this planet until another extinction event dealt them a fatal blow 180 million years later.

Overleaf: The Bitterroot Range of western Montana and eastern Idaho is carved from a mass of granite that formed as the Pacific Plate slid beneath western North America.

THE ROCKIES ARE BORN

The birth of the Rocky Mountains began with a birth of another sort. About 180 million years ago, the Atlantic Ocean sprang into being as the oldest part

of the Mid-Atlantic Ridge began to separate southeastern North America from North Africa. North America moved westward against the Pacific Ocean plate. The oceanic plate, being heavier than the continental rocks, slid down through a trench along the continent's western edge. In the resulting collision of titans, the volcanic chains and sedimentary strata along the continental margin became collateral damage, as they buckled, folded, and piled up in stacks that were shoved eastward.

Superhot water rising from the sinking oceanic slab melted large volumes of the continental crust above, creating magma. The magma rose—part of it erupted in a volcanic chain, the rest crystallized below the surface to become enormous masses of granite. The Bitterroot Range of eastern Idaho and western Montana is the easternmost extent of these structures. The sedimentary strata deeply buried and compressed by the collision metamorphosed into gneisses and schists. This large area of metamorphic rock is exposed in the Monashee and Selkirk mountains of southeastern British Columbia and much of the mountains of northern Idaho.

Parts of these masses of granite lost the sedimentary strata covering them in a remarkable way. Instead of washing away in rivers, several large expanses of sedimentary strata simply slid off the rising granite. In one case, a huge slab of rock that covered the eastern Bitterroot Range—15 000 meters (50,000 feet) thick—slid eastward, probably on a gently tilted gangplank of molten granite, for at least 80 kilometers (50 miles), plowing over and into older rocks as it went. The displaced slab became the Sapphire Mountains, and the gap behind it is the Bitterroot Valley.

The eastern Pacific Ocean contained volcanic chains and large islands of continental crust, somewhat like those of Japan or the Philippines today. As North America swallowed up the crust of the intervening marginal ocean basins, these island chains eventually crashed into the larger continent. Because the islands were made of continental crust, which is lighter than oceanic crust, when they collided with North America they did not go under but stuck fast onto the continental shelf as the continent inched inexorably westward. These island blocks rode up over the continental shelf of North America and onto the continental plain, burying the land 15 kilometers (10 miles) deep in places.

To the east of this collision belt, the thick sheets of continental shelf sediments buckled like a carpet being pushed along a floor. The resistant limestone layers were too brittle to fold and broke off cleanly, sending the westward portion of the sheet sliding over its counterpart to the east. As the sheet moved eastward, pressure on the sheet below it caused the lower sheet to buckle and break ahead of the first sheet. This process repeated itself over and over again, each new thrust appearing on the east side of the last. This

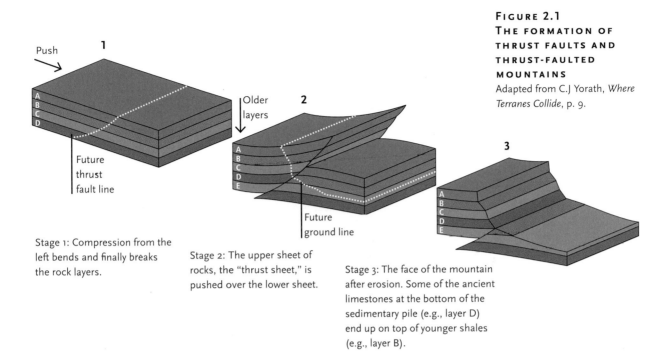

FIGURE 2.1
THE FORMATION OF
THRUST FAULTS AND
THRUST-FAULTED
MOUNTAINS
Adapted from C.J Yorath, *Where Terranes Collide*, p. 9.

Stage 1: Compression from the left bends and finally breaks the rock layers.

Stage 2: The upper sheet of rocks, the "thrust sheet," is pushed over the lower sheet.

Stage 3: The face of the mountain after erosion. Some of the ancient limestones at the bottom of the sedimentary pile (e.g., layer D) end up on top of younger shales (e.g., layer B).

was a huge event—from the Brooks Range in Alaska south to Montana and continuing south at various sites to Mexico.

Each of these thrust sheets has a slightly different character. In the Canadian Rockies, the rocks of the western ranges were laid down as muddy sediments in deep water and thus contain higher proportions of soft shale. The central ranges are characterized by towering cliffs of hard limestone, laid down in the shallow waters of the continental shelf. And the eastern foothills in Alberta are composed of sediments that eroded off the mountains building to the west. Remember, this was a long process—the thrust faulting had been going on for about 70 million years before it stopped 65 million years ago.

The tectonic shift that signaled the end of the thrust faulting in the northern part of the Rocky Mountains removed the mountain-building pressure that had been constantly applied to that part of the continent for 120 million years. Huge blocks of landscape fell back to the west, no longer being held up by the forces of collision. As the land stretched westward, long cracks appeared in the mountains of British Columbia. The greatest of these is the Rocky Mountain Trench, a remarkably straight valley that extends from northwestern Montana into northern British Columbia (and on into Yukon as the Tintina Trench). The southern half of this valley—almost 1 000 kilometers (620 miles) long—opened up like a trapdoor as the Rockies split in two. The western side hung in place like a hinge, but the eastern edge dropped more than a thousand meters (3,300 feet).

Overleaf: The Columbia Valley in the Rocky Mountain Trench

The Dillon Pinnacles tower above the Blue Mesa Reservoir of the Gunnison River. This impressive rock wall formed between 35 and 26 million years ago as volcanoes in the West Elk Mountains poured out lava and ash over much of southwestern Colorado.

Most of the American Rockies were still nowhere to be seen 60 million years ago. Then, from central Montana through Wyoming, Colorado, and northern New Mexico a flurry of mountain ranges rose out of nowhere, all east of the overthrust belt. These ranges were lifted by deep thrust faults that brought basement rocks to the surface. This was the Laramide orogeny, named after the Laramie Mountains of Wyoming and the Greek word for "mountain building." Geologists are still unsure of the exact process that produced all these mountains. One theory suggests that the Pacific Plate plunged steeply under the North American Plate in the Canadian part of the region but that farther south it slid more shallowly. Instead of disappearing into the mantle, this sheet of crust disrupted sections of the basement rock below the sedimentary layers far to the east of the Pacific coast. Rainfall was high at that time and erosion was rapid; the sedimentary rocks on top of the mountains disappeared as they rose, and the mountains lost 400 million years of sediments in just 10 million years.

After that event, things were geologically fairly quiet in the Rocky Mountains for the next 30 million years, except for localized volcanic activity and continual erosion. Huge volcanoes in the western Cascades of Washington, Oregon, and northern California ejected vast quantities of ash that drifted on the prevailing winds east to the Rockies. By about 20 million years ago, only the highest peaks poked above a mantle of ash, silt, sand, and gravel that extended in a gradually sloping surface to the Great Plains near the eastern borders of Montana, Wyoming, and Colorado. Some ranges completely disappeared. Winding rivers carried this debris away in valleys that bore no structural relation to the buried mountains beneath them. The climate was very dry through this entire period, so the rivers were not large enough to carry all the eroded sediments and ash out of the region. By the late Miocene, about 17 million years ago, the American Rockies were not a breathtaking sight at all; they were a few minor mountains rising above a high plain.

Then the American Rockies rose again. At the same time, the climate changed and rainfall increased dramatically. Rejuvenated by the power of the water volume and increased gradient, rivers sprang to life, cutting down into the debris as the land rose. They kept their winding paths even as they encountered long-buried mountains below. The Wind River cuts straight through the Owl Creek Mountains, then changes its name to the Bighorn—early explorers never imagined that the rivers on either side of the mountains could be the same. It also flows through the middle of Sheep Mountain, in one side and out the other. The North Platte slices through the Medicine Bows, the Seminoes, and the Granite Mountains. Throughout the American Rockies, the major rivers take paths that normal rivers should not take, evidence that they began to flow on a surface above the highest point on the rims of the canyons they eroded.

These rivers began the gargantuan task of digging out the Rockies and continue that work today. They have removed thousands of cubic miles of material from the Rockies and sent them to the Mississippi Delta. Their effectiveness has probably increased during the last 2 million years as the cool climate of the Pleistocene has brought increased precipitation and local glacial activity. This whole process is known in American geological circles as the Exhumation of the Rockies.

VOLCANIC ACTIVITY IN THE ROCKY MOUNTAINS

Several regions of the Rocky Mountains were formed by vulcanism rather than by faulting and uplift. About 53 million years ago, lava poured out of thousands of fissures to cover much of northwestern Wyoming, creating a high basalt plateau, which has since been carved by water and ice to form the Absaroka Range. Thirty million years later, southwestern Colorado was totally altered by three periods of massive vulcanism. Ash, lava, and breccia—chunks of broken volcanic rock in a hardened ash matrix—covered much of the region, forming the West Elk and San Juan ranges.

For the last 3.5 million years, there has been almost constant volcanic activity in the Wells Gray Park area in the Cariboo Mountains of British Columbia, caused by deep faulting at the eastern boundary of one of the volcanic chains that collided with North America eons before. Some of this volcanic activity occurred beneath the regional ice sheet, creating several tuya, or subglacial volcanoes.

The Yellowstone volcanic area is a resurgent caldera, a rare type of volcano that erupts at long intervals and in monstrous fashion. Yellowstone has erupted three times over the last 2.5 million years; the second eruption, about 1.8 million years ago, sent a huge ash cloud west to the Pacific Ocean, south to Mexico, and east to Missouri. The Yellowstone Plateau is still underlain by a large body of magma. The volcano is far from asleep. Most geologists assume that it will erupt again but have no clear idea when. Frequent small earthquakes rattle the region, and the thermal areas are hotter now than when first studied in 1872.

Overleaf: The Murtle River plunges over Helmcken Falls in Wells Gray Provincial Park, British Columbia. The falls are cutting a canyon through basalt formed a half million years ago when the valley was filled with molten lava.

Jackson Hole and the Tetons

One of the final touches in the building of the Rocky Mountains was one of the most spectacular. When the American Rockies had reached their greatest height, the area around modern-day Jackson Hole was surprisingly unspectacular—rolling hills quite distant from the mountain ranges that surrounded it on all sides. Then, about 8 million years ago, the earth's crust

The Tetons began to rise 8 million years ago, while the floor of Jackson Hole sank.

relaxed and stretched, opening an 80-kilometer (50-mile) fault that sent the western side of the region upward and the eastern side downward. The rising western block formed the Tetons, and the sinking eastern block became Jackson Hole. The tops of the higher Tetons are 1 800 meters (6,000 feet) above today's valley floor, whereas the bedrock valley floor is 7 300 meters (24,000 feet) below the peaks, filled with 5 500 meters (18,000 feet) of sediment.

YELLOWSTONE: A HOT SPOT

Although set in one of the most spectacular mountain ranges on earth, the landscape of Yellowstone National Park is at first glance unremarkable—much of it a high plateau covered primarily in a monoculture of Lodgepole Pine. But everywhere there are anomalies that do not seem to belong to our everyday world. Plumes of steam rise from the pine forest on the next hill. Around the corner sits a hillside that is pure white in high summer, with a herd of elk chewing their cud on a terrace of dazzling white travertine. Gigantic pillars of boiling water called geysers jet high into the air. The creek next to your trail is scalding. It is not surprising that Yellowstone became the first national park in North America.

It is also not surprising to hear that geologists consider Yellowstone a hot spot. But the term has a very specific meaning in scientific circles. Forty kilometers (25 miles) below the surface of the earth, lying underneath the solid crust, is the mantle, a region so hot that the rocks that form it are as soft as plasticine, kept partially solid only by the tremendous pressure exerted on them by the crustal rocks above. Scattered around the surface of the mantle are a few hot spots—sites that are hot enough to melt their way through the solid rock above them and create volcanic activity of all sorts. Since the earth's crust is literally floating on the mantle, a trail of volcanoes may be formed

on the crust as it drifts over the hot spot. The volcanoes become strung out like beads on a string, each bead older than the next. The Hawaiian Islands are a classic example, as are the Galápagos and Aleutian islands.

The Yellowstone hot spot began in southeastern Oregon about 14 million years ago. Volcanic fissures at that time

filled eastern Oregon and Washington with lava. As the North American plate moved west, the hot spot drew a track eastward across southern Idaho, a long progression of extinct volcanoes like the modern Yellowstone volcano.

Above: The Yellowstone River is named for the brightly colored

rock formations along its banks composed of volcanic ash that is locally altered by hot water and steam.

Opposite page: A minor eruption of Steamboat Geyser in the Norris Geyser Basin. This geyser has produced the largest geyser eruptions in the world, some as high as 115 meters (380 feet).

3 A Legacy of Ice

*The aerial tints of the snow, the heavenly azure of
the solid glaciers, the rainbow-like hues of their
broken fragments, and huge mossy icicles hanging
from the perpendicular rocks . . .*

—David Douglas, Athabasca Pass, May 1, 1827

A Legacy of Ice

CHAPTER 3

At the dawn of the Pleistocene epoch—a geologically brief 2 million years ago—the construction of the Rocky Mountains was almost complete. The mountains had risen to their present heights, then been sculpted by wind and water. But the sculpture was unfinished. Many of the American Rocky Mountain ranges were simply high, rounded plateaus, and valleys throughout the Rockies were narrow and shallow. There was not the same dramatic relief we see today in the mountains. What put the finishing touches on this continental masterpiece was ice—lots of it.

Glaciers

The climate cooled dramatically and precipitation increased. More and more snow fell throughout the Rockies, and less and less of it melted in the cooler summers. Permanent snowfields appeared along the mountaintops. This snow, altered by melting processes during the summer, quickly lost its fluffiness and became a more solid snow called firn. With each winter, the firn layer became thicker and the snow at the bottom of the pack solidified into ice. At a critical moment, the snowfield became so heavy that gravity took over and the ice began to flow. Glaciers were born.

When a glacier flows, it erodes the landscape in a manner much different from that of a river. Rivers cut through rock and gravel like a knife, whereas the mass and size of a glacier acts like a giant ice-cream scoop. Large valley glaciers grind their way down river courses, turning shallow, V-shaped valleys into much deeper, broader, U-shaped valleys. Alpine glaciers carve giant bowls, called cirques, into the mountain peaks. Alpine glaciers are more common on the northeast side of mountains, since that side is shaded during hot summer afternoons and snow melts more slowly there. Some small alpine glaciers are also fed significant amounts of snow by the prevailing westerly winds that sweep western mountain faces clear and deposit the snow on east-facing cirques.

If a peak has several alpine glaciers, the cirques they scoop out will have sharp ridges, called arêtes, between them, and if these arêtes meet at the top of the mountain, the peak will be sculpted into a spectacular horn. Although the huge continental ice sheets that covered most of Canada and the northern United States overran much of the landscape and rounded off a lot of its sharp edges, alpine glaciers had quite the opposite effect. They formed on these rounded mountains and ridges and produced a range of jagged peaks.

Alpine glaciers carve the granite spires of Bugaboo Provincial Park in the northern Purcell Mountains of British Columbia.

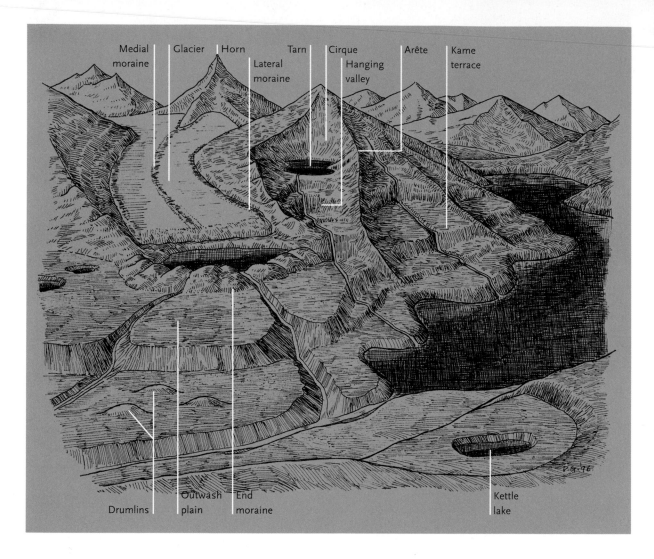

Medial moraine · Glacier · Horn · Lateral moraine · Tarn · Cirque · Hanging valley · Arête · Kame terrace

Drumlins · Outwash plain · End moraine · Kettle lake

FIGURE 3.1
GLACIAL FEATURES

Meltwaters of the Athabasca Glacier, Columbia Icefields, Jasper National Park, Alberta

Overleaf: The Robson Glacier, British Columbia

A GLACIAL ANATOMY

To understand in more detail how glaciers have shaped the Rocky Mountains, it helps to know a little more about how they work. An active glacier is always moving, flowing like a river in slow motion. The ice in an average valley glacier travels about the length of a football field each year; the rate in small alpine glaciers is much slower. The ice in most Rocky Mountain glaciers takes a century or two to flow from top to bottom. Since glaciers flow downhill, their lower edges, or toes, are established where the annual rate of melt is equal to the rate of accumulation at the head of the glacier. So, although the ice itself is always moving downhill, the terminus of the glacier may be advancing (if snow accumulation above exceeds melt at the bottom) or receding (if melt increases).

The ice in different parts of the glacier moves at different speeds, depending on how close it is to the friction of bedrock. Ice at the surface of the glacier flows faster than ice scraping along rock in the belly, and ice in the

center of the glacier flows faster than ice on either side. Whereas glacial ice can be surprisingly plastic if the flow is slow enough, it forms large cracks, called crevasses, where flow rates change abruptly, such as along its edges or where the glacier flows over a cliff. If the cliff is large enough, the glacier will have an icefall, a spectacular but slow-moving equivalent of a river's waterfall. Advancing glaciers have steep, breaking faces to their snouts, with many crevasses, since the ice on the surface is literally overrunning the deeper ice; retreating glaciers have shallow, smooth snouts. Glaciers can flow over smaller solid obstructions by simply melting their way around them. The high pressure on the ice above an obstruction causes the ice to melt (just as ice melts under the intense pressure of a skate blade), then refreeze beyond the obstruction.

Each summer the ice at the surface of a glacier melts to some extent, and streams of meltwater flow across the surface. If one of these streams encounters a crevasse, it naturally forms a waterfall, which goes deep into the bowels of the glacier and carves a vertical shaft called a moulin. These moulins move downhill with the glacier and may dry up if the shape of the glacier's surface changes enough to alter the stream flow. Deep, flowing moulins can bring huge amounts of water to the ice-rock interface at the belly of a glacier. If enough water accumulates, perhaps dammed by an under-ice ridge, the glacier can suddenly surge, sliding downhill on water instead of rock.

Water can also get under the ice if a glacier flows across a valley, blocking a river and forming an ice dam. The water backs up to form a glacial lake until it is deep enough to float the glacier. Then the lake rapidly drains, escaping underneath the floating glacier. This causes a sudden devastating flood, sweeping away the toe of the glacier. If ice keeps accumulating at the top of the glacier, this cycle of dam, lake, and flood continues. Glaciologists call these glacial events jökulhlaups, from their Icelandic name. One of the best-known Rocky Mountain glaciers with this characteristic is the Cathedral Glacier in Yoho National Park; from 1925 to 1984, there were seven jökulhlaups at this site, each causing huge flows of debris into the Kicking Horse Valley.

ICE, ROCK, AND FLOUR

As glaciers flow down a valley, the tremendous pressure of ice breaks the bedrock below, and the loosened chunks of stone are carried along by the belly of the glacier. These rocks act like sandpaper, scouring the bedrock into sand and crushing the sand into rock flour. A stream coming out of an active glacier has a distinctive color—it is white, filled with rock flour. This white fades to a powder blue farther downstream as nonglacial streams add their water to the flow. The fine silt sinks to the bottom of glacial lakes, but enough remains in suspension to give these lakes an unearthly sky-blue color.

Opposite page: Moon over Moraine Lake, Banff National Park, Alberta

This effect is common in tarns, the small lakes that sparkle in the bottom of a cirque vacated by a melting alpine glacier, but can also be seen in larger lakes that receive glacial meltwater.

Rocks also fall onto the surface of glaciers. In valley glaciers, these accumulate along the sides of the glacier, since most of the rockfall happens along the steep valley walls. If a valley glacier begins to shrink and recede, it loses height as well as length, and the rocks held along its side pile up in two long, high ridges on either side of the glacier. Other piles of rock and gravel are dumped at the snout of a glacier as the ice melts there each year.

These piles are called moraines, and they are common features of a postglacial landscape. The side ridges are called lateral moraines, and the ones at the snout are called terminal or end moraines. The latter may also form in a different way if an advancing glacier bulldozes its way through softer valley-bottom material, pushing a pile of debris ahead of it. Two valley glaciers that flow together downstream acquire a medial moraine where their lateral moraines meet within the larger glacier.

TWO MILLION YEARS OF ICE

The world began to cool during the late Pliocene, just over 2 million years ago, and has continued to be relatively cold through the Pleistocene and into the present. Yet the Pleistocene epoch was not a universally cold time; there were several long periods during which ice covered a great deal of the earth's

surface, but there were also times when the climate was warmer than it is today. Early glaciations are difficult to discern in today's landscape, since their effects have largely been erased by more recent glacial events. But it is generally agreed that at least nine major glacial advances occurred during the Pleistocene and late Pliocene and many more minor advances. Most of the trademark effects of glaciation we see in the Rocky Mountains today were created by the most recent major glaciation, which began about 75,000 years ago and ended about 12,000 years ago. Two advances occurred during that time—the first ended about 60,000 years ago, and the latest began about 30,000 years ago, reached its maximum extent about 15,000 years ago, then quickly waned.

These glacial periods were separated by warmer periods. We are probably in one of these interglacial periods now, though evidence suggests that the

The Alpine Forget-me-not was likely one of the plant species that survived the ice ages on nunataks—ice-free mountain peaks amid the ice sheets.

Overleaf: The Dutch Creek hoodoos in the southern Rocky Mountain Trench, British Columbia, were formed during a period of rapid ice melt that brought a mixture of glacial silt and outwash gravel into the Kootenay River valley.

Perhaps the most spectacular event at the end of the Pleistocene was the repeated formation and destruction of a huge lake in the Rocky Mountains of northwestern Montana and northern Idaho—Glacial Lake Missoula. About fifteen thousand years ago, when the last ice advance of the Pleistocene reached its maximum, British Columbia was essentially filled with ice to the tops of its mountains, and lobes of that ice field extended into the valleys of northern Washington, Idaho, and Montana. Ice flowing down the Purcell Valley into Idaho crossed the valley of the Clark Fork River just south of Sandpoint, creating a huge ice dam that filled the valley and blocked the river.

Over the next few years, the waters of the Clark Fork rose behind the dam, forming Glacial Lake Missoula. At its greatest extent, this lake extended east into Montana beyond Garrison, filled the Bitterroot Valley south beyond Darby, and flooded the Mission Valley north to Polson, where its shores were the southern edge of the glacial ice flowing down the Flathead Valley. Glacial Lake Missoula filled the valleys to an altitude of 1 265 meters (4,150 feet) above sea level, was 7 425 square kilometers (2,900 square miles) in extent, and held 2 171 cubic kilometers of water (521 cubic miles)—roughly the same volume as Lake Ontario.

As the water level rose to a height of about 600 meters (2,000 feet) at the ice dam, the dam began to float in the water. The floating glacier broke under the huge pressure from upstream, and in a matter of days Glacial Lake Missoula drained like a big bathtub that has had its plug pulled. Catastrophic floods streamed southwestward, carving canyons out of the bedrock basalt and washing all soils from what are now the scablands of eastern Washington. The floodwaters created huge temporary lakes in the Yakima, Columbia, and Willamette valleys and eventually emptied through the Columbia River into the Pacific Ocean. But the Purcell Valley glacier kept advancing and within a few decades had dammed the Clark Fork again; Glacial Lake Missoula was reborn and died another spectacular death a few years later. The cycle repeated itself more than thirty-six times over a period of three thousand years, each event smaller than the last as the Pleistocene came to a close.

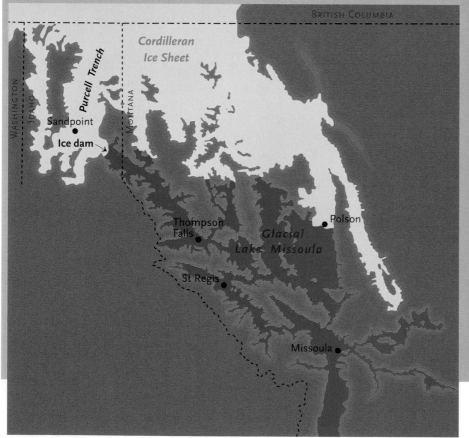

climate of the previous interglacial period, which occurred between 130,000 and 70,000 years ago, was considerably warmer than that of today. And anyone visiting Antarctica, Greenland, or Iceland could easily be convinced that the Ice Age lives on. There have even been several smaller glacial advances in the past 10,000 years. One of these was the Little Ice Age, which lasted from about AD 1600 to AD 1850 and dramatically lowered tree lines throughout the mountains of western North America.

In the Rockies, the advance of ice began in the mountaintops. In British Columbia, ice accumulated rapidly in the Coast Mountains and Columbia Mountains, spreading into adjacent valleys as a large ice sheet and coalescing with valley glaciers coming out of the Rocky Mountains. This coalescence eventually formed the Cordilleran Ice Sheet, which covered the western cordillera from central Alaska and Yukon south to northern Washington, Idaho, and Montana. A large continental ice sheet—the Laurentide— also spread south from ice accumulation centers in northern Canada and eventually met the Cordilleran Ice Sheet along the eastern flank of the Rockies. At the height of the most recent glaciation, 60 percent of the world's ice lay on North America.

Two million years of repeated ice attack changed the face of the Rocky Mountains. Every valley in the Canadian Rockies and most high-elevation valleys farther south were deepened and widened by valley glaciers. High, rounded ridges were carved into a sensational array of castellated peaks. But some of the most noticeable effects were caused while the ice was melting at the end of the last glaciation.

When the last ice advance was at its maximum, about 15,000 years ago, the Cordilleran and Laurentide ice sheets extended about 100 kilometers (60 miles) south of the present Canada–United States boundary. In the mountains, alpine glaciers were already receding while the larger ice sheets made their final push. The vast areas of ice to the north dramatically affected the climate of the ice-free regions. First, the ice caused a general cooling of the entire continent. Second, the mass of cool air over the ice blocked the strong westerly jet stream that now flows more or less along the Canada–U.S. border. The blocked jet stream was split in two, and the southerly branch coursed across the southwestern states. This split took moisture away from the wet belts of British Columbia, Washington, Idaho, and Montana and moved it south. Third, there was a prevailing high-pressure system over the Laurentide Ice Sheet, producing a clockwise air movement that brought cold, dry easterly winds to the Rocky Mountains south of the ice.

Most of the Rocky Mountains were covered with ice, in some areas more than 2 kilometers (1.2 miles) thick. Almost all of the life that we see in the Rockies today was gone. The ice-free peaks, or nunataks, were islands of life in the sea of ice, harboring patches of alpine grasses and flowers inhabited by hardy rodents and pikas and perhaps a lonely raven flying by.

An ecosystem map of North America during this period of maximum ice extent would show dense forests in the southeast, dry and cold spruce park- land south of the Laurentide Ice Sheet and along the eastern slopes of the

Rockies, and a region of prairie grassland south of the spruce. The American Southwest was mostly forested, thanks to the southern jet stream and the Pacific air it carried. Surprisingly, there was an ice-free area in northern Yukon and Alaska. This region, called Beringia, was a cold, grassy steppe that was too dry to produce large glaciers. It extended westward across the Bering Strait—dry land at that time because of the lowered sea levels around the world—to Siberia.

There were people in this landscape. Exactly when the first people arrived in North America has been a matter of intense debate, but it is now generally accepted that they were scattered across North and even South America by the time of the last glacial maximum. The habitats they lived in would look normal enough to modern biologists, but some of the animals they saw would be extraordinary, to say the least. Mammoths roamed the tundra grasslands, mastodons browsed on spruce and larch in the forests, and herds of camels and small horses grazed on the grasslands. And the cats that stalked these animals would certainly be cause for surprise today—saber-tooth cats, scimitar cats, lions, and cheetahs. The Short-faced Bear and Dire Wolf—both larger and more powerful than their modern counterparts—also roamed the land.

The end came quickly. As temperatures went up and precipitation decreased, most of the ice that had taken over 15,000 years to accumulate disappeared in less than 2,000 years. The vast ice sheets gushed water, forming large lakes. These lakes were filled with white glacial silt deposits, now a common feature of Rocky Mountain valleys. Rivers and creeks brought sand and gravel from the mountains into large valleys, where the sediments built up against the sides of the large valley glaciers to form kame terraces or were deposited into the glacial lakes as large deltas. These flat terraces and raised deltas are also characteristic sights in valleys today, marking the height of valley glaciers or their associated lakes. Mountains of stagnant ice blocked natural watersheds, forcing some rivers to take courses radically different from those of today. Water from the upper Fraser River, one of the main watersheds of the Canadian Rockies, flowed for a time down the Columbia River valley.

The end came quickly for many species of large animals as well. By the time the ice had disappeared from the landscape, two-thirds of the large mammal species in North America had vanished with it. Gone were the giant beavers, ground sloths, lions, camels, horses, mammoths, and mastodons. The reasons for their demise are unknown, but almost certainly the arrival of humans was a major factor. The populations of some species may have declined as the climate changed, but the presence of intelligent hunters likely pushed most of them into oblivion. The timing of recent mass extinctions of large animals is closely tied to the arrival of humans in several parts of the world—Madagascar, Australia, and North America. Some survived—the Bison and the Pronghorn are examples—perhaps through migratory habits that brought them respite in regions empty of people between warring tribes of hunters.

RETURN OF LIFE TO THE MOUNTAINS

As the ice melted, life reclaimed the mountains. The pattern of immigration reflected the pattern of ice melt: northern species moved out of Beringia into the northern Rockies, the spruce forests spread from the plains into the foothills and up the mountainsides, and the western coniferous forests marched into the deep valleys left by the ice. Moose and Grizzly Bears came south from Beringia, and songbirds migrated a little farther north each year from their tropical homes. Some species spread out from nunataks amid the Cordilleran Ice Sheet as the ice level dropped and alpine tundra expanded. Life on these mountaintop islands was tenuous. Brown Lemmings lingered on some Alberta nunataks such as Plateau Mountain until as recently as a thousand years ago but are now found nowhere in the Rockies.

Brown Lemming

The climate did not just get warm at the end of the Pleistocene, it got very warm. From nine thousand to six thousand years ago, the climate was significantly warmer than it is today. The tundra habitats that formed quickly after the ice left were just as quickly replaced by forests of spruce and pine. Tree lines formed on the high mountains, then moved uphill over the centuries as the climate became warmer. Summer droughts intensified in the northern Rockies, but the summer monsoons brought more rain to the southern Rockies. As conditions in the northern valleys became too warm and dry for forests, recurrent fires established grasslands and sagebrush steppes there, forming a lower tree line below the Ponderosa Pine. This lower tree line moved uphill as well, and some mountains were soon grass from top to bottom. To the east of the Rocky Mountains, the grasslands of the Great Plains extended north to the Arctic Circle.

The cycle turned between six thousand and four thousand years ago, and conditions became cooler and wetter for several millennia, similar to conditions today. There was a brief warm period from AD 700 to AD 1100, but about AD 1650 the climate became much cooler. Glaciers began to advance in the mountains, and high forests reverted to tundra. This was the Little Ice Age. In places you can still find the stumps and logs of these forests high above tree line, and remains of Alpine Larch can be seen 90 kilometers (60 miles) beyond the present northern edge of that tree's range.

Overleaf: Alpine glaciers have carved much of the Rockies, producing broad valleys, sharp ridges, and jewel-like tarns such as this unnamed lake below Mount Edith Cavell, Jasper National Park, Alberta.

A Wall of Ice

The ice fields of the Rockies were a serious barrier to the movement of animals and plant seeds alike, and the dry plains east of the mountains further separated the forest plants and animals of the southwestern and southeastern parts of the continent. The flora and fauna of Beringia were totally cut off from their counterparts south of the ice. Throughout the Pleistocene, many species grew apart, differentiating genetically into eastern and western, southern and northern forms. With each glaciation, some of these differences grew stronger; with each warming period, some of the differences vanished as disjunct populations were reunited. Some of these forms became so different that they would not recognize each other as the same species if they met again. As the ice melted, many of these forms were reunited in today's Rockies.

The wild sheep at the northern end of the Rockies are Stone's Sheep, a subspecies of Thinhorn Sheep. This species spent the Pleistocene in Beringia and moved south into northern British Columbia as the ice melted. As their name suggests, Thinhorn Sheep rams have rather slender, spreading horns, in contrast to the massive, tightly curled horns of their close relatives the Bighorn Sheep. Bighorns evolved south of the continental ice sheets in the mountains of western North America, and they have not yet met Thinhorn Sheep; there is a gap in the Rockies of northern British Columbia between Pine Pass and Stone Mountain without any sheep at all. What will happen if and when they do meet is anybody's guess.

A number of species that now occupy the Rocky Mountains and other western mountain ranges have closely related forms, or sibling species, as they are called, on the eastern flanks of the Rockies. Birds provide some good examples, including the flickers and juncos.

Flickers are colorful woodpeckers found across the continent. In the east, flickers have yellow wings and tails and a red patch on the back of the head, and males have a black mustache. In the west, they have bright salmon-red wings and tails and lack the red patch on the head, and males have a red mustache mark. The two types meet along a line just east of the Rockies now, but in the northern Rockies the boundary between them swings over the mountains and extends west through central British Columbia. Along this line, or suture zone, as biologists call it, the two types interbreed quite freely, producing intergrades with a potpourri of characteristics—red wings with red head patches, yellow wings with red mustaches, or orange wings and tails, for instance.

Dark-eyed Juncos—small sparrows with distinctive black hoods that nest in coniferous forests—are perhaps the most common birds in North America.

To unravel the mystery of past climate change, scientists use a variety of disparate sources. Tree rings are an obvious source of information for climates in the past few centuries. Cores of ice from immense glaciers provide a longer record of annual snowfall at high elevations and latitudes, and mud samples from ancient lake bottoms reveal species patterns in pollen, algae, and insects that are important clues to past ecosystems. But in arid environments, paleoecologists turn to an unlikely source for information about ecological change through the millennia—the middens of pack rats, or woodrats, as they are more properly called.

Woodrats are large mice common throughout the mountains of western North America. As most rural residents know, woodrats have a penchant for gathering things and storing them in their bulky nests, or middens. Around homes and cabins, silverware, coins, and other shiny objects often disappear from shelves overnight. Woodrats have traditional nest sites in small caves and crevices in walls of rocky canyons, sites that have been used by generations of these rodents for thousands of years. They bring plants into the nests for bedding, as well as seeds and other food for winter meals. This material collects at the bottom of the nest, where it mixes with urine and feces, which act as preservative agents. Over the years, the material turns into a rock-hard block of fossilized guano called pack rat amber, somewhat resembling a chunk of rich, nutty dark chocolate or toffee. It is a treasure trove for scientists.

Well-protected woodrat middens can be up to forty thousand years old. By sifting through the hard guano, identifying plant remains, and dating them with carbon-dating techniques, scientists can get a relatively clear picture of past environments. One study in the Bighorn Basin of southern Montana looked at the ratio of different species of junipers through the years. A northern species—the Common Juniper—was present from 10,000 to 8,200 years ago, suggesting a climate cooler than today's. The Common Juniper declined in abundance starting about 9,000 years ago, whereas the Rocky Mountain Juniper—a species adapted to warmer climates—increased. Starting about 4,400 years ago, the local climate became drier, signaled by the abundance of Utah Juniper and Pinyon Pine in the midden, plants typical of today's high deserts.

During the Pleistocene they diverged into no less than four forms. The Oregon Junco breeds in northwestern mountains, the Gray-headed Junco breeds in southwestern mountains, the White-winged Junco nests in the Black Hills of South Dakota, and the Slate-colored Junco breeds elsewhere on the continent. All but the White-winged meet in the Rockies, where they mix so freely that scientists now consider all four of them to be one species.

Fish simply swam upstream as river flows were re-established, but they too present interesting patterns. Over the centuries, as the great ice sheets melted, postglacial flow patterns changed constantly, and fish were able to cross divides as lakes near the height of land flowed first to the Pacific, then to the Atlantic or Arctic oceans, and then back to the Pacific. The White Sucker and Brassy Minnow, for instance, are species normally found in Great Plains drainages but were able to colonize the Fraser River as the glaciers retreated.

4 Climate

Climate

CHAPTER 4

THE CLIMATE OF THE ROCKY MOUNTAINS is more extreme than almost anywhere else on the continent. This fact is not surprising, considering the tremendous range in altitudes and latitudes in the mountains, but these extremes are also due to the effect the mountains themselves have on the local climate and that of the entire continent.

PATTERNS OF CLIMATE

The effects of altitude are most obvious and striking. Under normal conditions, for every 100 meters (300 feet) you ascend, the temperature of dry air will decrease by 1°C, meaning there is a difference of about 20°C (40°F) between the base of the Rockies and the tops of their highest peaks. This one physical law explains much of the diversity in mountain ecosystems. But remember that phrase "under normal conditions," for it is often difficult to find normal conditions in the mountains.

The effects of latitude are also obvious. The elevation of tree line is about 1 700 meters (5,500 feet) in northern British Columbia, and over 3 600 meters (12,000 feet) in southern Colorado. The trend toward lower temperatures at higher latitudes is mitigated somewhat by the long, warm summer days in northern British Columbia—about twenty hours long versus about sixteen hours in New Mexico.

In addition, the western slopes and the eastern slopes of the Rockies have different climate patterns, which also vary from north to south. The western slopes of the mountains almost always receive significantly more precipitation than the eastern slopes. Northern and western areas receive precipitation more or less equally through the year but with an emphasis on winter rain and snow, whereas eastern and southern areas get most of their precipitation from summer rains. Eastern slopes have much greater extremes in temperature, with colder winters and hotter summers than those in western valleys.

In fact, the eastern Rockies have recorded some of the lowest temperatures in North America outside the Arctic—Rogers Pass in central Montana hit −57°C (−70°F) one chilly January day in 1954, still the coldest day on record in the contiguous forty-eight states.

THE GREAT WALL

At the latitudes of the Rocky Mountains, the prevailing wind direction is westerly. These winds come off the Pacific Ocean, driven by two major weather centers, the North Pacific High and the Aleutian Low. The North Pacific High is influential in summer, when warm, tropical air descends over the eastern Pacific Ocean near San Francisco. The warm air creates a high-pressure center turning clockwise, creating westerly winds off its northern edge. In winter the flow is dominated by the Aleutian Low, a huge system rotating counterclockwise over the North Pacific.

As winter storms track across the Pacific on the mid-latitude jet stream, they are spun eastward along the bottom of the Aleutian Low into North America. There they immediately encounter the Coast Mountains in British Columbia and the Cascade Range in Washington, Oregon, and northern California. As moisture-laden air rises over these ranges, it cools and loses most of its capacity to carry water. Torrents of rain lash these

Prevailing westerly winds blowing across Mount Rundle, Banff National Park, Alberta, bring warm, moist air from the Pacific Ocean to the Rockies.

Overleaf: The western slopes of the Rocky Mountains, such as these in Vermilion Pass, Kootenay National Park, British Columbia, are generally snowier than the eastern slopes.

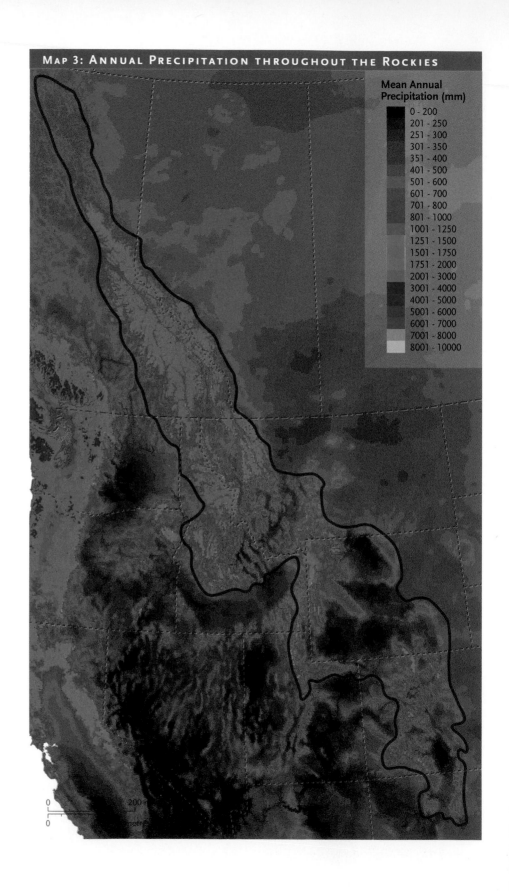

Mean Annual Precipitation (mm)

0 - 200
201 - 250
251 - 300
301 - 350
351 - 400
401 - 500
501 - 600
601 - 700
701 - 800
801 - 1000
1001 - 1250
1251 - 1500
1501 - 1750
1751 - 2000
2001 - 3000
3001 - 4000
4001 - 5000
5001 - 6000
6001 - 7000
7001 - 8000
8001 - 10000

coastal ranges, while their higher elevations are buried under world-record depths of snow.

The air continues inland, bringing only moderate rainfall or snow flurries to the intermontane valleys, but picks up additional moisture there from large lakes and forests. Finally the air reaches the Rockies, often twelve hours or so after it passed the coast. The western slopes of the northern Rockies, including the Columbia Mountains of British Columbia, fill with snow in winter storms. The snowiest place on record in British Columbia is not in the coastal ranges but in the Selkirk Mountains, where Mount Copeland near Revelstoke received 24.5 meters (80 feet) of snow in the winter of 1971–72.

The amount of snowfall dramatically decreases as the systems cross the Continental Divide—Lake Louise receives almost twice as much snow as the town of Banff, only 57 kilometers (35 miles) to the east. As the cool, dry air flows down the eastern slopes of the Rockies, it becomes denser and warmer, allowing it to hold more moisture; by the time it reaches the Great Plains, the great Pacific storm brings little more than a few wisps of rain or snow.

In this way, the mountains of western North America act as a great wall, keeping the Pacific rains away from the interior plains and creating the vast prairies where rainfall is inadequate for tree germination. The Rocky Mountains are the last and greatest obstacle for this westerly flow, and they are a barrier for airflows from other directions as well. During the winter, frigid polar air regularly moves south from another high-pressure center, the Polar High. This huge dome of cold air sits over the Mackenzie Valley of northern Canada.

Being cold, the air is dense and heavy and so flows southward out of the Polar High at ground level. As it encounters the northern Rocky Mountains, it usually stays on their eastern flanks, flowing south in pulses that people on the eastern side of the Rockies experience as cold waves. The first of these usually reaches the northern Rockies in November, sending surface temperatures tumbling far below zero. Each wave seems to go farther south, and by late December or January frigid air has reached eastern Montana and Wyoming. Very strong waves will be deep enough to flow over the mountain passes and fill the western valleys with Arctic air.

As the Polar High intensifies through the winter, the mid-latitude jet stream is deflected more to the south as it crosses the Rocky Mountains. This movement draws Arctic air southward along the eastern slopes of the mountains, intensifying the difference in temperatures on either side of the Rockies. Spring thus comes earlier to the western valleys in the Rockies, reaching Prince George in central British Columbia by mid-March, long before Alberta begins to thaw. Early spring blizzards are common in the eastern Rockies as cold, polar air collides with warmer, moist air moving east from the Pacific or north from the Gulf of Mexico.

Winter temperatures along the eastern slopes of the northern Rocky Mountains can be among the lowest on the planet. The mountains shut out most of the moderating flow of warm air from the Pacific, and the Polar High regularly sends frigid air south to Colorado. But several times each winter, this area experiences one of the most spectacular (and welcome) changes in weather—the chinook wind.

Chinooks arrive abruptly, their appearance announced only by a high arch of clouds over the mountains and a sudden increase in wind speed. The temperature rises rapidly, often increasing 20°C (40°F) or more in a matter of minutes.

Deep snow disappears without much trace of meltwater, since the water is absorbed by the dry, howling wind. Local residents eagerly await chinooks as respites from weeks of cold weather.

A chinook is created when warm, moisture-laden air is carried by high westerly winds over the Rocky Mountains. As a Pacific storm system passes over the ocean, it picks up moisture that has evaporated from the relatively warm water. This moisture contains latent heat—the energy used to evaporate it in the first place. If the winds carrying the moist air are strong enough, they push the air up over the mountains. As the air rises, it expands and cools, losing most of its ability to hold water. The moisture in the air condenses and falls as rain or snow, depending on the temperature. As the water condenses, it releases its latent heat into the air. So as the air passes over the Continental Divide, it is not only dry but warm. It then flows rapidly down the eastern slope of the mountains, and as it descends, it becomes denser and even warmer. At the bottom of the slope, the high wind brings dry air that is much warmer than the thin layer of cold Arctic air above the ground.

Chinooks can occur anywhere on the east side of a mountain range in western North America, but they are most common along the abrupt Rocky Mountain Front in northern Montana and southern Alberta. This region lies along the path of the mid-latitude jet stream, the rapidly moving river of air that carries storms eastward from the Pacific coast. Crowsnest Pass in southwestern Alberta has thirty to thirty-five chinook days each winter.

Chinook-like winds occur in other mountainous areas of the world, most notably in the Alps, where they are called foehn winds. The rapid drop in air pressure associated with these winds has been shown to cause an increase in migraines and is even blamed for cases of temporary insanity.

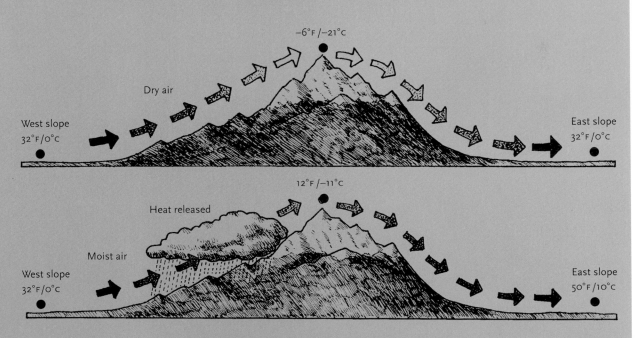

Opposite page: Chinook arch over Waterton Lakes National Park

	ELEVATION (M)	(FT)	MEAN JANUARY MINIMUM TEMPERATURE (°C)	(°F)	MEAN JULY MAXIMUM TEMPERATURE (°C)	(°F)	ANNUAL PRECIPITATION (MM)	(IN)	ANNUAL SNOWFALL (CM)	(IN)	MONTH WITH HIGHEST PRECIPITATION
Mackenzie, BC	690	2264	−16	4	22	71	655	26	326	128	December
Revelstoke, BC	450	1476	−8	17	25	78	946	37	425	167	December
Cranbrook, BC	939	3081	−12	11	26	78	383	15	140	55	June
Jasper, AB	1003	3291	−14	7	23	73	620	24	168	66	December
Lake Louise, AB	1524	5000	−21	−6	20	68	569	22	304	120	May
Waterton River, AB	1281	4203	−11	13	23	73	808	32	384	151	July
Sun Valley, ID	1774	5820	−18	0	28	83	441	17	307	121	January
Kalispell, MT	913	2995	−10	14	27	80	472	19	165	65	June
Missoula, MT	982	3223	−9	17	28	83	409	16	118	46	May
Yellowstone, WY	1902	6240	−12	10	27	80	380	15	180	71	June
Jackson, WY	1866	6123	−15	5	28	82	429	17	172	68	May
Vail, CO	2469	8100	−16	2	24	75	513	20	103	41	July
Denver, CO	1612	5290	−10	15	31	88	432	17	110	43	August
Park City, UT	2134	7000	−12	11	24	76	983	39	146	57	January
Taos, NM	2161	7090	−12	10	30	86	312	12	74	29	August

This deflection of the jet stream south has recently been shown to be the major factor warming Western Europe in winter. After the airflow brings cold air to central North America, it swings northward again, carrying warm, subtropical air from the Atlantic Ocean north to France and Britain. If the Rockies were not there, the jet stream would flow more or less straight out of the west, bringing air off the North Atlantic about 9°C (16°F) cooler than the southwesterly flow that Europe experiences.

SUMMER SUN, SUMMER MONSOONS

As the Aleutian Low drifts north with the sun in summer, its influence on western North America fades. The North Pacific High grows in intensity in summer and moves northwestward from southern California into the Pacific. It can block the flow of Pacific storms for weeks on end, bringing clear, hot weather to the Rockies, especially the western slopes. Summer is the driest season in many of the western valleys, but it is the wettest season in northern, eastern, and southern regions.

This difference is again the result of the Rocky Mountains themselves. In late spring and summer, a high-pressure system develops over the middle of the Great Plains, spinning clockwise, as all Northern Hemisphere highs do, and producing southwesterly winds on its western side. These winds bring warm, moist air from the Gulf of Mexico north to the eastern slopes of the Rockies. This humid air, lifted by the afternoon sun or by the mountains themselves, cools and releases its moisture in spectacular summer thunderstorms that can drop 5 or 10 percent of a site's annual rainfall in one hour. One such storm over Estes Park, Colorado, in July 1976 dropped 25 centimeters

Previous pages: Summer thunderstorms such as this one over Goat Peak, Montana, are common on the eastern slopes of the Rocky Mountains, since warm, humid air is cooled as it rises over the mountains.

(10 inches) of rain, sending a flash flood through Big Thompson Canyon that killed 139 people. Eastern Colorado and New Mexico, and to some extent eastern Utah and Wyoming, thus have dry winters and rather wet summers, a phenomenon known as the North American Monsoon. It is restricted to the eastern and southern edges of the Rockies, since the humid air loses all its moisture as it rises and cools over the mountains.

EXCEPTIONS TO THE RULES

I remember reading a guidebook that explained how to predict short-term local weather by noting the direction clouds are traveling and comparing that with the direction of winds at ground level. I was excited by this simple set of rules until I read the caveat at the end of the guide: "These rules do not apply in mountainous areas." Mountains complicate weather patterns in many ways—they block storms, redirect winds, and even turn temperature conventions topsy-turvy.

Inversions are one of the most common exceptions to weather rules in the mountains. When cold Arctic air spreads into the Rockies, it fills the valley bottoms, since it is denser and heavier than local air. If conditions are calm, the warmer local air lies over the cold air, and so temperatures on the mountaintops are considerably higher than temperatures in the valleys. These inversions can be quite stable in winter, since the lower layer of cold air cannot be warmed adequately while the ground is covered with snow and ice. The trapped cold air is easy to spot in urban areas, where smog forms a brown haze below the upper warm air. If the cold valley has a large open lake or river, a layer of low cloud forms in the valley bottom, while the mountain slopes above are bathed in winter sunshine.

Inversions can contribute to winterkill of trees on mountain slopes. If the temperature rises quickly, the trees lose moisture through transpiration but cannot replace it, since the water in the ground is still frozen. This phenomenon creates bands of red, dying trees at mid-elevations. Chinook winds can have a similar effect.

At the northern end of the Rockies, inversions have a long-term effect as well. Valley bottoms that are regularly filled with Arctic air, especially in the fall or early winter, have a permanent cover of willow, alder, and birch shrubs, since the growing season is too short for the spruce trees that are common on the mountain slopes above. Valleys farther south in the Rockies also have short growing seasons, though the effects are not as dramatic—the average period between last frost and first frost in Jackson Hole is only forty-five days.

5 On Top of the World

...mountains for David were made to see over,
stairs from the valleys and steps to the sun's retreats.
—EARLE BIRNEY, *DAVID*

On Top of the World

CHAPTER 5

ONE HOT JULY DAY, I left the Ponderosa Pine woodlands of the Bitterroot Valley and climbed a steep ridge to Trapper Peak, the highest point in the Bitterroot Range. I sweated up through the Lodgepole Pine and Subalpine Fir forests, drawn by the promise of the alpine ridge, its cool breezes and exhilarating views. Soon the forests opened to parklike stands of Whitebark Pine and Alpine Larch, then patches of snow and the tumbled boulders of the peak. A sea of granitic mountains filled the western skyline, green hills and golden grasslands to the east. This was the big picture.

It is not surprising that mountain peaks are often considered sacred places the world over. We usually view them from below, their summits bathed in the light of a pink dawn or golden sunset, their snows shining in the noonday sun. They beckon us upward, and when we are fortunate enough to stand on top of them, we see the world before us. Prairie people often joke that mountains get in the way of the scenery, but the view from their peaks is unlike any other vista, inviting big thoughts. As I rested against the rocks of Trapper Peak, I could imagine the rising magma that created this range. I could almost see the Sapphire Mountains sliding off that sea of magma to their present home in the east, leaving the Bitterroot Valley in their wake.

But although mountaintops may fulfill some of our spiritual needs, they are very difficult places to live. Only the hardiest of plants and animals can survive the almost never-ending chill winds to flourish in the short bursts of life-giving warmth. This is a place where that enduring life-form, the tree, struggles to survive. Life is small here, inconspicuous, but startlingly beautiful on close inspection. The alpine tundra is also the ecosystem that unites the Rocky Mountains. From Taos, New Mexico, to Toad River, British Columbia, the valleys change from desert to subarctic taiga, but the mountaintops are much the same. There are subtle differences, but the cushions of Moss

North

South

Krummholz line

Tree line

Forest
line

**FIGURE 5.1:
GENERALIZED
MOUNTAINTOP
SHOWING
DIVISIONS OF
TIMBERLINE**

Campion, the stunted fir and spruce, the bright sun, and the incessant wind
are familiar elements from one end of the range to the other.

ABOVE THE TREE LINE

Mountaintops are defined by timberline, a surprisingly abrupt transition from
forest to tundra. Viewed from a distance, most western mountain ranges
look as if they were painted with a broad brush stroke of dark green below
and a paler tint above, the two colors separated by a perfectly horizontal,
straight-line boundary. A closer view reveals quite a bit of fuzziness to the
line, but it is about as clear-cut as an ecological boundary can be. Timberline
can be thought of as three separate lines: the forest line, the upper limit of
continuous forest; tree line, the upper limit of upright trees; and krummholz
line, the upper limit of even the most stunted trees. *Krummholz* is the
German word for "twisted wood," and it refers to the gnarled mats of spruce,
fir, and pine found on mountaintops.

Above tree line, it is too cold for trees to grow, but bitterly cold winters
are not the reason—minimum temperatures on Rocky Mountain peaks are
nowhere near as low as those in the vast boreal forests of northern latitudes,
where trees can obviously flourish. In fact, midwinter temperatures on mountain peaks are not all that different from winter temperatures in the valleys,
especially when cold Arctic air flows into the valley bottoms. The true killing
cold is the cold of the short summer.

Overleaf: Alpine tundra at
timberline, Wilcox Pass

The mean annual temperature at tree line is always below freezing, and frosts can occur any day of the year. Not only is the growing season short, but it does not get warm enough most years for much plant growth. Analyses of tree lines around the world have shown that the most important factor limiting tree germination and growth is the average soil temperature during the growing season. If this temperature is below 6 or 7°C (43 to 45°F), it is difficult or impossible for trees to become established. Cold soil limits root growth, one of the critical components of plant establishment. Air temperature is also important, since it affects the growth rate of the plant above the ground. The average air temperature is about the same as average soil temperature, though the air is warmer than soil during the day and colder at night.

Because average temperatures decrease with increasing latitude, the elevation of tree line also decreases as you go north, roughly at the rate of 100 meters per 100 kilometers (or 500 feet per 100 miles). Tree line in Colorado is at 3 500 meters (11,500 feet) elevation; at the Canada–United States border, it lies at about 2 300 meters (7,500 feet); and at the northern end of the Rocky Mountains, it is only about 1 400 meters (4,500 feet).

The Work of Frost

Above tree line, in the treeless tundra landscape, you can often pick out curious patterns of rock and soil. These are nearly always the work of the almost daily freeze-thaw cycle that goes on in tundra soils. In some areas, there is almost no soil visible, just a sea of jumbled rocks. This is a fell-field, or *felsenmeer,* formed by the action of frost on the bedrock and loose rocks. Water often saturates the ground and fills the cracks in bedrock, especially during fall rains or spring snowmelt. When this water freezes, the ice expands, cracking boulders from bedrock and lifting loose rocks in the soil. The result is a surface of angular rocks that makes for difficult walking. Small areas of finer gravels and sands absorb water and, upon repeated freezing and thawing, churn to the surface, forming roughly circular patches surrounded by larger rocks that are

thrown farther by the frost action. On steeper slopes, these rock circles move downslope to form vertical lines of rock, separated by soil and plants.

On slopes with few or no rocks, the soil often develops horizontal wrinkles less than a meter (3 feet) apart. These are terracettes, formed in spring when the soil is saturated with snowmelt. In this condition, the soil flows slowly downhill, wrinkling like a rug. The flat parts of terracettes are often stabilized on tundra slopes by plants such as mountain-avens; the dark-green plants accentuate the pattern by forming long parallel lines across the hillside.

Orange Sunburst Lichen and other crustose lichens cover an alpine rock.

Life at the Top
When you stand on a rock-strewn peak above the krummholz line, the landscape can appear almost lifeless, but if you take a close look (easy to do if you are

lying down for a well-earned rest), life is all around you, and it is spectacular in its own way. Tiny plants hug the ground to avoid the drying, chilling wind; fat bumblebees buzz along at ground level; big spiders wait between the rocks, their webs quivering in the wind.

Lichens

The most widespread form of life on the highest peaks in the Rocky Mountains is lichens. These are fungi that have evolved into primitive but very successful farmers—they raise algae within their own bodies. The algae take the abundant sunshine and turn it into sugars that the fungi can use for their own survival. All the algae need are water and nutrients, and the fungi pull these directly out of the air around them. Lichens have no need of soil to grow in; they only need a firm structure to grow on, and rocks fit the bill perfectly. The dark gray of most peaks in the Rocky Mountains is not due to dark rocks but to blackish lichens covering the pale stones.

Among the lichens that grow on rocks, the most common are the crustose lichens, so-called because they appear to be a hard, flat crust on the rock surface. They grow in circular rosettes around the point where the first spore or fragment of lichen landed on the rock surface. These rosettes grow slowly but surely and can live to great ages. Rock surfaces can be dated by measuring the diameter of the largest rosette and comparing it with rosettes of known age—for example, those found on many old gravestones.

One lichen that stands out in the crowd is the Orange Sunburst Lichen, which forms bright orange patches on boulders and cliffs. This lichen requires sites with high concentrations of nitrogen and so grows only where there is a regular supply of bird droppings or mammal urine. It therefore marks favorite lookout sites of pikas, cliff nests of hawks, and song posts of horned larks. Orange Sunburst Lichen also seems to require high concentrations of magnesium, so grows on dolomite and basaltic rocks but does not thrive on limestone. Other lichens, such as the dark mats of Blistered Rock Tripe and Velcro Lichen, grow on rocks rich in quartz.

Watermelon snow

Not all alpine algae are found in lichens; some of them grow in the summer snowbanks. Snow algae are unicellular plants that grow profusely in the cold waters of melting snow. Hikers encounter these algal blooms as watermelon-pink stains on snowfields. A scoop of the snow reveals a slight watermelon fragrance as well, but don't use this snow as a base for an alpine smoothie—the algae cause diarrhea in some people when eaten.

The algae's red color comes from carotenoid pigments, the same type of pigments that color red peppers and carrots. These pigments act as a natural

sunscreen to protect the algae from the intense light on these high-altitude snowbanks. The tiny, spherical red cells are actually the resting stage—the apla-nospores—of the algae, though they are still actively photosynthesizing. They remain on the snowbanks through the summer, usually ending as a reddish dusting on the ground in early fall when the snow has completely melted. In winter they are covered by a thick blanket of snow, but as the warm sun of summer begins to melt the snow, sending water down to the soil, the

Red stains on summer snow-banks are caused by blooms of microscopic algae that produce a red pigment to protect themselves from the intense sunlight— a natural sunscreen.

aplanospores burst open, each one releasing a single cell with two whiplike tails. These cells swim upwards through the snow until they reach the zone just below the surface filled with blue, filtered light. Here the cells reproduce, then form the aplanospore resting stage. As the snow melts, these spores concentrate at the surface, the red of the snow deepening as the summer progresses.

Tundra flowers

Flowering plants on the alpine tundra hug the ground, tucked into cracks between boulders, forming cushions on exposed ridges. Almost all of them are perennials, since the alpine summers are far too short for an annual plant to germinate, grow leaves, produce flowers, and set seeds in the few weeks between killing frosts. Even on established perennials, flower bud development can take four years from the beginning of bud differentiation to the opening of the flower. Not surprisingly, 80 to 90 percent of an alpine plant's biomass is below ground in the root system, and roots can take decades to develop fully in the cold soils.

Each summer, alpine plants grow a tiny amount, produce flowers if they can, and store as much starch as they are able to produce in their roots, rhizomes, or bulbs. The starch is essential for flower development, which must begin as soon as possible in spring to ensure that seeds can be set before the end of summer. Flowers on these tiny plants are proportionately large—close to the size of flowers on their low-elevation relatives—so the investment in their production is huge.

Moss Campion grows relatively quickly for an alpine plant yet still takes twenty-five years to reach a cushion diameter of 18 centimeters (7 inches). Some plants take years to produce flowers. The Alpine Sunflower, also known as Old-Man-of-the-Mountain, spends several years amassing starch in a large taproot. When enough energy has been stored, it produces large yellow flowers— the largest in the alpine zone—sets seed, and dies. A mass flowering often takes place across the meadows, presumably the result of a good year for growth the previous summer.

The cost of producing flowers every year is too much for many alpine plants, and asexual reproduction is common. New plants are produced from underground rhizomes, runners, and bulbs. One of the most interesting examples of this process is the Alpine Bistort, which produces bulblets on its flower stalk, miniature plants that simply fall off the parent plant and roll on the ground to—hopefully—a good spot to put down roots.

Summer is a stressful time for alpine plants. Not only do they have to produce flowers and seeds in record time and store enough starch for the following spring, but alpine ridges are desertlike environments. Summer is a rather dry season in much of the high Rockies. Once the snows have melted

Found in rocky environments throughout the Northern Hemisphere, Mountain Sorrel gets its name from the same root as "sour," a tribute to the high vitamin c content of its round leaves.

Alpine Bistort

Overleaf: Alpine Sunflowers bloom high in the southern Rockies.

Alpine plants have relatively small leaves and stems, but their flowers are often just as large as those of their low-elevation counterparts. This phenomenon is seen here in the Limestone Columbine, a species found only in the Rocky Mountains from southern Alberta to Wyoming.

from the rocky ridges and the meltwaters have drained away, moisture is in short supply. In addition, the constant winds continually carry moisture away from exposed leaves. Cushion plants such as Moss Campion reduce this loss by lying flat on the ground, closely packed together, so that the leaves remain in that narrow belt above the soil where wind speed is significantly reduced. Many alpine plants cover their leaves with tiny hairs that protect the leaf surface from the wind, giving the leaves a grayish look. Stonecrops store water in succulent leaves and stems.

One day in July 2003, I drove through a grassy valley in northwestern Montana and into a cloud of grasshoppers. Hundreds of bodies exploded on my windshield for a few minutes, and then I was through and could stop and wipe off most of the mess.

Although memorable, my experience was nothing compared with the Rocky Mountain Locust outbreak of 1875. That summer a swarm of locusts 2 900 kilometers (1,800 miles) long and 177 kilometers (110 miles) wide, consisting of an estimated 10 billion individuals, devastated crops throughout the newly settled western plains. The United States Congress commissioned a report on the problem, but by the time it was completed there were no locusts to battle. A few local outbreaks were noted over the next twenty-five years, but after that, nothing—the Rocky Mountain Locust was extinct.

The Rocky Mountain Locust, like locusts around the world, looked and acted like a regular grasshopper at low population densities. But when it became locally crowded, hormonal changes turned the insects into larger, darker locusts more interested in flying and feeding than mating. Hordes flew out of the green valleys of the Rocky Mountains and onto the grassy plains, eating almost all the plant life in sight. Some of these locust clouds were blown high into the mountains to perish on glaciers in Montana and Wyoming. The best repository of the locusts is the Knife Point Glacier in the Wind River Range of Wyoming. Today this record of past outbreaks is surfacing as the glacier melts; some of the locust bodies recovered date to infestations in the early 1600s.

How could such an abundant insect become extinct so quickly? Biologists surmise that between outbreaks the Rocky Mountain Locust lived in relatively small numbers in Rocky Mountain valleys that were settled in the late 1800s and were radically altered by continuous farming or flooded by reservoirs. Several other species of grasshopper still thrive in the Rockies and some cause widespread damage to grain crops, but none have the devastating migratory habits of the Rocky Mountain Locust.

Plants with softer foliage take refuge in rock crevices. Alpine Avens is one of the most common members of this community from Montana south. Mountain Sorrel, Jacob's Ladder, and Parry's Primrose can also be found in the lee of large rocks.

Alpine invertebrates

Insects and other invertebrates are everywhere in the alpine tundra, even on the mountain snowbanks. Iceworms slither through melting snow like small, skinny earthworms, eating snow algae as they go. Springtails, tiny wingless insects with a bizarre single jumping appendage on their abdomen, abound on the edges of snowfields, creating dark-purple or golden-yellow patches that look like jiggling sawdust when viewed from human height. And in the rock crevices cooled by summer snow and ice live rock crawlers, or grylloblattids.

Rock crawlers are primitive, wingless relatives of crickets and cockroaches that prey on small insects and spiders. First found on Sulphur Mountain in Banff National Park in 1913, they form their own insect order—the same taxonomic level as flies or beetles—and are one of the most recent orders to be discovered. Like many high-mountain insects, rock crawlers have a specialized metabolism that allows them to function best when the temperature is close to freezing; they quickly die if held at room temperature. They were previously thought to be restricted to alpine rocks near tree line, but recent surveys have found them at all elevations in mountains, as long as their scree and talus habitat has crevices deep enough to allow them to retreat into a cool environment in midsummer.

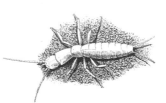

Rock crawler

Alpine flowers are pollinated by flies, bumblebees, and butterflies. The bumblebees stick close to the ground, tacking against the wind as they go from flower to flower. They take some time to warm up after a cold mountain night, shivering their shoulder muscles in the sun until their muscle temperature is high enough to take off. When they find a clump of flowers such as spreading phlox, they walk around on the plant, saving the energy needed for flight until they have to search out a new source of nectar.

Horsefly

Butterflies are conspicuous in most alpine meadows, their colorful wings flashing over the rocks and flowers. The resident alpine butterflies tend to be medium sized; smaller butterflies would have a hard time staying warm, and large-winged species would be tossed away in the constant wind. Many high-elevation species have darker patterns on their wings, especially at the bases, to absorb sunlight and heat into their bodies. And whereas most low-elevation species take only a year or much less to go through their life cycle, many alpine species take two years, overwintering as caterpillars the first year and as pupae during the second. When I was atop Trapper Peak, I noticed large numbers of Milbert's Tortoiseshells, strong-flying brown butterflies with fiery-orange bands on their wing edges. They were taking advantage of the July flower bloom, at a time when most lower-elevation flower sources have long since set seed. Although some butterflies move to mountaintops for food, many other insects are drawn to the peaks by another need—sex.

Tachinid

Next time you are resting on a mountain peak on a hot summer day, look around you. There are always insects there—more insects than you will find only a short distance downhill. They are there to meet others of their own kind—mountaintops are one of the most important singles bars in the insect world. This habit—called hilltopping by entomologists—presumably evolved because it is hard to find members of the opposite sex of the proper species when you are a tiny, inconspicuous fly or beetle. Some insects send out chemical attractants, and crickets and grasshoppers sing, but many species just fly uphill and keep going until they can't find any higher ground to fly to. Voilà—there is just the mate they're looking for, hovering beside the climbers' cairn on top of the mountain.

Sarcophagid

Horseflies are common hilltopping insects. In fact, male horseflies are almost impossible to find at lower elevations, where their female counterparts are busy biting animals to get the nutrition needed to form eggs, but are easily found on mountaintops. You can tell a male horsefly by taking a close look at his face—his eyes don't meet broadly on top of his head as female eyes do. And he won't try to bite.

Tachinid and sarcophagid flies are also abundant on mountaintops. Tachinids are the bristly parasitic flies that lay their eggs on caterpillars, allowing the larvae to hatch and consume the caterpillar from the inside. Sarcophagids look like striped houseflies. A few butterflies also look for mates on mountain peaks, notably the Anise Swallowtail and Western White.

Ladybird beetles come up to mountaintops to hibernate in large masses in rocky crevices. Bear biologists have discovered that grizzly bears search out these swarms in early autumn, to fatten up on the little red beetles.

Black Swift

Many insects end up on mountaintops accidentally. They are part of the aerial plankton, a vast, usually unseen movement of insects on the annual search to find new places to breed. Rising high into the air above their lowland habitats, they are caught by prevailing winds and carried into the mountains. If they are high enough, they make it through the passes and find new valleys in which to live. The unlucky ones are caught by downdrafts of cool air over mountain snowfields and crash-land onto the snow, where they quickly succumb to the chill. Birds take advantage of this bounty. Black swifts circle over peaks on hot summer days, feasting on windswept clouds of flying ants. For rosy-finches, the snowfields are a private refrigerator, providing a constant supply of insect food that simply has to be picked up every day.

Birds

Few birds make their homes above tree line. The only birds that normally stay there all year long are the ptarmigan. These small grouse feed on berries, seeds, leaves, and bugs in the summer, then survive the winter by nipping buds off the prostrate branches of dwarf willows. There are three species of ptarmigan—the Willow, Rock, and White-tailed. The first two are primarily Arctic species; the Rock Ptarmigan's range only barely reaches the northernmost tip of the Rocky Mountains, and the Willow Ptarmigan is found south to Jasper National Park, Alberta. The Rock Ptarmigan is found in grassy alpine tundra, while the Willow, as its name suggests, is found in shrubby subalpine habitats. The smallest of the three, the White-tailed Ptarmigan, is found through most of the Rockies.

All three molt into an all-white plumage in autumn. This plumage not only hides them from predators but provides extra insulation. Dark feathers are filled with pigment granules, whereas white feathers are hollow and do not transfer heat as readily, thus keeping in body heat. The birds further reduce heat loss in winter by spending most of the season beneath the snow, venturing out for only a few hours each day to feed.

In spring, ptarmigan molt back into their darker summer plumage, which allows them to blend in with their rocky surroundings. Male Willow Ptarmigan stop halfway through this molt in spring and court the females in a startling costume of dark head and neck and white body. By summer, though,

White-tailed Ptarmigans molt into a pure white plumage for winter, providing cryptic coloration against the snow as well as better insulation against the cold.

Opposite page: A Hoary Marmot snacks on a Cow Parsnip flower.

ptarmigan are all exactly the color and pattern of the lichen-covered rocks around them. I have sat down for lunch on a rock and only noticed fifteen minutes later that there were a dozen a few feet away!

Only a handful of songbirds spend their summers on the high peaks. Rosy-finches nest on rocky ridges near permanent snowfields. Like the ptarmigan, there are three species of rosy-finches in North America. The widespread Gray-crowned Rosy-Finch is found in the Rocky Mountains south to central Montana and all ranges to the west. The Black Rosy-Finch breeds in the more isolated ranges from southern Montana through Wyoming to northeastern Utah, and the Brown-capped Rosy-Finch breeds in the Rocky Mountains south of the Wyoming Basin. The latter two species, along with the Gunnison Sage-Grouse, are the only birds restricted to the Rocky Mountains. In winter they gather in flocks at lower elevations, feeding on weed seeds in open, windswept, gravelly habitats. Some Black and Gray-crowned rosy-finches move south in winter, so all three species can sometimes be found together from southern Montana to New Mexico at that time.

Another characteristic songbird of alpine tundra is the Horned Lark. As a family, larks evolved in Eurasia and Africa, where every open habitat has one or more lark species. The Horned Lark lives across northern Eurasia in tundra habitats, and it reached North America long ago via the Bering Strait. It is the only lark to have established a population in North America, where treeless habitats were open for the taking, and now almost every desert, prairie, beach,

A pika gathers food for its hay pile, a store of food for the long mountain winter.

and tundra habitat on the continent has its resident subspecies. Like all male larks, male Horned Larks sing their territorial songs from high in the air, then plummet to earth to a favorite stone perch. Since there are no trees or shrubs in their territory, larks nest on the ground, the tiny grass cup tucked in behind a rock or tussock for protection from the wind.

The American Pipit is also tied to the alpine tundra in summer. These birds, from another large Eurasian family, act a lot like larks but nest on steep slopes and usually feed in moister habitats, often along meltwater streams.

Small mammals

Perhaps because there are no trees to hide behind, small mammals are a very conspicuous part of the alpine environment. Marmots, the largest members of the squirrel family, are prominent in alpine habitats throughout the Rockies. In the northern ranges of the Rocky Mountains, the Hoary Marmot fills this niche; south of the Wyoming Basin, the Yellow-bellied Marmot replaces it at tree line. Throughout the Rockies, the Yellow-bellied Marmot is also a lower-tree-line species, found in sagebrush grasslands below the Ponderosa Pines and Douglas-firs.

Marmots live in families in burrow systems dug amid the alpine meadows. Young males are kicked out of the family after their first winter, so the families sharing burrows consist of an adult pair, their daughters from the previous year, and their new babies. The daughters occasionally mate and become pregnant but are so harassed by their mothers that they almost always abort their young. This odd family behavior is related to their winter survival strategy. Marmots spend the summer eating the lush green plant growth, adding 50 percent to their body weight in fat before retreating to their burrows in September for a long winter's sleep. Marmots are serious hibernators, lowering their body temperature to near that of the surrounding air and remaining in torpor until the following May. The young of the year have trouble accumulating enough fat to survive this deep sleep, so they keep their body temperature higher and curl up in the middle of the family group to stay warm. Families could not keep more than one set of young alive through the winter, hence juvenile pregnancies are discouraged.

Few animals symbolize the mountains as well as the Mountain Goat. Its long white fur, shiny black horns, and passion for barely accessible cliffs have made it an emblem of the western mountains. Mountain goats are not close relatives of the barnyard goat and are more technically termed goat-antelopes; their nearest kin are two species of Asian ungulates—the Serow and the Goral—which they left hundreds of thousands of years ago when they crossed the Bering land bridge and colonized North America. Another close relative is the chamois of the Alps. Mountain Goats are now found from the northern end of the Rocky Mountains to northern Wyoming. They were introduced into Colorado starting in 1948 and are now locally common there.

Mountain Goats are true mountaineers and are rarely seen away from the steep, rocky terrain that is their best defense against predators. Their hooves are widely cleft, with a soft pad between that gives them superb traction on the smallest of ledges, and their front legs are relatively close to their hind legs, allowing them to turn in very close quarters. Although their creamy white coats seem to stand out against dark rocks,

snow patches and pale rocks are common enough in the high mountains in summer to make goats hard to pick out from a distance. And in inaccessible terrain with few predators, camouflage is not an important strategy anyway.

Like their farm namesakes, male Mountain Goats are called billies, females are nannies, and their kids are, well, kids. Nannies and billies look very similar, both having dangerously sharp, curved black horns. Nannies' horns are curved more sharply at the top, though, whereas billies' horns curve more smoothly throughout their length. The nannies and kids often gather in groups, but aggression is common and mothers don't let yearlings and other young goats get too close to their kids.

The adult males lead solitary lives for most of the year. During the fall mating season, males battle each other by circling and jabbing with their horns, trying to prod the back ends of their opponents. Serious wounds are not unknown, and often the jousting animals fall from their rocky perches. Males roll in urine-soaked dust at this time of year, presumably making

themselves more attractive to the females.

Nannies rank highest in the social order, and the older nannies usually stake out the best winter range so that they can produce a healthy kid the following May or June. Eagles and cougars sometimes prey on the kids but have to be

lucky to avoid the nannies' sharp horns. Climbing falls and avalanches are probably the most common source of adult mortality. Like other herbivores, Mountain Goats cannot get all the necessary salts and minerals from their diet of grass and shrub twigs and so need to regularly go to mineral licks.

Marmots give a long, piercing whistle as you approach them—this is their "amber alert" predator warning call and gives them the nickname of "whistler." If a Golden Eagle flies over, they give series of shorter, more emphatic whistles to tell their family to get underground immediately.

Ground squirrels are similar in many ways to their larger cousins the marmots. Two species are common in the Rocky Mountains, the Columbian and

Golden-mantled ground squirrels. Like most members of the squirrel family, they are active during the day, and like the marmots they have loud chirping calls that draw attention to them. As their name suggests, they spend much of their time underground in burrows; they can spend up to nine months each year hibernating in their hidden homes. The Columbian Ground Squirrel is a meadow specialist, living in colonies in grassy flower meadows, whereas the Golden-mantled Ground Squirrel is usually seen in open forests. The Golden-mantled looks for all the world like a giant chipmunk but lacks the facial stripes of its much smaller relatives.

The other conspicuous small mammal of alpine slopes is the Rocky Mountain Pika. These are small relatives of rabbits and hares—they are often called rock rabbits—but lack the large hind feet, and their ears are barely visible. Pikas live in mountain rock slides next to meadows with abundant grass and flowers. They graze close to the rocks that are their protection from hawks and other predators, turning the grass near the rock slide into turf that looks like a golf green. But you also see them dashing across the slopes to clumps of high-stalked flowers, nipping them off, and carrying them back home stuffed in their mouths. In these long-distance forays, they are gathering food for winter—since they don't hibernate—which they store in "hay piles" hidden among the rocks. Pikas give a loud *enk!* call when potential danger approaches.

Two other small mammals are rarely seen, but their workings are often evident on the tundra. Heather voles scurry in runways hidden by low vegetation, but their winter nests—softball-sized clumps of dried grass—are often seen on the ground after the snow melts. Nearby you will see a neat pile of mouse droppings, the vole's winter outhouse. If you see a molehill in the Rockies, it is not the work of a mole, but of a pocket gopher. These rodents are like vegetarian moles, living in underground burrows from which they eat the roots of plants. In summer pocket gophers pile the earth from their diggings at the burrow entrance; in winter they pack the soil into snow tunnels dug on the surface of the ground. After the snow melts, these filled tunnels appear as raised, miniature highways of earth running through the meadows.

Mountaintop trees

Krummholz forms where the growing season is long enough to permit tree germination but the wind still kills back exposed twigs. Not only the cold winds of winter kill the twigs; often the warm winds of spring dry out the twigs while the roots are locked in frozen ground, unable to replace the lost moisture. The branches near the ground are protected by the snowpack, but the snow rarely lies very deep on mountaintops, since it is always being blown off by the wind. Any twig poking up through the snow is killed back, producing a green mat of low branches with scattered upright red-brown

Opposite page: Subalpine Firs are common members of the krummholz zone throughout the Rocky Mountains.

Pocket gopher

Golden Alpine Larches at tree line in Banff National Park, Alberta

twigs, the dead new growth from the previous summer. In slightly more protected areas, the tree can manage to establish a vertical trunk, but the only branches that survive are those on the lee side of the trunk, protected by the snow that crusts downwind of even the smallest trunk. This phenomenon produces one-sided, or flagged, trees.

Krummholz mats also protect themselves, since the twigs on the lee side don't suffer the same amount of wind damage, while those on the windward

side are slowly killed back. The snowpack presses branches to the soil, where new roots can form through a process called layering. Therefore the tree can literally move along the ridge, dying back on the windward side and growing through layering on the lee side.

If any tree manages to become established, it can protect others that germinate, producing tree islands. Large trees not only protect germinating trees from the wind but also provide shade from the intense sun, which actually

Overleaf: This ancient Limber Pine has survived several centuries of winters at tree line in Rocky Mountain National Park, Colorado.

inhibits photosynthesis in some species. Large trees also slow the loss of heat during clear summer nights, creating pockets of relatively warm air that allow growth to continue. Deep snowdrifts form behind tree islands in winter, providing an extra down blanket for young trees. Large drifts often last so long into summer that trees cannot germinate on their footprint except at the edges. A ring of young trees is thus formed and grows into a circle of mature trees known as a tree atoll.

Ribbon forests are another common pattern of tree growth in subalpine meadows. These forests apparently begin on parallel low ridges related to underlying rocks. Because these ridges become snow free earliest, tree germination is enhanced along their spines. As the line of trees grows higher, the snowdrift on their lee side becomes deeper and suppresses further spread of the forest, resulting in parallel lines of mature trees strung across the high ridges.

Few species of trees can survive the rigors of the subalpine environment, where their main competition is not other trees but the wind and cold. Two

The famed duo of Rocky Mountain explorers, Meriwether Lewis and William Clark, both have bird species named in their honor. Both birds are unique in their own way—the Lewis's Woodpecker is a woodpecker that looks and acts a lot like a crow, whereas the Clark's Nutcracker is essentially a crow that looks and often acts like a woodpecker.

Like its crow and jay cousins, the Clark's Nutcracker has a springtime habit of robbing other birds' nests to feed its own young, and like the Gray Jay, it can become quite a panhandler for food, especially in mountain parks. But in late summer and early fall, the Clark's Nutcracker specializes in eating large pine seeds, which it finds in the cones of Ponderosa, Limber, and Whitebark pines. Its long-term relationship—biologists call it coevolution—with Whitebark Pine is remarkable.

The Whitebark Pine is not an ordinary pine. Most pines have thick cones armed with nasty spines or a heavy coating of pitch to deter squirrels and other animals from eating the seeds, which are usually small with large wings so that they can fly far on the fall winds. Whitebark cones, in contrast, have no spines or heavy pitch and look like dark-purple flowers on the ends of branches. The seeds are very large and wingless, and the cones do not open fully to release the seeds when mature—if the cones did release the seeds, they would just fall to the ground and grow up competing with the parent tree. Instead, Whitebark Pines rely almost entirely on Clark's Nutcrackers to open their cones and gather, disperse, and plant their seeds.

The nutcrackers have a throat pouch with space to store up to a hundred pine seeds. When it is full, the birds fly off to a suitable place to cache the seeds for winter food, usually a windswept southern exposure with sandy soil, allowing the birds easy access all winter to their supply of seeds. It is no coincidence that this habitat is also ideal for Whitebark Pines. The birds land on the ground and bury the seeds in groups of five or six; then they take off and harvest more. An adult nutcracker will cache 30,000 to 100,000 seeds in this manner each fall.

How do they find them again? Studies have shown that Clark's Nutcrackers have remarkable spatial memories and outperform zoology graduate students time and time again in tests of finding buried seeds. They don't need to find all 30,000 or so seeds to survive, of course, and come summer the hillsides are dotted with clusters of tiny pine seedlings, a half-dozen or so in each group, depending on how many seeds the nutcracker planted. Some of these clusters survive to grow into the many-trunked form that is typical of Whitebark Pine.

As the number of mature Whitebark Pines dwindles because of blister rust and pine beetle infestations, there is growing concern about the future of both the pines and their nutcracker companions.

of the common subalpine forest species are often present at Rocky Mountain tree lines—Engelmann Spruce and Subalpine Fir—but some trees are mountaintop specialists.

The tree growing at the highest elevations of the central Rockies—from the Bitterroots and Salmon River Mountains to Banff National Park—is the Alpine Larch. Like all larches, this species has the unusual habit of dropping its needles in winter—it is a deciduous conifer. In summer you can pick out Alpine Larches from a great distance, their grass-green foliage standing out against the dark green of the firs and spruce below. But it is in autumn that they truly shine, splashing the peaks with bright gold against the first snows of September and October. The lack of needles in winter gives the Alpine Larch a tremendous advantage at tree line, where the prime enemy is the winter wind, which kills back the twigs of other tree species. These trees not only survive at tree line but seem to prefer the cold, northern exposures. They germinate well in rocky, infertile soils, do not tolerate shade, and grow only slowly, so are quickly overwhelmed by other species below timberline.

Alpine Larch twig

The other champions of the tree line are a trio of five-needled pines: the Whitebark, Limber, and Bristlecone pines. Whitebark and Bristlecone are upper-tree-line specialists in the northern and southern Rockies, respectively; the Limber Pine is found at the lower tree line, but in Colorado grows at the upper tree line as well. These are slow-growing, gnarled trees on mountaintops, but Whitebark and Limber pines can be good-sized trees in subalpine forests. Like most pines, they prefer full sun; Whitebark Pine takes the south side of mountain ridges where Alpine Larch is on the north side. These pines can grow to great ages; one Bristlecone Pine at 3 350 meters (11,000 feet) near Fairplay, Colorado, is more than 2,435 years old.

Whitebark Pine

Serious threats endanger the trees' continued survival, however. As I climbed through tree line on Trapper Peak, the trail wound up through a ghost forest of dead Whitebark Pines. During a series of warm, dry years, Mountain Pine Beetle epidemics spread upslope from Lodgepole Pine forests and killed most of the Whitebark Pines in Montana during the drought of the late 1920s and early 1930s. The stage has been set for a replay of this event, as vast areas of Lodgepole Pine have become infected. Mountain Pine Beetles also kill Limber and Bristlecone pines.

A more insidious threat is that of White Pine Blister Rust, a fungus accidentally introduced from Eurasia to Vancouver, British Columbia, in 1910. This fungus, like most rusts, has two hosts: five-needled white pines and shrubs in the genus *Ribes*—currants and gooseberries. It first infected Western White Pines but by 1960 had spread through most of the range of Whitebark Pine, and by the mid-1990s, 90 percent of the Whitebark Pines in northern Idaho and Montana had been killed. The fungus also affects Limber Pines and recently has been found on Bristlecone Pines as far south as the Sangre de Cristo Mountains in southern Colorado.

SUBALPINE MEADOWS

Between the krummholz line and the forest line is an in-between world of subalpine meadows, where groups of tall trees stand amid carpets of flowers, where mats of prostrate trees huddle beneath the wind and snow. Alpine and forest species mix here in a diverse and highly picturesque ecosystem. Subalpine meadows are formed by a number of forces—fire, snow, and history.

Hikers on mountain ridges are well aware of one of the most exciting and dangerous of natural events—high-elevation thunderstorms. I have huddled through such storms, seeking out the lowest hollow, hiding from the hail, and shuddering with every peal of thunder. Lightning strikes cause hundreds of forest fires each year, most of them small and quickly doused by another rainstorm. Others are larger, racing upslope until they run out of fuel at timberline. At high elevations, the forest can take centuries to reclaim areas lost to fire. A forest of silver snags stands for decades, then slowly becomes a meadow as the snags fall. Germination of replacement trees is extremely rare and growth is slow, depending on not just one good summer but perhaps a string of two or three to allow young trees to become established. And even then it might take a Subalpine Fir more than fifty years to reach a height of 2 meters (6 feet). Fire-carved meadows are thus temporary, lasting a century or two, but by then another fire has cut out a meadow nearby, so the subalpine meadow mosaic is permanent.

In mountain ranges with heavy snowfall, such as the Cariboos, Selkirks, and Monashees of British Columbia, high-elevation fires are much less common, and most subalpine meadows are sites where snowfall accumulates more deeply during the winter and stays longer in summer. These are often in natural bowls where cold air ponds, delaying melt until July or even August. By then it is too late for trees to germinate and become cold hardy for the first frosts, and the meadow fills with sedges, heathers, and huckleberries.

North of the Peace River in British Columbia, the subalpine zone begins to change dramatically in character. Above the last spruce trees is a zone of high willow and alder that extends up the mountainsides, gradually becoming shorter until they are knee-high krummholz themselves. The northern valleys often have two cold tree lines (as opposed to one upper, cold tree line and another lower, hot/dry tree line)—one high up on the mountainsides and the other just above the valley bottom. Like the snow bowls previously mentioned, this second, lower tree line is due to the ponding of cold air that brings early killing frosts to the valley. The valleys are therefore subalpine in character, with high willow and birch at low elevations, then a zone of White Spruce at middle elevations, and another willow zone above that before the open tundra is reached.

Some alpine meadows are artifacts of history. During the Little Ice Age, starting about AD 1650, tree lines throughout the world were depressed by 100 meters (300 feet) or more. Since the world's climate began warming again more than a century ago, forests have been slowly moving uphill, reclaiming lost ground. This advance does not happen in a straight, horizontal line but snakes up snow-free ridges or along patches of more fertile soil, encircling meadows that are now below tree line.

Flower Blooms

In the short mountain summer, subalpine meadows fill with flowers, all rushing to bloom and set seed before the late-August frosts. The flowers tend to bloom in two distinct waves, one during and immediately following snowmelt, and the other two or three weeks later, once the soil has dried. The showiest member of the first wave is the yellow Glacier Lily, which forms spectacular golden carpets on meadows throughout the Rockies in early summer. The small white flowers of the Spring Beauty can be quite

Overleaf: A female Rufous Hummingbird incubates her eggs in a walnut-sized nest decorated with lichens.

noticeable through sheer numbers at this time as well. From Montana north, the early-summer meadows are often filled with the large creamy flowers of Western Anemone, which turn into moplike seed heads later in the summer. Globeflowers have blooms similar to those of the anemones but grow in moister situations, often next to the shiny yellow flowers of Snow Buttercups. The leaves of all three species, like the leaves of many of their relatives in the buttercup family, contain ranunculin. This is an innocuous chemical itself, but it readily hydrolyzes to form an extremely irritating oil, protoanemonin. This chemical blisters the tongue and throat if eaten, an obvious deterrent to grazing animals. Plants in the buttercup family have long been used in folk medicine to raise hot blisters when applied as poultices.

As the first flowers are setting seed in mid-July, a second, more colorful bloom wave spreads across the subalpine meadows. Blue lupines, larkspur, and monkshood; red paintbrush; pink daisies and primroses; yellow cinque-foils, sunflowers, and arnica—all add a rainbow palette to the high-mountain summer. Whereas the earlier white flowers of the first bloom wave were pollinated mainly by flies, these colorful flowers also attract butterflies and hummingbirds, drawing both up from their forest breeding grounds to get their sugar fix in the mountain meadows.

Birds of the Mountain Meadows

The open, shrubby habitats of the subalpine are ideal for a number of sparrows. White-crowned Sparrows are common in tree line willows throughout the Rocky Mountains, whereas Fox Sparrows find the thick skirts of the timberline conifers ideal. The Brewer's Sparrow has two distinct subspecies, one found in the arid sagebrush grasslands in the valleys and plains, the other in the tree line krummholz of the Canadian Rockies. These birds, perhaps the plainest members of a plain family, have glorious canarylike songs of trills and buzzes. Some scientists consider the two subspecies separate species, pointing out the radically different habitats they use and the pitch of their songs. One expert reported that the song of the timberline race "sounds like the sagebrush race on helium." Golden-crowned Sparrows sing their mournful whistled song from high willows in the northern Rockies, whereas American Tree Sparrows are really a subarctic species that breeds in mountain thickets south to the northernmost peaks of the Rocky Mountains.

By the time the subalpine flower meadows are in full bloom in late July, adult hummingbirds are moving south in large numbers. They need to refuel regularly, and many of the subalpine flowers, especially columbine and paint-brush, provide high volumes of nectar—high-octane fuel for these buzz bombs of the bird world. So the first step in hummingbird migration is not to fly south but to fly up—up to the nearest alpine ridge and follow the wildflower

GOLDEN EAGLE MIGRATION

On March 20, 1992, biologists Peter Sherrington and Des Allen counted 100 Golden Eagles migrating northwest near Mount Lorette in the Kananaskis Valley, Alberta. Two days later, Sherrington saw 250 Golden Eagles flying over the same site in one afternoon. Until then, it was thought that Golden Eagles did not migrate in large numbers; most birds seen passing the few North American raptor watch sites were smaller hawks. The 1992 sightings prompted Alberta naturalists to set up regular raptor watches at Mount Lorette and other sites in the Alberta Rockies. These counts reveal a major migration route of Golden Eagles going north in spring and south in the fall; each season about four thousand are seen making the trip.

The existence and extent of the route has since been confirmed and elaborated by satellite telemetry of eagles breeding in central Alaska. The Golden Eagles are flying between their breeding sites in Alaska and Yukon and their wintering grounds in the southern Rockies and beyond—some go as far as northern Mexico. The dependable wind currents along the northwest-trending ridges of the Rocky Mountains provide a highway for the eagles. The movements peak in Alberta from mid-March to early April and again in late September and October. Large numbers can be seen south of Alberta as well; the Bridger Mountains of Montana have proved to be another hot spot for watching Golden Eagle migration in fall.

bloom south. An old wives' tale has it that hummingbirds migrate south on the backs of geese, but that story has two fatal flaws. One is that hummingbirds migrate before the geese. Even the young have left by early September, whereas geese don't migrate through the Rocky Mountains until early October. Another problem is that geese migrate to the central and southern United States, settling in for winter well north of the winter home of the hummingbirds in the western Sierra Madre of Mexico.

The bird life of the high-mountain meadows really comes into its own in late summer and early fall, when many species use the ridges as highways

south to wintering ranges in Central America. Most migrant birds avoid mountain ridges during spring migration if they can, since the snow-covered slopes offer no food, and a change in the weather could prove fatal. In August and September, however, the mountain winds provide reliable lift and the abundant berries in the open woodlands provide the needed fuel for migrants. Flocks of American Robins go by, joined by smaller numbers of Northern Flickers and more secretive thrushes.

One bird family that really takes advantage of mountain ridge migration is the hawks and eagles. These birds glory in the masses of air rising over the Rockies, carried by the prevailing winds. Some, like the Sharp-shinned Hawks and Merlins, hunt the migrating songbirds on their way south. Next time you are on a sunny mountain ridge in September, look up—you'll be surprised how many hawks go by.

MOUNTAIN SHEEP

One of the most exciting wildlife adventures I had as a boy occurred while I was stalking a small group of Bighorn Sheep with my brothers and my father. We were crawling along on all fours at the top of a cliff, with a steep slope above us and a creek far below. As we crested a small ridge, we could see the three rams below us. But before my father could get his camera ready, we heard a thundering from the slope behind us. Turning around, we saw another ram charging toward us, head down. All I could think of was getting knocked off the cliff by a large set of horns. We all stood up together and the ram, perhaps suddenly realizing we were two-legged humans instead of four-legged sheep, skidded to a halt only a few feet away. My father managed to get one picture, but unfortunately he was still shaking with excitement when he pressed the shutter.

My fascination with wild sheep has remained, and I am always happy to see these magnificent animals while hiking in the mountains. There are two species of mountain sheep in the Rockies: the Bighorn Sheep throughout most of the range north to the Peace River, and the Thinhorn Sheep north of the Peace River. Even without the range difference, they are easily distinguished. The Bighorns are a brownish color and the rams have massive, tightly curled horns, whereas the Thinhorns are patterned in blackish-brown and white and the rams have thinner horns that flare out from their heads.

Mountain sheep are grazing animals and need access to grasslands to survive. Like Mountain Goats, they also require rugged escape terrain nearby. Sheep are typically found in small herds, the adult rams forming bachelor herds separate from the ewes and younger animals for most of the year. In fall the rams join the ewes for the rutting season. The rams battle regularly for position in the herd by showing off the size of their horns to other rams; if that fails to impress the other ram, they will charge at each other and crash their horns together in a literally stunning collision. The dominant male guards females that are ready to mate and makes most of the mating attempts, but younger males regularly sneak in and mate when they can.

The following spring, the rams retreat to higher-elevation meadows to take advantage of rich summer grazing, while the ewes find suitable ledges on steep cliffs to give birth to their lambs in safety. By summer the ewes have re-formed their flocks and gradually move upslope as well if local conditions allow it.

Bighorn Sheep were quite common when the Rockies were first settled by white immigrants in the 1800s. Overhunting quickly reduced numbers, and by 1950 many herds had vanished altogether. Since that time, wildlife managers have worked hard to bolster the sizes of existing herds and to reintroduce the species to sites where they had been eliminated.

Healthy populations are now found throughout the Rocky Mountains except at low-elevation sites where grassland habitats and migration corridors have been irrevocably altered by development.

The most recent serious threat to Bighorn Sheep populations has been contact with domestic sheep. Domestic sheep carry several diseases and parasites for which wild sheep have little or no resistance. In particular, pneumonia caused by *Pasteurella* bacteria has caused dramatic population declines in many herds, and it often takes many years for the numbers to recover.

. . . David spotted
Bighorns across the moraine and
*   sent them leaping*
With yodels the ramparts redoubled
*   and rolled to the peaks*
And the peaks to the sun . . .
        —Earle Birney, *David*

Left: Bighorn Sheep

6 High Forests

High Forests

CHAPTER 6

THE SOUL OF THE ROCKY MOUNTAINS may lie in the rock and ice of the high peaks, but the heart of the range is in the subalpine forests of dark-green fir, spruce, and pine that cloak its mountain slopes. These are the forests we escape to from the busy world below. We hike through them in summer with the warmth of the July sun at our backs, the flutelike song of the Hermit Thrush slipping through the trees and the scolding chatter of squirrels sounding in the spruce. Too few of us walk or ski through them in the dead of winter, when the forest seems to be fast asleep under a bright blanket of snow. And there is surely no better aromatherapy session than a stroll through a forest of Subalpine Fir on a warm spring day.

Subalpine forests in the Rocky Mountains are a mosaic of old and young forests. Mature subalpine forests are dominated by two species of trees from one end of the Rockies to the other—Engelmann Spruce and Subalpine Fir. Two other species, Lodgepole Pine and Trembling Aspen, predominate in younger forests growing in after fires or other disturbances. At the southern end of the Rocky Mountains, subalpine forests are found above 2 835 meters (9,300 feet) elevation. Like tree line, this boundary descends as you go north, and subalpine forests reach the valley bottoms at the northern end of the range.

The subalpine forests of the Rockies are similar to the vast boreal forests of northern Canada and Alaska, and in fact the forests at the northern end of the Rockies blend into the taiga, or boreal forests, of northern British Columbia. But the two types of forest differ in several important ways. The winters in the mountain forests, while cold, are not nearly as cold as those in the boreal forest, where temperatures regularly drop to −40°C (−40°F), a chill rarely if ever encountered through most of the Rocky Mountains. But summer days are long and hot in the boreal forest, and summer nights are short and warm, so plants and animals can grow quickly at that time. In contrast, summer days in the mountains are relatively short and rarely more than

While checking spruce cones, you may notice that many of the brown, conelike structures on the spruce twigs are not cones at all. If you look closely, you will see that the scales are dried, swollen needles. These are galls—old homes of the Cooley Spruce Gall Aphid. This effect of the aphids superbly illustrates the fact that cones themselves evolved from simpler structures at branch tips.

If you break a gall apart, you will see small chambers at the base of each needle, each of which held several aphids when the gall was fresh. These aphids started as parthenogenetic eggs—unfertilized but viable, and all female—laid on the soft new twig. The young aphids suck plant juices from the stem, exuding chemicals that stimulate the growth of the gall around them. They later mature into winged adults that fly off to found a new generation of woolly aphids on Douglas-fir trees. This generation does not produce galls. The cycle is complete when the progeny of those aphids return to the spruce forests. Cooley Spruce Gall Aphids are therefore found only in mountain forests where Douglas-firs are growing nearby. Other species form galls in areas that lack Douglas-fir, but they either stick to spruce throughout their life cycles or alternate with larch or pine hosts.

Another infection that affects Engelmann Spruce is Spruce Broom Rust. This fungus produces a tangle of small branches on the spruce tree—hence the name broom. The stunted needles on the branchlets are bright gold instead of green and are shed in the fall. When the rust matures, a strong, musky smell fills the forest and flecks of orange spores cover the needles. Most rusts alternate between two unrelated hosts; the spores of Spruce Broom Rust waft through the forest, infecting its other host, Kinnikinnick.

warm, and summer nights can be downright cold. Mountain life must adapt to these fluctuating temperatures throughout the year.

Although only four species of trees dominate subalpine forests, the smaller plants are much more diverse and can tell you a lot about local conditions. Drier sites throughout much of the Rockies are covered by Grouseberry, a small relative of blueberries and huckleberries. Its pale green stems, tiny leaves, and purple-red berries make it easy to identify; the berries are very tasty but so small that it would take hours to pick enough for a pie. The Black Huckleberry is larger and has much bigger berries; if you buy a huckleberry ice-cream cone from a roadside stand, this is the species you are licking. The delicate runners of Trailing Raspberry indicate moist, nitrogen-rich sites, whereas the small dogwood flowers and red berries of the Bunchberry cover areas of nitrogen-poor soil.

FORESTS OF SPRUCE AND FIR

Engelmann Spruce

Both boreal and mountain forests are dominated by spruce, fir, and pine species. Engelmann Spruce is the common subalpine spruce throughout the Rockies, though from Montana north it shows increasing signs of hybridization with White Spruce, its boreal forest equivalent. Engelmann Spruce is often seen in krummholz form at tree line but, especially in the northern Rockies, can also grow to huge size in river bottoms. It can be a pioneer species after a fire, alone or with Lodgepole Pine, but young spruce are common in the understory of many Lodgepole Pine forests, suggesting that on dry sites it germinates best given some shade. In most sites it grows together with Subalpine Fir, but the fir is always a shade-germinating species and so gradually replaces spruce as the older trees fall.

Engelmann Spruce is easy to recognize from a distance by its blue-gray needles, small, hanging cones, and long lower branches covered with drooping, pendant branchlets, which give the tree an untidy appearance. At closer range, its bark is covered with large flakes, and its needles are painfully sharp if you try to grasp a branch to steady yourself on the trail. You can separate the two closely related spruce species with care by looking at their cones: White Spruce has stiff, rounder, smooth-edged cone scales, whereas those on Engelmann Spruce are papery, wavy-edged, and more pointed.

Spruce Beetles can cause widespread mortality in Engelmann Spruce forests. Like Mountain Pine Beetles, these insects attack mature, live trees, and the infestation can spread over large areas if climatic conditions are right. A small infestation in the northern end of the Cariboo Mountains was clear-cut between 1980 and 1986 to control the beetles, but as usual, harvesting did little to control the outbreak. Eventually a series of small cutblocks had merged into a monstrous clear-cut about 50 000 hectares (125,000 acres) in size, the largest clear-cut in the world. Spruce Beetle outbreaks are a natural component of the environment here—a fur trader had noted a large outbreak in the same area in 1836. Many of the trees affected in the 1980s were probably given a boost of sunlight and growth as the mature trees around them died off 150 years before.

Young trees are not the only organisms that benefit from Spruce Beetle epidemics. The American Three-toed Woodpecker is a spruce specialist, flaking the bark off spruce trunks in a never-ending search for tiny bark beetles. When beetle numbers reach epidemic proportions in an area, these woodpeckers fly in from miles around to take advantage of the feast. As you walk through one of these patches, there is a constant tapping sound from all the feeding woodpeckers, and the normally gray trunks of the trees appear reddish-brown, since the woodpeckers have flaked off all the old bark. The woodpeckers cannot control the beetle populations once an infestation reaches epidemic levels, but they probably help keep beetle numbers low in most areas.

A male American Three-toed Woodpecker at its nest hole in a spruce trunk

Subalpine Fir

The other important tree species in mature subalpine forests is the Subalpine Fir. Its symmetrical, spirelike form makes it easy to identify, even from the fast lane of a highway. At slower speeds on mountain trails, you will see the upright, purplish cones—looking somewhat like candles on a Christmas

My close encounter with Caribou came on an end-of-summer day on Tonquin Ridge in Mount Robson Provincial Park, British Columbia. I was resting beside a snowfield when I saw a half-dozen Caribou on the rocks a few hundred meters away. They began trotting in my direction, and eventually the biggest male passed so close that I was spattered by the snow flying from his large hooves. These elegant members of the deer family are symbols of the North; their other name is reindeer, evoking images of the North Pole. They occur south to Banff in the main range of the Rocky Mountains and into the northern tip of Idaho in the Selkirk Mountains.

Caribou are the only deer in which both males and females bear antlers. They have unusually large, round hooves—a friend of mine describes them as "small frying pans." These hooves have a dual purpose, acting as snowshoes when the animals are walking across the deep late-winter and spring snowpacks and serving as snow shovels when the Caribou are searching for food on the ground.

But the feature that sets Caribou apart from all their deer cousins is their main diet—lichens. Caribou forage on alpine tundra for ground lichens (such as reindeer lichen, or reindeer "moss," as it is often called) in the summer, then migrate into old-growth subalpine forests during the winter to feed on horsehair lichens hanging from the trees. It is the abundance and distribution of the latter food that is most critical to the Caribou. As high-elevation logging increases throughout the mountains, Caribou winter range is being degraded at an alarming rate. Increasing backcountry recreation, especially the use of snowmobiles, may also be affecting Caribou populations, not only through direct harassment, but also through indirect effects such as the easy access into high-elevation forests that hardened snowmobile trails provide for Wolves.

The other threat to Caribou comes indirectly from their cousin, the Moose. Moose populations increased dramatically over the past century, in part because of the logging that has created the shrub habitat they prefer. At the same time, Wolf populations have been allowed to increase back to their natural levels, fuelled in part by increasing prey in the form of Moose. As the availability of Caribou winter food decreases and Caribou populations decline, Wolf populations are increasing as the Moose also increase. Since Wolves feed on Caribou whenever they find them, the Moose population is keeping Wolf numbers at a level that can be catastrophic for the declining Caribou.

tree—that are typical of the true firs, as well as the smooth, gray bark. The needles on most twigs are arranged in brush-cut fashion—closely bunched and turned upwards. Some Engelmann Spruce twigs can look somewhat like this, but remember that spruce needles are sharp to the touch, whereas fir needles are smooth and blunt. This brush-cut form has a distinct function. The dense cluster of needles reduces wind flow around them, creating a warmer microclimate during cold mountain nights, and reduces water loss during winter. And the vertical stance of the needles reduces the intense direct sunlight they receive during the day—intensity that inhibits photosynthesis instead of promoting it.

Hair Lichens

Subalpine Fir and Engelmann Spruce forests are usually draped in hair lichens—festoons of cream and dark-brown strands of hairlike material hanging from the trees. These lichens do not harm the trees; they only use them as a support to get up into the moist air currents, which bring them water and nutrients, and to the light, which allows them to photosynthesize.

Horsehair lichens are important winter food for Caribou.

There are two main types of hair lichens—the cream-colored Witch's Hair Lichen and the dark-brown horsehair lichens. Both are indicators of old forests, and horsehair lichens are important winter food for Caribou. Hair lichens can be tremendously abundant, with up to 3 300 kilograms of lichen per hectare (2,900 pounds per acre). Witch's Hair tends to grow lower on the tree, whereas horsehair lichens grow mainly on the upper half of trees. Lichens need to be wet to actively grow; horsehair lichens do this mainly in the spring when the air is moist from melting snow, and Witch's Hair is more active during summer rains. Hair lichens break off and disperse on the high- mountain winds; snowfields can look like barber shop floors over long distances from the nearest lichen source.

Beargrass, a member of the lily family, grows for years before sending up a spectacular flower stalk. The grasslike clump of leaves then dies.

Owls of the Subalpine

The Boreal Owl is a locally common predator in Rocky Mountain subalpine forests. This small owl, only the size of an extra-large coffee cup, specializes in eating voles—short-tailed mice related to lemmings. Boreal Owls are sit-and-wait predators; they perch low in a tree and wait for ten or twenty minutes, listening intently for the sound of a vole scampering along its runway just below the surface of the snow. They have very large heads relative to their body size, and those heads are all ears. Boreal Owl ears are also asymmetrical; the left and right ears are different sizes and shapes, and one points up and the other points down. This asymmetry allows the owls to accurately pinpoint the direction of any sound—they could catch mice in complete darkness if they had to. Boreal Owls nest in large woodpecker holes, an increasingly rare commodity in high forests and one that undoubtedly limits their distribution and numbers in the Rocky Mountains.

The Great Gray Owl eats voles and pocket gophers. This is the biggest owl in North America based on weight. It has a face the size of a dinner plate, an indication of its hearing expertise, since the round faces of owls are their external ears. It is amazing to watch a Great Gray Owl peering intently at a meadow covered with 50 centimeters (2 feet) of snow, then flying out over the meadow, plunging through the snow head first, and emerging with a vole or pocket gopher.

FORESTS OF FIRE

I drove into Glacier National Park, Montana, on a hot afternoon in late July 2003. As I pulled up to the ticket kiosk, I could see a mushroom cloud on the north horizon that could only be a major forest fire. The next morning the MacDonald Valley was thick with smoke, and I only escaped it by crossing Logan Pass and the Continental Divide. Two days later park officials evacuated the west side of the park as fires consumed a large part of the

Overleaf: The large feathered disks that form the face of Great Gray Owls act as very sensitive sound gathering devices, allowing them to detect mice under deep snow.

In early July 1974, I was hiking near the Continental Divide in Mount Robson Provincial Park, British Columbia, when I heard a remarkable bird song, a song I had never heard before, although I had been seriously birding for ten years. It was loud and canarylike, seemingly out of place in the spruce forests around Yellowhead Lake. I finally tracked down the singer, a beautiful pink bird atop an Engelmann Spruce—a male White-winged Crossbill. Although my fellow park naturalists were envious of my sighting, I didn't have much time to gloat. Within two weeks, White-winged Crossbills were singing in various parts of the park, and by early August there were thousands of them, their songs ringing throughout the Canadian Rockies. They were still reasonably common through 1975 but by 1976 had all but disappeared from the region, not to return in numbers for almost ten years.

There are two crossbill species in North America—the White-winged and the Red Crossbill. They are finches with a difference: the tips of their bills are crossed like the points of fine tweezers. This feature, which looks as if it would hinder attempts to feed on anything, is an adaptation for extracting seeds from immature cones. They insert their closed bills between the scales of a cone, then pry the scales apart by moving the lower mandible sideways. When the gap is large enough, they extract the seed with their tongue.

Crossbills rely so heavily on conifer seeds that they roam the continent in search of areas with good cone crops. One year they could be the most common bird species in Rocky Mountain forests, and the next almost all of them are gone, feeding on spruce seeds in New Brunswick or pine seeds in California. Where cone crops are heavy, crossbills can breed year-round;

park's Lodgepole Pine forests. Fires blazed everywhere from central British Columbia to Wyoming that summer, one of the driest on record.

The winter of 1987–88 was unusually dry as well in Yellowstone National Park, with only 31 percent of the normal snowfall. Heavy spring rains gave park managers renewed hope that the forests would not be too dry for the summer, but there was almost no rain in June and the drought index stood at severe. A few lightning fires started in June and July, but they remained small and park staff began to think that the fire season would be no more than ordinary. But August was very dry with severe winds and the drought index climbed to extreme, and by the middle of the month a quarter of the huge park was engulfed in flames. By the time the fires were brought under control in late fall, 321 272 hectares (793,850 acres) of the park—36 percent of its total area—had gone up in smoke.

What caused this holocaust? As usual in the natural world, it resulted from a combination of events. Fifty years of fire suppression had increased the fuel load in forests throughout western North America. Forests that normally have an open understory were thick with shrubs and small trees, and the ground was thick with needles and dead branches. The dry winter and summer combined to create tinder-dry fuel in all parts of the forest. An unusual configuration of the jet stream not only blocked summer rains that normally come from the southwest but brought dry lightning storms that set most of the fires and constant westerly winds that fanned the flames. But the

forest was also primed for fire in a historical sense. Research has shown that fires of this magnitude have occurred in the Yellowstone area about six times in the last two thousand years, or about once every three hundred years, and the last such event had occurred around AD 1700.

Lodgepole Pine

Subalpine forests have evolved with periodic fires—large, all-consuming conflagrations that forest scientists call stand-replacing fires. The tree species at the center of the fire processes in the forests of the high West is the Lodgepole Pine. Ecologists call Lodgepole Pine a seral species, meaning it is a pioneer after fire, logging, or other events that clear the trees from a section of forest. It needs full sunlight to germinate, so young pines are almost never found growing in the shade of their parents. But after a fire, the ground is covered with Lodgepole Pine seedlings, and within a few decades there is a dense forest of pines, all growing tall as fast as they can to keep ahead of their neighbors in the race for sunlight. This intense competition creates the polelike form of the Lodgepole Pine—a ramrod-straight trunk with live branches clustered at the crown. In some circumstances, the trees are growing so close together that none of them can gather enough nutrients and light to grow quickly and a doghair forest of densely packed skinny trees is formed.

In these forests, century-old trees can have trunks only a few inches in diameter.

To double-check its identification, you only need to count the needles in each bunch—Lodgepole Pine is the only subalpine pine in the Rocky Mountains with two needles per bunch. And unlike other local pines, Lodgepole Pines retain their small cones on the tree instead of letting them fall to the ground. On many trees, these cones never open under normal conditions but stay tightly closed for years, waiting for intense heat to open them. That heat source is usually a forest fire. This cone form, called serotinous, is most common in Lodgepole Pine forests at low or moderate elevations where stand-replacing fires are common. As you approach tree line, fires are less frequent and often burn along the ground in open situations, allowing older

BEARS

One summer weekend, I camped near the Great Divide in Mount Robson Park, British Columbia. At lunchtime, I took down the garbage bag in which I had carefully stored my food, hung beyond the reach of bears. A sudden shower struck my campsite as I ate my sandwich, so I hurriedly stuffed the food bag under a log and retreated into my small tent. A few minutes later I heard a rustling sound in the food bag. Thinking that a squirrel was after my bread, I flew out of the tent to scare it away, only to find myself face to face with a large Black Bear. It gave a loud *whooof* and ran up the hill.

Confident that it was as frightened of me as I was of it, I yelled and waved my arms to make sure it left the area. Instead, it turned and ran down the hill toward my camp and slid to a stop right in front of me, whoofing and champing its teeth. I had nowhere to retreat to other than the lakeshore a few meters away, so I simply stood there and watched the bear eat my bread. After it had its fill and

wandered away, I packed my gear and left as well.

Few animals engender such excitement and fear in the Rocky Mountains as the two species of bears that inhabit the mountains. Black Bears are by far the more common of the two, found in all types of forests throughout the Rockies. Grizzly Bears are restricted to the Canadian Rockies, northern Montana, and the Yellowstone area. The two species have similar habits and appearance, but there are several important differences. Grizzlies are larger than Blacks, the males averaging about 200 and 115 kilograms (440 and 250 pounds) in weight, respectively. Grizzlies are usually dark brown with a frosted or grizzled appearance but can be pale blonde; Black Bears are usually black or cinnamon-brown. With a little practice, you can identify Grizzly Bears at a distance by the high hump over their shoulders.

Both species are predominantly vegetarian. In spring they graze on grasses, horsetails, and other green vegetation; one June day I

watched a female Black Bear with two tiny cubs gorge herself on Dandelion stalks in Pine Pass, British Columbia. They continue eating plants in summer, switching to stalks of Cow Parsnip and Fireweed in many areas, then to berries as they become available. Berries are the staple diet of both bears in the fall. Blueberries and huckleberries are important in subalpine habitats; Buffaloberries (also known as Soopolallie) are favored in many montane forests. The latter are tiny red berries that grow on large bushes; a Grizzly Bear can eat more than fifty thousand a day.

Grizzly Bears have much longer claws than Black Bears and use them to dig for Glacier Lily bulbs in spring and the starchy roots of sweet-vetches in the fall. They also dig for ground squirrels and marmots in spring and fall. In the American Rockies, the seeds of Whitebark Pine are another important part of the Grizzly Bear diet. These seeds are so critical to bears in the Yellowstone region that years

of low cone crops invariably lead to high numbers of hungry bears invading lowland habitats they normally avoid.

Insects are an important part of their diet as well. Both species eat ants whenever they find them, ripping apart rotting logs or overturning large rocks in their search for ant nests. Grizzly Bears move high into rocky alpine areas in summer to feed on swarms of Army Cutworm Moths. These moths migrate into the mountains to mate in summer, then return to the fields and pastures of the Great Plains in the fall to lay their eggs. Grizzly Bears also seek out masses of ladybird beetles that gather on mountain peaks in late summer.

Spawning salmon and trout are important sources of protein wherever they are easily available in the Rockies, but many spawning populations have drastically declined or disappeared altogether, especially in the Bitterroot Range of Idaho. Grizzly Bears have also disappeared from the Bitterroots.

Bears mate in the summer, but the implantation of fertilized eggs is delayed. If the female is in good physical shape in the fall, the egg implants in the uterus and pregnancy begins. The tiny cubs are born after only two months of gestation, while the female is still in the middle of her winter sleep. Black Bear cubs stay with their mother for the next year; Grizzly cubs usually remain with their mother for two years. Since the females do not breed while they have cubs, Black Bear females breed every second year and Grizzly females breed every third year.

Attitudes toward bears in the Rocky Mountains have drastically changed over the past century. Watching bears feed at garbage dumps was once a common tourist activity and was even encouraged in some parks. The daily feeding of the bears was one of the most popular attractions in Yellowstone. But things changed dramatically as wildlife biologists realized how detrimental these activities were. Garbage dumps accessible to bears have been removed from all parks and in many communities throughout the Rockies, forcing the bears to rely on more natural food sources away from humans.

Grizzly Bear populations are healthy throughout the Canadian Rockies and stable or increasing in the two areas of the American Rockies where they occur—the Yellowstone region centered in northwestern Wyoming and the Glacier National Park region in northwestern Montana. There are more than a thousand Grizzlies in Montana and Wyoming, and plans to reintroduce them into the Bitterroot Range have been shelved because of local concerns about bear interactions with people and livestock. Most conservation planning in the Rocky Mountains uses the Grizzly Bear as a centerpiece, assuming that if the needs of this large predator are met, then those of other animals will be met as well. These plans concentrate on the development and maintenance of habitat corridors to allow bears to move along the spine of the Rockies, especially between the population isolated in Yellowstone and the large population farther north.

trees to survive. Here most of the Lodgepole Pines bear cones that open when the seeds are mature, since the seeds have a good chance of landing in a sunlit meadow, and the tree may die from old age before a fire comes through to open serotinous cones.

Lodgepole Pine can be found in vast monocultures where large fires have burned forests in the past few centuries, but more often the subalpine forests of the Rocky Mountains are a mosaic of tree species and ages. Even the immense fires of 1988 in Yellowstone burned the forest in a patchy manner. The smaller fires that started earlier in the summer were less intense than the late-summer fires, burning more on the forest floor and less in the tree crowns. The fires of August were more catastrophic, but even at their most severe they only completely consumed half the landscape in their path, severely burning another 30 percent and leaving 20 percent of the area with only a light surface burn.

This mosaic created by the patchiness of fire is an essential element in the long-term ecology of subalpine forests. As the Lodgepole Pine forests mature, some trees fail in the competition for light and fall to the ground, creating a more open forest. Engelmann Spruce and Subalpine Fir seedlings germinate in the shade of the pines and begin the slow journey to the open sky. After two or three centuries, the pines reach maximum size, and the firs and spruce challenge them for height. The pines begin to die from old age or a variety of diseases. Occasionally the pines are selectively eliminated from huge areas of forest by one of the most important forces shaping these forests—the Mountain Pine Beetle.

Mountain Pine Beetles

Mountain Pine Beetles are tiny—the size of a grain of rice—but have a disproportionate effect on Lodgepole Pine forests. The adults attack mature pines in summer, preferring those greater than 25 centimeters (10 inches) in diameter. They bore through the thin outer bark into the nutritious cambium layer. When they begin feeding in a tree, the beetles release pheromones, simple volatile chemicals that attract other beetles. When the tree becomes crowded with beetles, the males emit another pheromone that deters other beetles from landing. The tree attempts to fight back by exuding copious pitch, but only the healthiest of trees growing in ideal conditions can withstand the onslaught of many beetles. Infested trees can be easily identified by the numerous pitchy holes scattered on their trunks; by spring they are essentially dead, and their red needles identify them miles away. The beetles bring in another killing agent with them, spores of the Bluestain Fungus, carried from their natal trees. The combination of the voracious beetle larvae and fungal infection girdles and kills the tree. The following

A typical mature Lodgepole Pine forest in Kootenay National Park, with an understory of young Engelmann Spruce and Subalpine Fir.

summer, the larvae mature and emerge as adults, which fly off to find more suitable trees. In the Rocky Mountains, these trees are rarely very far away.

Serious pine beetle epidemics usually begin during drought periods when trees are stressed and summer temperatures ideal for larval growth, and end a decade or so later when a cycle of higher precipitation begins. The beetles went on a rampage during the dust-bowl days of the 1930s and again in the dry 1970s. By the end of the 1990s, conditions were becoming right for yet another epidemic, and this one has proved to be the largest ever. In 2004 more than 7 million hectares (17 million acres) of British Columbia Lodgepole Pine forests were overrun by beetles, almost twenty times the size of the 1970s epidemic. The beetles created havoc south to Colorado, where 250 000 hectares (600,000 acres) were affected in 2002.

Large pine beetle infestations speed up the succession processes in most forests. Young firs and spruces, released from the shade of the pines, grow quickly into a climax forest—one in which the species composition remains the same barring any major disturbance. Even on dry sites where Lodgepole Pines are climax species, outbreaks can enhance the diversity of these forests by creating a mosaic of unevenly aged stands. The forest industry, however, is unwilling to wait for the fir and spruce forests promised by widespread beetle attack. The usual way the forest industry deals with pine beetle infestations is

to immediately log the infested trees. The result is large clear-cuts that more often than not grow back into monocultures of Lodgepole Pine, ammunition for a new beetle explosion.

In the short term and on a small scale, techniques using pheromones to capture or at least divert beetles searching for new trees are effective. The best way to reduce pine beetle epidemics is to employ silvicultural practices that produce a high diversity of tree species and ages. Careful thinning of uninfected pine stands, for instance, speeds the growth of spruce and fir seedlings, produces vigorous pines, and increases wind flow to disperse beetle pheromone trails.

But in the end, only a shift in climate will stop the beetles. An early-winter cold snap can significantly reduce the numbers of overwintering beetles, but it has to be very cold—a week of −40°C (−40°F) temperatures is needed. Wet summers allow the pines to fight the beetles and slow the reproductive activities of the insects. Unfortunately, most climate models predict the opposite for the near future in the Rocky Mountains—warmer winters and longer, hotter, drier summers. As long as huge areas of the West are covered with dense stands of Lodgepole Pine, the Mountain Pine Beetle will continue to flourish.

Mountain Pine Beetle

Red Squirrels

Lodgepole Pine forests have a notoriously low species diversity, but one mammal that is always present is the Red Squirrel, whose incessant chatter ensures that you know it is there. These tree-dwelling squirrels specialize in eating conifer seeds, although like their chipmunk relatives, they also eat a lot of bird eggs and nestlings in season. They also methodically harvest mushrooms, hanging them on tree branches to dry for long-term storage. But the bulk of their winter food consists of conifer seeds.

DWARF MISTLETOE

Most of us think of mistletoe as a cluster of green leaves hung in houses at Christmastime, inviting good-luck kisses. The most common form of mistletoe in the Rocky Mountains is much less conspicuous and much more interesting. The Western Dwarf Mistletoe is a tiny plant that grows on the branches of various western conifers, including Lodgepole Pine. It is yellowish green and leafless, deriving all its water and nutrients from the host tree and growing slowly for five or six years before producing seeds.

Although most mistletoes disperse by producing berries that birds eat and then defecate onto a new branch, the dwarf mistletoe has evolved a unique method to move its seeds around. The sac around the seed gradually builds up water pressure until the outer wall suddenly gives way, shooting the seed out at speeds of up to 80 kilometers per hour (50 miles per hour). The seeds can travel up to 20 meters (65 feet), though most go less than half that distance before hitting a neighboring branch. The sticky seed then sprouts to infect the new host. Dwarf mistletoes do not kill their host trees but can reduce their vigor and growth rate. Because of their seed-spitting travel, mistletoes are much more prevalent in dense, young forests than in older, thinned forests.

Red Squirrels survive the winter on their store of cones, hidden underground in middens.

Red Squirrels spend much of the late summer and fall clipping cones off treetops, gathering them up on the ground, and storing them in large underground middens. Their stores of cones allow Red Squirrels to remain active all winter, and you can hear their loud calls on any calm and dry day no matter what the temperature. You often come across their dining tables in the forest, usually a favorite log or stump littered with the central stalks of cones. They extract the seeds by chewing on the cone as we would a corn-on-the-cob, starting at the big end and discarding the scales as they come off. Pine cones are relatively tough and woody compared with other cones, so squirrels dwelling in pine forests have significantly larger jaw muscles than their wimpier cousins living in fir or spruce forests.

Trembling Aspen

The second tree species that rises like a phoenix from the ashes of forest fires is the Trembling Aspen. Like the Lodgepole Pine, it is found throughout the Rockies but generally grows in moister situations. Small patches grow in wet swales, but it dominates postfire forests in the wetter parts of the Rocky Mountain Trench and in Colorado, where summer rains are common.

Unlike the pine, however, aspens only rarely reproduce from seed. Instead they sprout from the ground; the root systems of burned trees send up saplings. This habit produces aspen copses whose trees are all genetically identical—clones of the original tree. You can often pick out these clones in the fall, when each copse has its own time to turn color. A large grove of aspens will show clumps of green, yellow, and orange, each color representing an individual multi-stemmed clone. Live trees send up saplings from their roots as well, and these clones can become very large; one clone in Utah covered 43 hectares (106 acres) and had about 47,000 separate stems. The clones are very long-lived as well, since the plant lives on long after a single trunk dies; some have undoubtedly survived for many thousands of years.

Trembling Aspen leaves

Trembling Aspens are easy to identify by their smooth white bark and gray-green leaves. The leaves have flat stalks, which cause the leaves to tremble in the slightest breeze. The smooth bark is noticeably green under a powdery white coating, which apparently acts as a sunscreen. The tree can photosynthesize through the sensitive bark when leafless, an obvious advantage in a tree having to put up with the short mountain summers.

Aspens are especially susceptible to heart rot, a characteristic that makes them a favorite target of woodpeckers looking for trees in which to excavate their nest holes. Around my home, Trembling Aspens make up only 5 percent of the forest cover but contain 25 percent of the woodpecker nests. The abundance of woodpeckers draws a great diversity of animals to aspen copses, since many other birds and mammals use old woodpecker holes for their homes.

Throughout the Rocky Mountains, but especially in Yellowstone National Park, many groves of Trembling Aspens have not been reproducing successfully for years—ungulates, especially Elk, have been eating the new shoots before they reach maturity. Elk populations in much of the Rockies are likely much higher than they ever have been, thanks to the protection offered by parks and the elimination of carnivores. The carnivores may be the key to the problem—aspen shoots stopped producing trees in Yellowstone around 1920, the year that the last of the local Wolves were killed. As well as reducing Elk populations, Wolves also apparently change the Elks' behavior so that a herd never stays in an area long enough to permanently damage the local aspens.

Few animals engender such intense human feeling as the Wolf, feared as a top predator, revered as a symbol of wilderness. As the American West was settled in the 1800s, Wolves were essentially eradicated from the landscape, dramatically altering the Rocky Mountain ecosystem south of the Canadian border. Because they hunt in packs, they can kill game much larger than themselves, including Moose, Elk, and even Bison. Wolf packs consist of eight to fifteen animals, each led by an alpha male and female—the top dogs. Only this pair of Wolves mate within the pack, producing four to six pups each year.

Recent attempts to reintroduce the Wolf to the American Rockies have been spectacularly successful. In 1995, 17 wolves were moved from northern Alberta to Yellowstone National Park, followed the next year by 16 wolves from northeastern British Columbia. The project was supposed to continue for five years but was so successful that the introductions stopped after two years. Placed into wolf heaven—a national park full of prey with few other top predators and no human hunters—the packs bred in spectacular fashion. Instead of only one breeding female per pack, the Yellowstone packs had up to three females producing pups each year. The packs soon became unusually large—up to 29 animals. The present Wolf population in Yellowstone is about 170 animals, and there is still strife and instability within the packs as the Wolves sort themselves out in this new situation.

A similar introduction into Idaho has been just as successful. Numbers in Glacier National Park, Montana, have risen as well, so the Wolf seems well on its way to a new lease on life in the American Rockies. Whether this trend will continue is unknown. One of the important factors governing long-term success is how well the wolves can survive outside their wilderness enclaves. Population stability may depend on the existence of relatively safe corridors between Yellowstone, Idaho, and Glacier, routes in which they are not regularly shot and that have a minimum of large highways. Wolves regularly travel great distances—one Montana animal traveled to the Okanagan Valley in British Columbia, a straight-line distance of about 400 kilometers (250 miles), before being shot; another wandered from Yellowstone to northern Colorado and back.

MUSKEG FORESTS OF THE NORTH

In the northern half of the Canadian Rockies, sphagnum bogs become progressively more common in valley bottoms, hinting at their importance in the taiga forests of the Far North. The bogs are circled by Black Spruce— small, scrawny trees with clubbed tops—and grass-green Tamaracks, the larches of the bogs. Black Spruce also grows on upland sites, but it does best in peaty soils. Its shallow rooting habit allows it to grow in the very wet bogs

Opposite page: These fiery-colored Trembling Aspens in the San Juan Mountains rely on periodic fires to maintain their dominance; they sprout from roots after a fire and grow rapidly to form these colorful stands.

Sapsuckers are especially tied to aspen stands. There are four species of these highly specialized small woodpeckers in the Rocky Mountains. The Red-naped Sapsucker is found throughout the Rockies, the Red-breasted and Yellow-bellied occur on the western and eastern sides of the northern end of the range, and the Williamson's is seen throughout the American Rockies. All of them have a fascinating feeding strategy. They drill a series of small holes, called wells, in the bark of trees, then return regularly to lap up the sugary sap flowing out of the holes. Other animals, including squirrels, ants, wasps, and hummingbirds, come to sapsucker wells for the sugary treat. Williamson's Sapsuckers drill their sap wells on coniferous trees, whereas the other three species primarily use deciduous trees such as birch and willow. All four of them prefer aspen trees for nesting. Each pair excavates a new hole each year for nesting, usually using the same tree, so you can find large aspens with ten or more sapsucker nest holes in them.

Left: Red-naped Sapsucker

as well as in areas of patchy permafrost. Moss often grows up around the lowest branches, stimulating them to send down roots and establish a new trunk through layering.

Boggy habitats are usually buggy habitats, especially attractive to biting flies. A summer camping trip in the Rocky Mountains would not be complete without the whine of the mosquitoes in the tent after the flashlight is turned off or the incessant buzz of a large horsefly circling your legs on a mountain trail. Female mosquitoes, horseflies, deer flies, black flies, and no-see-ums all need a blood meal to boost their egg production. The males ignore humans altogether and spend most of their time looking for females of their own kind or simply waiting for them to show up at a prearranged meeting place.

Although biting flies can be pests anywhere in the Rockies, they really come into their own in these boggy forests, because their eggs and larvae need to develop in water. Mosquitoes can breed in almost any body of standing water, including ponds, marshes, large puddles, or even tree holes. After mating, the female mosquito begins her search for a blood meal. She flies toward increasing carbon dioxide concentrations, since all animals exhale that gas. If the animal is warm-blooded, she first senses the heat given off by its body and then finally sees the target and lands. The most effective mosquito repellant, DEET, interferes with her detection of body heat.

When black flies land on you, they scurry around looking for a good place to feed and usually settle on areas with thin skin that are somewhat protected.

I always get nailed at the base of my beard or under my collar. Because black flies use a "slash and lap" method for blood feeding and employ an effective anticoagulant, their bites are often very messy events with blood flowing freely. DEET is less effective against black flies, since they run around on your skin until they find a spot you missed—on your eyelid or inside your ear, for instance—and bite away.

You are usually beset by black flies near a picturesque mountain stream, since the larvae develop in running water. In the stream, the larvae glue themselves to rocks and use large brushes on their heads to filter out the tiny plankton rushing by.

The tiny flies known as no-see-ums are biting ceratopogonid midges. The adults are large enough to see but small enough to scramble through regular mosquito netting. Their bites are fiery and out of all proportion with the biter's size. The larvae are small, clear worms that live in a variety of aquatic habitats.

The largest—and most painful—biting flies in the Rocky Mountains are the horseflies and deer flies. They are close cousins but can be distinguished with a careful look at their beautiful, iridescent eyes. Horsefly eyes are striped, whereas deer fly eyes are spotted.

Mosquito

Black Fly

SEASONS

Spring is a long season in the subalpine zone; the warm sun gradually melts deep snows, but stretches of fine days are interspersed with wintry blizzards. Migrant birds move up from the valleys as early as late March or April, the males singing heartily to defend territories still blanketed by snow. The long-distance migrants, flying in from Central America, arrive in May and early June. Most of the snow has gone by then, and the spring flowers bloom for a short time before summer sets in.

The insect world comes alive in June, when warm days awaken creatures that have spent the winter as eggs, caterpillars, pupae, or hibernating adults. The green forest is buzzing with flies, wasps, beetles, and other six-legged animals busy gathering nectar, eating pollen, chewing leaves, or eating other insects. By July, most of the birds have fledged young from their nests and are busy growing a fresh set of feathers in preparation for migratory flights.

Autumn comes quickly and, like spring, lasts for several months as August frosts and September snowstorms alternate with glorious sunny days. Three-quarters of the birds are gone. Half the bird species, the insect eaters such as flycatchers, vireos, swallows, and warblers, have gone to the tropics. Another quarter have made shorter migrations, some to Arizona, some to Texas, some just downslope to the nearest valley bottom, where the snows don't last more than a few weeks. Bears fatten themselves on fields of blueberries and huckleberries,

Spruce Grouse in the Rocky Mountains, like most other members of the grouse family, have a fascinating courtship display. Elsewhere in the boreal forest, Spruce Grouse males simply fan their tails, then make a noisy fluttering flight up to a low branch to attract the local female. But Spruce Grouse in the mountains look and act differently and are often considered a distinct species, the Franklin's Grouse. These males have all-black tails that they fan to show off the white spangles on the feathers above and below. They make the same fluttering flight up to the branch, but on their descent, they crack their wings together over their heads twice, to make a very loud double-clap that is audible for a great distance. Listen for this short-term applause at dawn on spring mornings.

Opposite page: The Mountain Chickadee is the common chickadee of conifer forests throughout most of the Rockies.

and deer and Elk move downslope to wintering grounds that have less winter snow.

Winter is a quiet time in subalpine forests. The plants are dormant, waiting for the warmth of spring to thaw the soil so that water can be drawn into roots. Many of the animals are hibernating, not so much to avoid the frigid winter temperatures as to avoid starvation. A deep layer of snow covers the ground and blankets the trees. The only sound you might hear over the swishing of your skis or snowshoes is the croaking of a distant raven or the twittering of a roving flock of chickadees and kinglets. Winter is a time of sheer survival, and the animals that remain active are working hard to just stay alive.

The birds that remain find food as best they can. The finches roam the forests searching for seeds; the woodpeckers, chickadees, and nuthatches probe tree bark for insects; the jays and ravens scavenge for anything edible; and the hawks and owls carefully watch the whole process and try to pick off the unwary.

Grouse are almost impossible to find in winter. Their strategy is to sit quietly in trees all day, noiselessly eating needles or buds. Ruffed Grouse feed on willow buds, and Spruce Grouse sit in spruce trees. But not just any spruce tree—these grouse choose the same tree year after year, a tree that is one of the most productive in their territory despite the fact that the grouse have eaten most of the needles off its young twigs. The needles of these chosen trees are more nutritious than the needles of adjacent spruces, and the piles of toothpaste-like grouse droppings that accumulate under them over the winter help keep them filled with nutrients.

Many mountain birds store food in the summer for winter survival. Chickadees and nuthatches store insects and seeds in bark crevices all summer, a behavior that becomes more frenetic in the last warm days of autumn. Jays do much the same—if you have ever wondered how that Gray Jay could eat the piece of bread it stole from your picnic table so fast, know that it didn't eat it at all but stuffed it bit by bit into some secret hiding place. These birds (also known as whisky-jacks or camp robbers) can nest very early in the spring because of their ample winter stores.

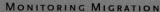

Like canaries in a coal mine, songbird populations are used by conservation biologists as an index of the health of our ecosystems. Birds are easy to see and identify, and there is an army of willing volunteers available to count them. One technique is to count birds as they go by on their annual migrations, and a network of observatories has been set up across North America to do this. The observatory at Mackenzie, British Columbia, in the northern Rocky Mountains, has been operating since 1995. The species with the most serious decline over the past decade is the Rusty Blackbird, a denizen of wetlands in the boreal forest whose population has declined 24 percent per year. The most common songbird encountered at Mackenzie is the tiny Ruby-crowned Kinglet; 3,083 have been banded over ten years.

Left: One of the most common birds in the subalpine forest, the Ruby-crowned Kinglet is a short-distance migrant, moving to the Pacific coast and southern states for the winter.

For these small birds, the most critical part of the winter is the long, cold nights. They cannot store much fat on their tiny bodies—a kinglet weighs only a fifth of an ounce—and must maintain a high body temperature. To survive, they roost communally in sheltered spots. I have seen a small flock of chickadees disappear into a mistletoed clump of pine; kinglets often burrow up into branches covered by a thick layer of snow, where they snuggle with other members of their flock. Research has shown that kinglets reduce heat loss by 23 percent if they roost in pairs and by 37 percent in a ménage à trois. This is one reason why they travel in flocks all day—it could be fatal for a kinglet to find itself alone as dusk falls.

Snow Insects

Boreus

You might be surprised how many insects you can see on a winter's day if you simply look down at your feet while skiing or walking through the snow. As long as the temperature is not too low—around freezing is best—several types of insects are active in mountain forests. One looks superficially like a pale brown spider, walking purposefully with long legs across the snow, until you notice that it has only six legs. This is *Chionea,* a wingless crane fly that gets its name from the Greek word *chion,* meaning "snow"; these insects are commonly called snow flies. *Boreus,* a wingless scorpionfly named after the Greek god of the north wind, hops away like a tiny grasshopper. And if you are walking or skiing along a mountain stream, you will often see small dark stoneflies scurrying about on the snow, freshly emerged from their underwater nymphal stage.

I first traveled through the northern end of the Rocky Mountains on my way to Yukon in 1980. Of the many memories of that trip, I most clearly remember the long northern days and the abundance of animals. Snowshoe hares were almost constantly in view; I saw dozens of lumbering Porcupines and a Lynx padding off into the aspens; families of Great Horned Owls perched on roadside spruces in the long twilight; and ptarmigan were abundant in the subalpine willows. When I returned to the same roads seven years later, I found them almost empty of wildlife. I saw no Porcupine, no Lynx, no ptarmigan, one pair of owls, and only one or two hares. Yet this was not another ecological disaster; it was merely the natural ten-year cycle of the snowshoe hare population, a cycle that rules the subalpine forests throughout much of the Rockies.

During the low portion of the population cycle, hares can be hard to find for four or five years, and then the population begins to climb rapidly for two or three years, peaking at densities about fifty times that found in the low phase. Hares are everywhere at this point, the normally nocturnal animals feeding brazenly by roadsides during the day. Predators are everywhere as well, especially the hare specialists—Lynx, Great Horned Owls, and Northern Goshawks. Other species also thrive during this period, taking advantage of the fact that most of the predators are concentrating on hares and temporarily disregarding burgeoning populations of squirrels, grouse, and ptarmigan. The hares maintain these high numbers for two years; then, in the winter of the third year, 95 percent of the hares die and the population is at the low level again.

A long-term study in southern Yukon looked at many possible causes for this cycle and concluded that it was the high numbers of predators that eventually drove the hare population down and then kept them there for several years. And what allows the hare numbers to increase? The obvious answer seems to be the disappearance of predators after the hare population crashes. Lynx, Great Horned Owls, and other hare predators turn to grouse, ptarmigan, and squirrels immediately after the crash but eventually move out of large areas altogether as all prey numbers dwindle. After predator numbers drop, the hares literally begin to breed like rabbits.

This breeding boom is not driven by an increase in food but seems to be caused by relief from stress when the predators leave. There is also an intriguing but controversial finding that points to an increase in precipitation in northern forests every ten years. This pulse of precipitation is significantly correlated not only with the hare cycle but also with records of sunspot activity kept for hundreds of years by European astronomers. Sunspot activity may affect rainfall patterns, which in turn would affect plant growth and boost the hare population to unusually high levels.

What are these insects doing? Shouldn't they be hibernating through winter? There is little for them to eat on the snow, and they probably do most of their feeding during their summer life in the leaf litter and mosses on the forest floor. But the snow makes a nice surface for small legs to walk on, and winter probably provides the flightless *Chionea* and *Boreus* with their best opportunity to disperse away from their natal area. It also provides a good place to find mates. Stoneflies certainly use the snow as a mating ground. These insects typically live very short lives as adults after a long life as nymphs underwater. All they need to do upon becoming adults is fly a short distance—most have rather short wings—find a member of the opposite sex, and mate. Other stoneflies are easy to see against the snow, and there are few insect-eating predators about to disturb their activities.

Avalanches

Steep mountain slopes and deep snow combine to create one of the most powerful forces that shape mountain forests—avalanches. The deep mountain snowpack is not a uniform mass but is built in distinct layers, each one laid down by a separate snowfall. These layers normally have different characteristics; new layers are usually soft, whereas old layers can have a hard, crusty surface and a loose, grainy interior. Some of these layers are bonded strongly to the layer below, but others are only loosely held.

Prolonged periods without new snow can create a layer of large hoarfrost crystals on the snow crust, and these crystals provide a very poor bonding surface when buried by a new layer of deep snow. Cold, dry weather can sublimate water out of the snowpack itself, slowly turning the firm snow into a thick layer of gravelly crystals, another possible source of weakness. As the snowfalls accumulate, the weight on each bonding surface increases. If the weight, or shear force, on a surface is greater than the bonding force, the slope will fail and a mountainside of snow will roar to the valley bottom.

Avalanches carry catastrophic power, and their tracks are easily visible at the height of summer—vertical grass-green swaths through the dark conifers. Deciduous shrubs, especially alder, dominate avalanche track vegetation, since these plants can regrow from suckers if the main stem is snapped off by the avalanche. If a conifer trunk is broken off at the ground, the tree dies. Since most of the snow on avalanche tracks is swept to the valley bottom, these cleared areas are often the first places where green grass and herbs appear in the spring. This new growth attracts bears, ground squirrels, and marmots waking from their winter sleeps.

Avalanche tracks form vertical streaks on these mountains in Kootenay National Park, British Columbia

7 Forests of Rain and Snow

Forests of Rain and Snow

CHAPTER 7

ON THE WESTERN SLOPES of the northern Rocky Mountains is a sinuous network of valley forests that has as much in common with the great temperate rain forest of the Pacific coast as it does with the dry forests of the continental interior. Lying in the path of the continental jet stream, these mountain slopes wring water out of Pacific storms just as the coastal ranges do. Stretching from the north end of the Cariboo Mountains in British Columbia to central Idaho and continuing south in patches to a few moist canyons in the Tetons, these warm, wet forests are remarkable for their large trees, their great diversity, and their antiquity.

These wet interior forests receive less precipitation than most of the coastal forests in the Pacific Northwest, but because of two factors—summer rain and snowfall—their productivity and appearance is very similar to that of their coastal counterparts. The coast receives much of its rainfall in winter, which is only a minor part of the growing season there. In contrast, the wet interior forests receive significant rainfall in summer, when it is needed most by trees and other plants. And they get prodigious amounts of snow. In one of the wetter parts of the interior forest, Revelstoke, British Columbia, receives 946 millimeters (37 inches) of precipitation annually, almost exactly the same as Seattle, Washington, which is at the dry end of the coastal rain forest spectrum. The big difference is that Revelstoke gets almost half its annual precipitation in the form of snow—an average of 425 centimeters (167 inches) per year. That snow melts in spring to saturate the ground just as plants are beginning to grow.

The moist summers and steep mountain slopes combine to create a diversity of microclimates within this zone, which in turn fosters a tremendous diversity of tree species. I remember one campsite in the Elk Valley of British Columbia where I counted ten species of trees within ten paces of my tent, almost an impossibility in any other forest type in the Rockies. These included

Interior wet forests include a greater diversity of tree species than other forests in the Rocky Mountains. But what exactly is diversity and why is it important? The simplest definition and most important attribute of diversity is species richness—the number of species found within a given area. The size of that area is all-important. Although it is clear that the species richness in an old-growth forest is much greater than that in a young forest, foresters often point out that plants and animals are often more diverse in a two-year-old clear-cut than in the old forest. But these newly logged habitats are filled with species that are common in backyards, old gravel pits, and other disturbed habitats all too common in the modern landscape. Very few if any of these species are found in old forests and, conversely, few of the species in old forests are found in clear-cuts. To maximize species diversity, therefore, we must maintain a mosaic of forests of all ages, including ancient forests, and in significant amounts.

Right: The Pacific-slope Flycatcher is found along shady streams throughout the northern Rocky Mountains but is most abundant in moist, old-growth forests.

trees of the dry forests, such as Ponderosa Pine; trees of the wet forests, such as Western Hemlock; and trees of subalpine forests, such as Engelmann Spruce.

The increased summer moisture in these forests inhibits the spread of lightning fires, so large conflagrations are very rare. In the wetter parts of these forests, fires occur about every three or four centuries instead of every one or two centuries as in Subalpine Fir forests or every few decades as in Ponderosa Pine forests. And some sites, especially those at the base of mountains and in gullies, have not been burned for more than a millennium. This stability creates forests of great antiquity, forests much older than the individual trees that grow in them. This stability in turn promotes diversity of plant and animal life.

TREES

These forests are a melting pot of trees, home to almost every species in the region, but a half-dozen are found only in these wet forests. The primary indicator for this forest is the Western Hemlock, easily recognized by its drooping tip and finely furrowed bark. Young hemlocks are very tolerant of shade and are often the only tree species growing in the understory of these dark forests. Like all trees adapted to wet conditions, hemlocks have no taproot. Instead, they send their shallow roots out like a mat below the surface of the soil. They are also biochemically adapted to the local conditions, using ammonia as their prime source of nitrogen as opposed to nitrates, which are almost nonexistent in these leached, acidic soils.

Western Redcedars, with their elegant sweeping branches and massive reddish trunks, grow alongside Western Hemlocks in wet sites. Their scalelike needles lack the waxy coating that most conifers have, so they are intolerant of any drought that reduces groundwater availability. Redcedars are very tolerant of water tables close to the surface and often dominate the saturated soils on flat valley bottoms. Old trunks are noticeably buttressed at the base to reduce the chance of windthrow. Redcedar roots spread out like a thick mat just below the surface of the soil, a fact known to gardeners with redcedars near their vegetable patch.

Redcedars are very long-lived trees, commonly exceeding five hundred years in age. Old trees can be very large; some are among the largest trees in the Rocky Mountains, with trunks 50 meters (165 feet) in height and 3 meters (10 feet) in diameter. They contain an arsenal of chemicals that makes them resistant to most insect and fungal attacks. Over their long lives, however, fungi eventually begin to detoxify the heartwood, and older trees are often completely hollow, making them valuable wildlife trees. The decay resistance and straight grain of redcedar wood has made it a favorite of homebuilders for the past century, and older stands are now rare.

A century ago, much of this wet forest was ruled by the Western White Pine. Forty percent of the trees over much of this area were pines, their tall trunks bearing long, armlike branches of soft gray needles and large banana-

Western Redcedar

PACIFIC YEW AND TAXOL

Pacific Yew is a small tree, which usually grows in the shady understory of moist forests. Its parallel rows of dark-green needles make its twigs look superficially like Western Hemlock or Grand Fir, but the needles are pointed instead of blunt. And instead of bearing its seeds in cones, it has small, bright red berrylike fruits called arils. Although they look appetizing, the arils of many species of yews contain alkaloids that cause cardiac arrest, so it is best not to tempt fate by eating one. Yews also differ from other evergreens in having male and female trees; only the female trees have arils. For decades, yews were ignored by foresters as being trash trees suitable only for specialized products that demanded strong, supple wood, such as archery bows and canoe paddles.

In the 1960s, it was discovered that Pacific Yew produces a very interesting chemical—taxol. The tree uses this compound to fight off fungi and other agents of decay that are prevalent in these moist forests, but what brought taxol to the attention of biochemists was its promise as an anticancer drug. The only problem facing pharmaceutical companies was how to obtain enough taxol—the bark of 360,000 trees was needed to produce a single year's supply. For several years, yews were harvested at completely unsustainable rates, but fortunately a synthetic technique was devised that could produce the drug much more cheaply and at no cost to the environment. This technique has the added benefit of producing similar compounds that promise to be even more effective than taxol.

shaped cones. Many of the largest trees were removed by logging that started in 1880. Then, in 1910, White Pine Blister Rust was accidentally introduced from Europe to the port of Vancouver, British Columbia. It quickly spread through the Northwest, killing most of the mature Western White Pines in its path, and now these pines make up only 2 percent of the forest cover.

The rust attacks the tree trunks, girdling them and killing all growth above. Sometimes the lower branches of the trees survive but do not reproduce, since the cone-bearing branches are the highest on the tree. Like most rusts, White Pine Blister Rust alternates host plants; the alternate hosts for this species are currants and gooseberries in the genus *Ribes*. During the Depression and for a decade or more thereafter, several make-work programs sent out crews to try to eradicate currants and gooseberries from affected forests. After these manual-removal methods proved futile, foresters turned to herbicides but eventually gave up. Recently, rust-resistant trees have been produced in nurseries and will be planted in the forests in an attempt to defeat this alien pathogen.

Stately Grand Firs grow with Western White Pines in the southern part of this forest. Their dark-green foliage, smooth gray bark, and symmetrical growth pattern identify them at a distance, and the horizontal placement of their needles separates them from their high-altitude cousin, the Subalpine Fir.

My favorite tree of these moist forests is the Western Larch. Unlike its relatives, which commonly grow stunted in harsh alpine or bog environments, the Western Larch grows to immense sizes. It does retain the larch characteristic of turning gold in September and October, dropping its needles for the

Above: Western Larch needles turn gold in autumn.

Western White Pine

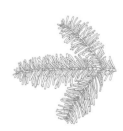

Grand Fir

winter, and then regrowing its soft, light green foliage in the spring. Western Larch is a seral species, pioneering on bare soils left after forest fires or logging. It grows quickly and dominates other species in the forest for several centuries before rotting from within and eventually falling. In drier sites with more frequent ground fires, it can form gorgeous parklike stands of large trees underlain by Pinegrass, orchids, and lilies. In slightly wetter sites, where stand-replacing fires are more common than ground fires, it tends to occur as smaller trees in denser forests.

Mountain Hemlock

Like the Trembling Aspen, mature larch is favored by woodpeckers excavating nest cavities because of its firm outer bark and softer heartwood. Larches have even harder outer bark than aspen, providing better protection for cavity-nesting birds against marauding bears. Williamson's Sapsuckers nest almost exclusively in Western Larch when it is available, and smaller birds such as chickadees and nuthatches then use the sapsucker holes. Northern Goshawks and Great Gray Owls like the open nature of these stands, and the owls often nest on the broken tops of very old larches.

Yellow Cedar

In the snowiest parts of these wet forests grow two other trees—Mountain Hemlock and Yellow Cedar. Yellow Cedar is very rare in this region, but Mountain Hemlock can be quite common at higher elevations, where more than half the annual precipitation falls as snow. Mountain Hemlock is intolerant of frozen soils and so can grow only on sites where the snow falls so deep and early that the ground is insulated from freezing.

SHRUBS

Sir Sandford Fleming, one of the pioneer railway builders of the 1800s, described hiking through the Illecillewaet Valley of the Selkirk Mountains thus:

> The walking is dreadful, we climb over and creep under fallen trees of great size and the men soon show that they feel the weight of their burdens...The dripping rain from the bush and branches saturates us from above. Tall ferns sometimes reaching to the shoulder and Devil's Clubs through which we had to crush our way make us feel as if dragged through a horsepond and our perspiration is that of a Turkish bath...The Devil's Clubs may be numbered by millions and they are perpetually wounding us with their spikes against which we strike...We wade through Alder swamps and tread down Skunk Cabbage and Prickly Aralias, and so we continue until half-past four, when the tired-out men are able to go no further.

The Devil's Club Fleming mentions is a plant you do not forget once you have been introduced. Its broad leaves, which resemble those of a giant maple, spring from crooked stems that are completely covered in wicked spines. Even

the undersides of the leaves are spiny. The stems have a nasty way of springing back when stepped on, hammering hundreds of thorns into bare legs and arms. The spines have a mild irritant as well, so the pain lasts for a few days.

Skunk Cabbage grows in the wettest, most nutrient-rich spots in redcedar forests. It has large leaves as well but is most spectacular in spring, when its huge yellow flowers shine like lanterns in the dark forest. The air around them is filled with a pungent odor that attracts tiny rove beetles to the spike of tiny flowers framed by the large yellow bracts.

Shrubs in the heath family—rhododendrons, huckleberries, and their relatives—do well at higher elevations in these forests. White Rhododendron forms thickets on steep slopes; its small white flowers are a bit of a disappointment considering some of its spectacular relatives. It is also known as mountain misery, since its long branches sweep downhill and create a

Devil's Club leaves catch the evening sun in Glacier National Park, Montana.

Overleaf: Thimbleberry leaves turn brown in autumn in the wet forests of the Columbia Valley near Golden, British Columbia.

challenge for hikers trying to fight their way upslope to the mountain meadows. False Azalea, also known as fools-huckleberry, is similar to the rhododendron in leaves and growth form but has small, bell-like flowers that look similar to those of its huckleberry relatives. Heaths favor these snow forests because they are biochemically adapted to two characteristics of the acidic soil here— the lack of nitrates and the abundance of free iron. Like hemlocks, heaths can use ammonia as a source of nitrogen when nitrates are in short supply, and they need a lot of iron.

OLD-GROWTH FORESTS

Although old-growth conditions can be found in any type of forest, they are especially spectacular in these rain forests. A standard definition of an old-growth forest is one that is made up of trees more than 250 years old, but these forests have characteristics other than pure seniority. The older trees in them are obviously large, often more than 50 meters (165 feet) high. Much of the unique life in old-growth rain forests is found in this high canopy, where moss and lichens drape the branches, fed on by insects and other animals that never set foot on the ground. The canopy microclimate is benign, cooled and humidified in summer by evaporation from the needles and leaves.

The structure of old forests is also radically different from that of young forests. A forest only a few decades old may have good-sized trees, but they are all of the same age and height, creating a dense, unbroken canopy that allows very little light through to the forest floor. The dark understory is almost lifeless, since few plants can tolerate the deep shade. As the forest ages, trees fall, creating gaps in the canopy. These gaps bring life-giving light to the forest floor, allowing plant life to flourish. Small seedling trees, held in check for decades by the low light, shoot upward to create a multilayered canopy. Standing dead trees can take decades to fall. As they slowly rot from within, woodpeckers excavate nest cavities in the weakened trunks, and these are used in turn by many other birds, mammals, and insects. Even after these snags fall to become logs on the forest floor, they can provide a century of low-cost housing for a myriad of animals, from salamanders to small carnivores. Almost one-fifth of the biomass of an old-growth rain forest is dead wood. Young forests—especially those that regrow after clear-cut logging— lack all this structure and the resulting diversity of older forests.

The canopy of old rain forests is heaven for arboreal lichens. The relatively constant climate, slow-growing trees, bare branches, dappled sunlight, and regular breezes provide exactly the right conditions. In younger forests, arboreal lichens are almost entirely absent. Their ability to disperse into young forests is rather limited because it depends entirely on the wind blowing broken lichen fragments across the landscape, and the conditions they find

Skunk Cabbages can increase the temperature of their flower stalks to enhance the release of a pungent odor that attracts beetles to pollinate the flowers.

In all my years of hiking through the mountains of western North America, I have never seen a cougar. I have come across freshly killed deer surrounded by cougar prints, and I have even seen prints across the top of my driveway, but I have never glimpsed this elusive big cat—often called the Ghost of the Rockies. The cougar, also known as mountain lion or puma (a name from the language of the Incas), is one of the most widely distributed mammals in the New World, found from the northern Rocky Mountains south to Tierra del Fuego. It is called a mountain lion because of its large size—a male can weigh up to 68 kilograms (150 pounds)—but it is actually more closely related to the Cheetah than the Lion.

Its long tail and unspotted coat are unique among wild cats in the Rockies, although the young have a spotted coat for their first two years.

Cougars prefer to hunt ungulate prey such as deer, Elk, Moose, and Bighorn Sheep but will also take smaller mammals such as Snowshoe Hares or Porcupines when other prey is scarce. An adult male or a female with cubs needs to kill a deer about once every eight to ten days. Cougars are generally solitary animals. Males maintain territories up to about 800 square kilometers (300 square miles) from which they exclude all other males. Breeding adults are promiscuous and polygamous; both males and females mate with multiple partners in a single season. The young are generally born in summer or fall.

Hungry cougars occasionally attack humans, but such incidents are rare. Most serious attacks are against children; one of the best defenses against a cougar is to appear as large as possible. Brandishing a large branch or canoe paddle is often enough to send a cougar away. Humans have a much greater effect on cougars than cougars do on humans. Even in areas where the animals are protected from hunting, most cougar deaths can be attributed to humans, primarily by vehicles, ranchers protecting livestock, and illegal hunting.

there—dense stands with little light or airflow around all but the uppermost branches—are anathema to their needs.

Lichens, perhaps more than any other group of organisms, are prime indicators of very old temperate rain forests. Diversity of lichen species begins to increase when a forest reaches about 150 or 200 years old and doesn't peak until the forest is more than 500 years old. Most of these forests are now managed on about 100-year logging rotations, a strategy that may have very negative consequences for the growth of future trees. Recent studies have found that lichens play an important role in the nutrient cycles of these forests. Lungwort Lichen is perhaps the most important of these lichens, and not just because it makes up the lion's share of lichen biomass. The cyanobacteria (formerly known as blue-green algae) cells it farms within itself can take atmospheric nitrogen and turn it into the nitrates organisms need, much as bacteria in clover roots do. Lungwort Lichen is therefore one of the most important sources of nitrates in this nutrient-poor environment.

One animal with a direct dependence on lichens is the Northern Flying Squirrel. This big-eyed squirrel glides through the forest at night, feeding on

Opposite page: Witch's Hair Lichen and Western Hemlock are characteristic species of the wet coniferous forests from central British Columbia south to Idaho and Montana.

arboreal lichens in winter and mushrooms and truffles in summer. Flying squirrels build nests in tree cavities, lining them with a thick layer of soft Witch's Hair lichen.

LIFE IN THE SOIL

Although it may not be apparent on the surface, these wet forests can be a tough place for trees to grow. In wet forests, nutrients do not stick around very long. They are quickly leached away by snowmelt and rain, so trees and other forest plants must absorb them rapidly before they are lost. Because fungi readily absorb nutrients, trees and many other forest plants team up with fungi in partnerships that benefit both organisms. These partnerships are not restricted to wet forests—they involve almost every tree in the world—

The Fly Agaric is one of the highly poisonous *Amanita* mushrooms.

but they play an all-important role here. Many of these fungi fruit as conspicuous and familiar mushrooms, such as amanitas and agarics, but most fruit underground. The most famous of these fungi are the truffles.

The vegetative part of the fungus, called the mycelium, is a mat of fine hairs that spreads through the organic layer of the soil. At every turn, these hairs encounter tree rootlets, and if the species combination is right, the fungus and rootlets combine to form a partnership called mycorrhizae—literally, "fungus root." The fungus provides nutrients and water to the roots, and the roots provide sugar to the fungus. Without this partnership, trees can barely stay alive, let alone grow to great heights.

The mycorrhizal partnership is much more complex than this description suggests; most partnerships also contain nitrogen-fixing bacteria (*Azospirillum*) and a yeast culture. The bacteria provide nitrates for both the fungus and the tree, and the yeast stimulates bacterial growth and fungal germination. All these elements are neatly packaged in the droppings of rodents that have eaten truffles or underground mushrooms. For whereas aboveground mushrooms can spread their spores on the wind, those species that fruit underground are totally dependent on mammals to spread their spores.

Other fungi prosper in this environment not by helping the trees but by eating them, a good strategy in an ecosystem where 98 percent of the biomass is in wood. Honey Mushrooms are common, ordinary-looking mushrooms, the fruits of a large mass of rhizomorphs that grow like shoestrings underground, searching for tree roots to feed from. Honey Mushrooms thrive on the wood of dead stumps but will also invade and kill live trees.

The main target of fungi in the forest is dead wood. Although there is plenty of that around, it is a monotonous, high-carbohydrate diet, and fungi have to snack on other things for a more balanced existence. Many of them consume the bacteria common in decaying wood, first killing them with natural antibiotics—most of the antibiotics we use were first discovered in soil fungi. Others lure nematode worms and other tiny animals with chemical attractants, then catch them with an amazing arsenal of harpoon cells, inflatable nooses, and exploding poison sacs.

Insects team up with fungi in attacking dying trees. Beetles bring fungi with them, often intentionally, when they cut through the protective bark. Tiny ambrosia beetles cannot digest wood, so they farm fungi by collecting fungal spores in special cavities in their bodies and then seeding the spores throughout their galleries in the heartwood of newly fallen trees. The fungi digest the tree, and both the adult and larval beetles eat the growing fungi.

Other insects move in after fungi and bacteria have softened the wood of a dead tree or log. Carpenter ants chew long, elaborate galleries in the wood to provide a home for their colony. Whereas ambrosia beetles are farmers, carpenter ants are ranchers, tending herds of aphids that suck sap from healthy trees nearby and then gathering the honeydew excreted by the tiny bugs. The ants even gather aphid eggs in late fall and shelter them in their colony over winter, then "plant" them on vegetation in spring. Carpenter ants are eaten in turn by woodpeckers, especially the big Pileated Woodpecker, a crow-sized species with a big red crest. You can recognize Pileated Woodpecker workings by their elongate, rectangular or oval shape, which often exposes the galleries of a carpenter ant colony. In Western Larch forests, carpenter ants are also harvested by Williamson's Sapsuckers, which glean them off the branches while the ants are tending their aphids.

Orchids, such as this Sparrow's-egg Ladyslipper, are especially tied to mycorrhizal relationships; their seeds will not germinate unless invaded by the right kind of fungal hairs.

Carpenter Ant

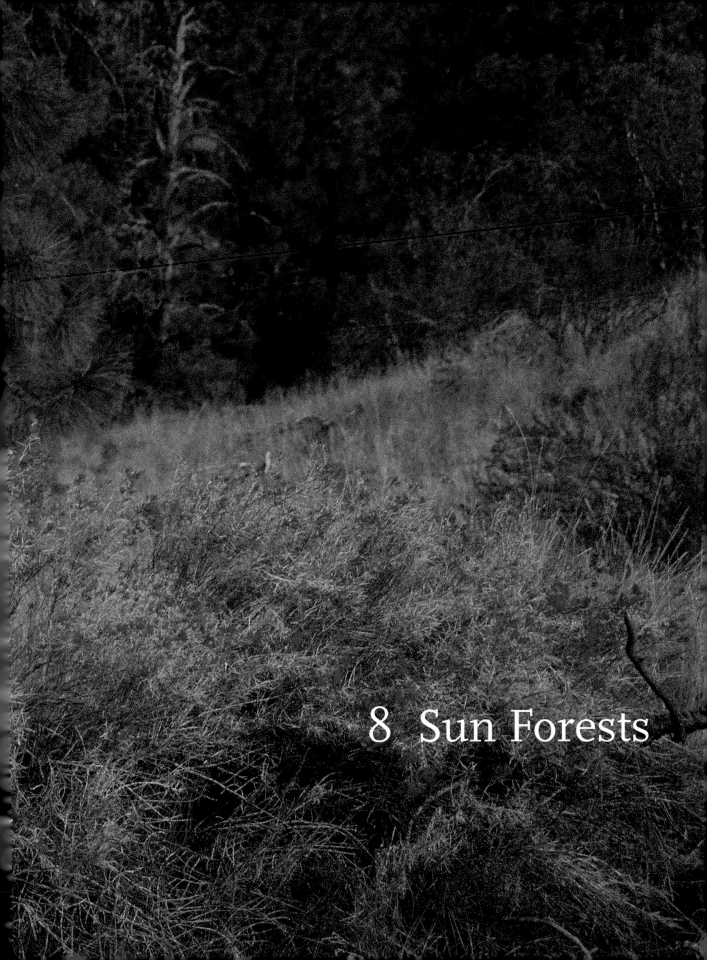

8 Sun Forests

*Ponderosa pine ... seems to have a penchant for
dramatic and lightning-prone settings. It is a tree
that swims in memory, and surfaces in dreams.*
—DON GAYTON, *LANDSCAPES OF THE INTERIOR*

Sun Forests

CHAPTER 8

BELOW THE FORESTS OF SPRUCE AND FIR and above the valley grasslands
of sagebrush and cactus lies a band of drier forests. These forests are a
transition between hot and cold, dry and wet, open and closed. The widely
spaced trees and grassy understory of these woodlands invite exploration on
foot. Often called montane forest, this is my home habitat. I grew up hiking
through these fragrant, sunlit groves, listening to the strident buzz of cicadas
on hot summer afternoons and the mellow whistles of poorwills as dusk fell.
These forests are found at elevations of 400 to 1 200 meters (1,300 to 4,000
feet) in British Columbia, climbing to 1 800 to 2 700 meters (6,000 to
9,000 feet) in Colorado.

Montane forests are dominated by two species of trees in the Rocky
Mountains—Ponderosa Pine and Douglas-fir. In wetter sites along creeks
in the southern Rockies, Blue Spruce can be common. This species is very
similar to the Engelmann Spruce found at higher elevations but has longer
cones—about twice as long as Engelmann cones—and the needles are often
much bluer, as its name implies. The two species hybridize extensively at
intermediate sites, where it can be impossible to positively identify them. At
the south end of the Rockies, thickets of Gambel Oak often mark the lower
edge of this forest, and woodlands of Pinyon Pine and Utah Juniper merge
with the high deserts of the Colorado Plateau.

Goldilocks would have loved these forests—not too hot, not too cold; not too
wet, not too dry. Snowfalls are light, and by March or April grass is growing and
flowers are blooming. Summers are hot but not as scorching as in the grasslands below. Like most environments in the Rocky Mountains, montane forests
are shaped by fire and have been greatly altered by the mix of fire suppression
and logging over the past century.

DOUGLAS-FIR FORESTS

Descending through subalpine forests, the hiker first encounters montane forests on south-facing slopes, where old, square-topped Douglas-firs tower above the spruce. The dark subalpine forest floor opens into green swaths of Pinegrass, and the big branches of the Douglas-firs glow with chartreuse Wolf Lichen. The Douglas-firs are easy to recognize by their deeply furrowed bark; a quick look at the cones, with their unique three-pronged bracts, clinches the identification.

Wolf Lichen on trunk of Douglas-fir

Douglas-fir has difficulty germinating under hot, sunny conditions, so at lower elevations it gives way to Ponderosa Pine as the dominant tree species or simply to open grassland. Douglas-fir can still be found in hot valleys, growing in shady canyons or on boulders and talus. In the last two places, the rocks act as umbrellas, sending the meager rainfall to the cracks between them, where the shallow roots of the Douglas-firs drink up the runoff.

Many of the old Douglas-firs carry witch's brooms—large clumps of tangled twigs, the legacy of attacks by dwarf mistletoe. These growths can

Douglas-fir

reduce the vigor of the tree but provide nesting platforms for hawks, owls, and ravens. Northern Saw-whet Owls often roost in the shadowy recesses of the twisted branches.

Mammals

Opposite page: Wolf Lichens provide a colorful accent in moister montane forests.

Old-growth Douglas-fir forests are important winter range for Elk, Mule Deer, White-tailed Deer, and Bighorn Sheep. Smaller animals are conspicuous in summer, especially Yellow-pine Chipmunks. Like many of their relatives in the squirrel family, chipmunks break the mold of the normally secretive nocturnal mammals. They are active throughout the day, and their strikingly striped faces and bodies, loud calls, and hyperactive personalities make them easy to find in the forest.

ELK

The Elk is a relative newcomer to North America, emigrating from Eurasia across the Bering land bridge in the later stages of the Pleistocene Ice Age. It is considered the same species as the Eurasian Red Deer but is much larger than its Old World cousin. The name Elk is confusing to Europeans, since there it refers to the Moose; many people prefer the name Wapiti for the North American

Elk, a Shawnee word meaning "white rump." Elk are large deer, the males weighing 300 to 500 kilograms (660 to 1,100 pounds) and the females weighing 200 to 300 kilograms (440 to 660 pounds). The males have massive antlers, which begin growing in April and are shed late the following winter.

Elk are grazing animals that live in herds. Grass is the most important food for most

herds, though they heavily browse shrubs and trees such as willows and aspens in winter and commonly eat broad-leaved herbs as they move to higher elevations in summer. In late summer and fall, dominant males guard harems of up to thirty females. At this time, the males produce loud bugling sounds, which attract females and advertise the male's fitness—it takes a lot of energy

to produce these loud bellows, and only a healthy male could keep giving them constantly throughout the rut. In winter, Elk gather in larger herds of a hundred or more. The winter herds disperse in spring as the females seek out wooded locations to give birth to their spotted calves.

Like many large mammals, Elk have disappeared over much of their former range in North America, and the Rockies are their stronghold. Most large parks in the mountains are home to substantial herds, though many leave the parks for lands at lower elevations in the winter. Some of these herds have become habituated to humans and are commonly seen in the residential areas of park townsites. Their presence creates problems, especially during calving season, when mothers are very protective of their newborns. Officials in Banff have begun chasing Elk out of the downtown area in part to reduce the chance of injury to town residents and visitors.

A Northern Pygmy-Owl

Townsend's Warbler

Chipmunks live in underground burrows, usually at the base of a tree, where they bear their young and add to their storehouse of winter food. They harvest seeds all summer long; I remember one that stored sunflower seeds from our bird feeder under our living-room couch one day when we left the front door open. Some have separate summer homes, usually in an old woodpecker nest or other tree cavity. Chipmunks sleep through the winter but not as deeply as their ground squirrel and marmot cousins. This light sleep uses up their fat reserves more quickly, forcing chipmunks to wake up regularly in winter to refuel from their food pile.

Birds

Douglas-fir forests can seem quiet and empty at noon on a summer's day, but a walk through them at dawn reveals a lively community of birds. Male Western Tanagers, looking decidedly tropical with their bright yellow bodies

FLAMMULATED OWLS

If you go out on a warm late-spring night into the lower part of the Douglas-fir forests—where they are interspersed with large Ponderosa Pines and groves of Trembling Aspen—you might hear a soft *boo-boot!* coming from the forest. This is the call of the Flammulated Owl, a tiny insectivorous owl found only in the montane forests of western North America. Measuring only about 15 centimeters (6 inches) long and weighing 60 grams (2.1 ounces), these owls migrate from the mountain forests of Mexico and Central America each spring to raise their young in the Rocky Mountains. They were once considered almost mythically rare, but in the 1970s, biologists discovered that Flammulated Owls were locally common in older montane forests and could be found by listening at night for their calls.

I clearly remember my first encounter with the species. My parents had discovered a calling male in the pine-fir forests above their home, so I returned home as soon as I could get a day off from my summer job. I stood in the dark, anxiously listening for the soft hoots, but all I heard was a rather menacing *khaaah!* Thinking that I might at least see an interesting mammal, I started up the slope but within a few steps realized the sound was coming from above me. Turning my flashlight upwards I saw a tiny ball of fluff perched on a branch—a hungry owlet screaming for food! A few minutes later one of its parents flew in and stuffed a moth in its mouth, and my lifelong interest in owls had been born.

and scarlet heads, sing raspy robinlike songs from high in the trees. Tanagers are indeed from a family of tropical birds and come north each year to feed on caterpillars and other insects before returning to their Central American homes for a winter diet of berries. Townsend's Warblers sing their high, sibilant songs in the northern Rockies, their striking black-and-yellow bodies usually hidden from view. This is another species that winters in Central America—many of the songbirds of the Rocky Mountains are best considered tropical species. These birds dash north in spring to take advantage of the long summer days, abundant insects, and lack of snakes to raise their young before returning in early fall to their southern homes.

One way to liven up the bird community in a quiet afternoon forest is to imitate the whistled call of the Northern Pygmy-Owl. These small predators—little bigger than sparrows—are daytime hunters, preying on small birds and mice. Being diurnal, they lack the two main owl adaptations for night hunting:

a big round face for sound reception and soft, silent wings. An imitation of their steady *kook—kook—kook* calls, about one every two seconds, rallies all small birds in the forest to find the tiny owl. Within minutes all the chickadees, nuthatches, warblers, finches, and jays are crowded around you, calling derisively. If you are lucky, a small owl might appear as well.

This behavior, called mobbing, seems rather counterintuitive at first. Why would a small bird fly toward a deadly enemy? The answer is that the owls catch most of their prey by surprise, so if the small birds can find the owl, they can save themselves by watching the owl's actions. The loud calls also let the owl know that the entire neighborhood knows where it is, so it might as well go somewhere else to hunt. This is a learned behavior—small birds will only come in to the call of a pygmy-owl if they have previously encountered a mob scene.

Reptiles

Although forests are not the first places that people might think of going to see reptiles, there are some interesting species among the Douglas-firs. One is the Rubber Boa, one of only two true boas in North America. Unlike its tropical relatives, the Rubber Boa is not a huge snake; it is rarely more than 60 centimeters (2 feet) long. It is sometimes called the two-headed snake

The Rubber Boa is a small, inconspicuous constrictor found in montane forests from southeastern British Columbia to northern Utah.

because of its unique body form—the tail is short and blunt, matching the boa's rounded head. Rubber Boas use this tail while consuming their favored prey—baby mice. While it eats one mouse and constricts one or more other ones with its coils, the snake distracts and fends off the frantic mother mouse by striking at her with its tail, imitating the motion most snakes make with their heads. Adult boas can have seriously scarred tails because of this habit. They are long-lived snakes; one marked snake is known to be more than thirty years old and was a scarred adult when first found. Rubber Boas are normally nocturnal, hiding beneath rocks or logs during the day.

Rubber Boas share two adaptive behaviors with most other northern reptiles—they hibernate and give birth to live young. I learned of the latter habit of northern snakes when I picked up a large garter snake to photograph it and a small copy of the adult slipped out and onto my arm. Garter snakes are perhaps the most common reptiles in these forests. Predators of mice, birds, insects, amphibians, and small fish, both the Common Garter Snake and Western Terrestrial Garter Snake are often encountered in summer meadows. They normally hibernate in small groups, but at some sites, perhaps where suitable underground cavities are rare, they amass in amazing numbers. In spring the males emerge from the hibernacula first and wait around the entrance for a week or two for the females to come out. As each female emerges, it is wrapped in a writhing mass of males competing for mating rights.

PONDEROSA PINE WOODLANDS

Ponderosa Pines are easy to identify by their orange, jigsaw-puzzle bark, long needles, and large, egg-shaped cones. No other Rocky Mountain tree displays such features. Like many forest zones, Ponderosa Pine woodlands can also be identified by smell. The bark of the tree contains pure vanillin, the same chemical as the popular flavoring, and on warm summer days the unmistakable aroma of vanilla wafts through the pines.

Ponderosa Pines form pure stands at the lower tree line at scattered locations throughout the western valleys of the Rocky Mountains and also on the eastern slopes south of the Wyoming Basin. Limber Pine replaces it at the windswept lower tree line on the east slope from Wyoming north to Alberta. Below the lower tree line, soils are too hot and dry in summer for tree germination, and the hills are covered with grasses and shrubs. Just above this line, Ponderosa Pines can grow in conditions unfit for almost any other tree. Unlike most other Rocky Mountain conifers, Ponderosa Pines have a substantial taproot. After one year of growth, a seedling may be only 7 centimeters (3 inches) high, but its taproot is over 50 centimeters (20 inches) long. The lateral roots of old trees can extend up to 46 meters (150 feet) from the tree, so open woodlands with scattered trees are underlain by an almost complete mat of pine roots. Young seedlings can withstand ground temperatures of up to 72°C (162°F), but they may be greatly damaged by temperatures above 55°C

ABERT'S SQUIRRELS

If you look high in the canopy of a Ponderosa Pine forest in the southern Rockies, you might see a large round nest built of sticks, the home of an Abert's Squirrel. These large, tassel-eared squirrels, like Red Squirrels, feed on the pine seeds, but the Abert's Squirrels also chew on pine twigs, eating the soft, nutritious inner bark. This activity can be quite damaging to some trees, depending on the size of the tree and the extent of the damage. The trees fight back by producing mildly toxic chemicals called monoterpenes, which deter the chewing to some extent. The pines also produce large cone crops every few years, thus overwhelming the squirrel population, which couldn't possibly eat all the seeds that year.

Pygmy Nuthatch on
Ponderosa Pine bark

(131°F). Shade or a series of relatively wet summers substantially improves the survival of seedlings at lower tree line.

Ponderosa Pine woodlands are usually so open that the understory is very similar to that of the grasslands below them. Bunchgrasses cover the ground, interspersed with shrubs such as Antelope-brush and Mountain Mahogany. Saskatoon bushes bloom en masse in spring and produce sweet berries in July. Arrowleaf Balsamroot flowers turn entire hillsides butter-yellow in spring, and Mock-orange blossoms fill the warm June evenings with their sweet scent.

Birds

Several birds are strongly associated with Ponderosa Pines, perhaps attracted by the open structure of both the forest itself and the old trees. Pygmy Nuthatches are rarely seen more than a stone's throw from the pines. These tiny birds roam the forests in small flocks, keeping track of each other with shrill piping calls. They use their sharp beaks to probe the rough bark for insects, reach into ripe cones for the big seeds, and dig nest holes in the soft wood of dead pines. In winter Pygmy Nuthatches travel in flocks of 20 or more birds and roost communally in tree cavities to stay warm. As many as 120 birds may share the same cavity. The ones on the bottom are so squashed by the ones who arrive later that they have to spend the night in torpor, an almost breathless sleep similar to hibernation.

Pygmy Nuthatches forage more out on the pine branches than their relatives, the White-breasted and Red-breasted Nuthatches, which search for food on the tree trunks. White-breasted Nuthatches are also found in open Douglas-fir forests and oak woodlands. They are much larger than the Pygmy, about the size of a small sparrow, and give a nasal chuckling call. Red-breasted Nuthatches are found in almost all coniferous forests and are easily recognized by their loud *enk-enk-enk* call. All three nuthatches feed on insects in summer; during periods of bounty, as when flights of ants appear, they store excess food in the deep cracks of pine bark.

In winter other woodland birds, such as chickadees, kinglets, and creepers, join the nuthatch flocks. These birds move through the forest together for protection from predators—it is always good to be part of a crowd when a pygmy-owl appears. The Mountain Chickadees and Golden-crowned Kinglets glean food from the outer branches, the nuthatches crawl up and down the trunks, and the Brown Creepers methodically spiral up the trunks, probing the cracks with their long curved bills.

The Lewis's Woodpecker prefers open pine woodlands—really grasslands with scattered big pines. It is a very unusual woodpecker; the only behavior it shares with its relatives is excavating holes in old trees to nest and roost in. Lewis's Woodpeckers feed in summer by sallying out from high perches to catch large flying insects in midair, sometimes spending twenty minutes or more in the air, as if they were overgrown swallows. They have a crowlike flight, rowing steadily through the air in a manner totally different from the normal bounding flight of woodpeckers.

In late summer, Lewis's Woodpeckers switch from insects to fruit and nuts, gathering berries in the woodlands or moving to orchards to feast on apples. If oaks are available, such as in some older suburban residential areas, they concentrate on acorns in the fall, pounding hundreds of them into cracks on tree snags for winter use. If winter food is not abundant locally, they are forced to migrate to southwestern oak woodlands.

Western Bluebirds also prefer the open Ponderosa Pine woodlands. They nest in cavities made by woodpeckers in the big pines and forage by perching on low branches and flying to the ground to catch grasshoppers and other sizable insects. Like the Lewis's Woodpecker, they turn to berries in late summer and will spend the winter in Rocky Mountain valleys if food is plentiful. They are especially fond of Russian Olive berries in winter.

Calliope Hummingbirds are the most common hummingbirds in Ponderosa Pine forests north of Wyoming. They arrive in April as they follow the blooming of Wax Currants northwards. Calliope Hummingbirds are the smallest birds north of Mexico, weighing about the same as five extra-strength aspirin tablets, but their character is bigger than life. They are often the first on the scene to mob pygmy-owls, buzzing the predator like oversize bees.

The males have a spectacular display, in which they fly to a height of 10 meters (30 feet), then dive toward the ground, pulling up at the last second to return to the same height. At the bottom of the dive, they spread their tail feathers to produce a loud *ptzing*, which must impress any females nearby. Like all male hummingbirds, male Calliopes are all show and no family values—they simply mate with any female excited by their displays and take no part in nest building or raising of young. The female builds a walnut-sized nest of plant down on top of a Ponderosa Pine branch, often just below another branch, which provides protection from the rain.

From Wyoming south, the Broad-tailed Hummingbird takes over from the Calliope as the most common of its family in montane forests. Male

Broad-tailed Hummingbirds have specialized wing tips—their outermost primary feather is narrowly tapered—that produce a cricketlike trilling when they fly. This sound is essential to the birds' ability to maintain territories against intruding males and thus ensure their success at mating with local females. They also put on diving displays, but the trilling flight to the top of the dive is a key component of their show.

Nightlife

As the western sky darkens on a summer evening, the Ponderosa Pine forest awakens to a natural nightlife that's one of the liveliest on the continent. Common Poorwills begin calling their name from open ridges—a rich, whistled *poor-will, poor-will*—while a Flammulated Owl gives a series of soft, ventriloquial *boo-boot* calls from the pines and firs upslope. An adult Great Horned Owl chimes in with a loud *HOO-hoo-hoo-HOOO*, wakening one of its fledged young, which replies with a hungry *khheee-ik!* A pack of Coyotes

The blue in the plumage of this male Western Bluebird results from light reflected off the fine structure of the feathers, whereas the rusty-red color of the breast is created by a pigment that absorbs blue light.

Opposite page: Calliope Hummingbirds, the smallest bird north of Mexico and the Caribbean, are common in the dry forests of British Columbia and Montana.

begins yipping and yowling from the grasslands below, and a Northern Flying Squirrel chitters, then launches itself into the air, gliding to the next big pine trunk and landing with an thud.

Common Poorwills are insect-eating specialists, cousins to the eastern Whip-poor-will. A poorwill sits on the ground, looking up at the twilit sky with large eyes, waiting for a moth to fly by. When it does, the bird flies up and catches it in a monstrous mouth and then returns to its perch. If you see a poorwill in a flashlight beam or the headlights of a car, its eyes reflect like big ruby lasers. During the day, these birds are much harder to find, their mottled gray-brown plumage blending perfectly with the pine twigs and dead leaves. I have seen hundreds of poorwills at night—they are common around my home—but only once have I flushed one off the ground by day. Poorwills call and hunt insects all night if the moon is out but quickly become inactive when it gets truly dark.

The masters of after-dark insect hunting are the bats, and there are plenty of them in these warm forests. They fly largely unseen and unheard by humans except for the descending buzz as they home in on and catch a moth. One species, the spectacular Spotted Bat, does produce clicks in our hearing range and can be heard most summer nights in the Ponderosa Pine forest—listen for a high-pitched *tsip-tsip-tsip-tsip* coursing overhead. Spotted Bats hunt in regular routes at treetop level around forest openings, and their huge ears and the low frequency of their echolocation call allow them to detect moths at great distances.

Male bats lead solitary lives all summer, but females of most Rocky Mountain species mass by the hundreds or even thousands with their young in nursery colonies. These big maternity wards are always in warm locations; attics of old buildings or large hollow pine snags are favored. One Little Brown Bat nursery colony in northern British Columbia was in a cave heated by an underground hot spring.

Spotted Bat

CRICKET THERMOMETERS

The loud daytime buzzing of cicadas is replaced at night by the trills of ground crickets and the measured peeps of tree crickets. Crickets sing by rubbing a file on one front wing over a scraper on the other. Each of the tree cricket species that live in the Rocky Mountains has a different song. Male Snowy Tree Crickets synchronize their chirps, producing a loud chorus that presumably attracts females from a great distance. This species is sometimes called the thermometer cricket, because observers in eastern North America have calculated that the frequency of its chirps is directly related to temperature—you can get a good estimate of temperature in degrees Celsius by counting the number of chirps in seven seconds and adding 5.

Mountain-dwelling Snowy Tree Crickets may not follow exactly the same rules, but you could make your own thermometer by counting the number of chirps in a given time over several evenings while recording the temperature. The closely related Riley's Tree Cricket also chirps but apparently not in a synchronized chorus. Its chirps are slower than those of Snowy Tree Crickets—about ninety per minute at 21°C (70°F).

The relatively large young—at birth up to a third of their mother's weight—are born in May and June. They usually stay at home, hanging from the rafters, while their mothers go on feeding flights. By late summer, they are strong enough to fly on their own, and in September the colonies disperse, the bats returning to hibernation caves, sometimes hundreds of kilometers away. There the females find males calling for them in the dark, and mating takes place with a minimum of courtship and absolutely no pair bonding. Since the young must be born in spring to survive, female bats use a rare technique to delay fertilization. They store live sperm all winter, feeding them at special cells in their uteruses.

FIRE AND THE FOREST

Douglas-fir and Ponderosa Pine have a different strategy from that of Lodgepole Pine for living with fire. Because montane forests are warmer and drier than those in the subalpine zone, fire returns much more often than it does to the cooler forests above—every ten or twenty years is common. So mature Douglas-firs and Ponderosa Pines have thick, corky bark that allows them to survive most ground fires. The fires create the open, parklike woodland with scattered large trees—called "veterans" because of their past brushes with fire—so typical of montane forests.

High-intensity fires do occur in montane forests, removing all trees, young and old, from large parts of the landscape. When such a fire burns through a Douglas-fir forest, Ponderosa Pines are often the pioneer species that germinate in the intense sun of the burned clearings. In the relatively moist conditions at these elevations, Ponderosa Pines grow to great sizes, their massive red trunks dwarfing those of their relatives on the drier slopes below. But pine seedlings are not adapted to growing in the shade of their parents, so the understory of these forests eventually becomes carpeted with Douglas-fir seedlings and a mixed forest is created.

Conditions are different in a pure Ponderosa Pine forest at lower elevations. Large Ponderosa Pines seem to encourage ground fires by producing quantities of highly inflammable fuel—old pine needles. Like all conifers, Ponderosa Pines shed their needles periodically. The needles are filled with natural preservatives and in the dry climate decay very slowly. As a result, a deep layer builds up under older trees. This layer can be extremely deep; as a boy, I often used to build forts with my brothers by piling needles into walls almost a meter (3 feet) high. In summer, this layer is so dry and the volatile chemicals in the needles are so inflammable that any spark will start a ground fire. Fueled by the dry grasses among the pines, the fire clears the open forest of any small trees and shrubs that might compete with the large pines for the precious water supply. The larger trees may be blackened by the fire, but they

Humans have been inextricably linked with fire since the dawn of humankind. We may not often ponder our relationship with fire, but recent summers of devastating wildfires in the Rocky Mountains have brought that ancient connection to prime-time news and banner headlines.

Fire ecologists divide forest fires into two main types—low-intensity, or stand-maintaining fires, and high-intensity, or stand-replacing fires. Low-intensity fires generally occur in fall and spring, burning low on the forest floor and killing small trees, shrubs, and dry grass but leaving large live trees to create an open, parklike forest of Douglas-firs or Ponderosa Pines. High-intensity fires happen at the height of summer, when the forest is tinder dry and the humidity is low. Ignited by lightning or a careless human, they quickly leap off the grass and brush and into the tree crowns. Afternoon winds, common on hot summer days, send them roaring through the forest, killing almost everything in their path and leaving a moonscape of black snags and white ash.

Evidence from tree rings and historical sources suggests that low-intensity fires were once common in the dry forests of the Rocky Mountains, burning any given patch of woodland every five to thirty years until the late 1800s. After that time, low-intensity fires essentially vanished from the forests, not just in the Rockies, but throughout western North America. Why? Fire suppression in the style of Smoky the Bear did not become effective until about 1940. Overgrazing by cattle, which were brought into the mountains by the thousands in the late 1800s, may be part of the reason, as the cows ate most of the grass that helped fuel these ground fires. But more and more evidence links historical low-intensity fires to the environmental management practices of aboriginal people.

The indigenous peoples of western North America regularly used fire as a tool to create habitat for berry-producing shrubs in high-elevation forests and to enhance habitat for other food plants, such as Glacier Lily, Arrowleaf Balsamroot, and Spring Beauty. The fires also improved game animal forage and protected villages from high-intensity wildfires. Some tribes had families who were the firekeepers for the community, directing the time and place of annual burns. To clear the underbrush from a mountainside or valley, large fires were usually set in the late fall, when the lowland grass was still dry but the first snows would keep the fire from spreading into thick forests at higher elevations. Areas were normally burned every ten or fifteen years but as often as every three years on sites where fuel, in the form of dried grasses, shrubs, pine needles, and dead branches, accumulated quickly, and where open habitats such as berry patches were the desired result. In the second half of the nineteenth century, indigenous peoples were confined to reservations and their traditional practices severely disrupted.

High-intensity fires, in contrast, continued unabated until fire suppression efforts significantly dampened their frequency in the middle of the twentieth century. Early logging quickly removed most of the large, fireproof trees from the landscape, and the forest filled in with thick stands of young trees and a shrubby understory. In these dry forests, organic material does not decay very quickly, and the production of leaves and branches vastly exceeds the decomposition rate. Fuel loads quickly build up. Without periodic ground fires to clear away this fuel, the forest is soon ready for a major firestorm.

So what can we do? Prescribed burns are being set more frequently by forest managers to reduce the likelihood of firestorms, but in many areas there is simply too much fuel in the forests to safely do this. Lower branches, small trees, and shrubs must be removed mechanically before fire can be used to complete the job. These projects can be expensive but generally cost only a fraction of the amount spent on fighting a major forest fire. Public concerns about air quality during prescribed burns and fears about runaway fires must also be addressed, but the greater fear of seeing whole communities razed by fire may allow land managers to reintroduce fire as the important ecological tool it was to indigenous firekeepers for centuries.

This fire in the Sawback Range of Banff National Park, Alberta, was set by habitat managers to create a more diverse, natural landscape after decades of active fire suppression.

usually survive. They can even survive more serious blazes that burn right through the bark on one side of the trunk and destroy up to half of the crown.

But if the fire burns all the big pines, only the grasses and some shrubs will survive, sprouting from root systems protected from the blaze. At the lower tree line, it may take decades for conditions to be right for pine germination, and if another ground fire occurs within a decade or two of that, any young pines will be destroyed and the grassland will be maintained indefinitely.

Gambel Oak is the common scrub oak of southern Rocky Mountain hillsides.

Previous pages: This burned forest in Jasper National Park is a typical sight in the montane and drier subalpine forests of the Rocky Mountains, where frequent fires maintain a mosaic of open meadows, young growth, and older forests.

GAMBEL OAK WOODLANDS

At the fire-maintained boundary between grass and forest in the southern Rocky Mountains is a woodland dominated by the Gambel Oak. These green woodlands turn fiery orange and red in autumn, tumbling down mountainsides in colorful torrents that hint at the flames that maintain them. For like the Trembling Aspen at higher elevations, Gambel Oaks reproduce most commonly by sending out suckers from their roots, creating clonal thickets of small trees after a fire. The oak thickets are home to a community of animals quite different from that in the pines around them.

Gambel Oaks also reproduce by seed. In spring the branches carry green male catkins, which produce pollen, and tiny green female flowers. The acorns mature in the fall; every few years, a bumper crop of acorns is produced, often after a very low yield the previous year. A wide range of wildlife

species eats the acorns. Wild Turkeys forage through the oak woodlands but usually return to Ponderosa Pine forests in the evening to roost high in the larger trees. Rock Squirrels—a woodland species of ground squirrel—feed on the acorns as well but are really food generalists, eating everything from flower bulbs to carrion.

THE PYGMY FOREST
A unique ecosystem forms where the Rockies merge with the Colorado Plateau and the Great Basin. Below the Ponderosa Pines and above the sagebrush is an open woodland of Pinyon Pines and Utah Juniper. These trees are often barely more than shrub height, but they can live for centuries and have trunks up to 1 meter (3 feet) in diameter. Pinyons, with their almost spherical form, are easy to identify; and their large, edible seeds form the

Western Scrub-Jays are conspicuous residents of oak and juniper woodlands in the southern Rockies.

Overleaf: The large seeds of the Pinyon Pine are an important source of food to many animals.

basis of one of the important food chains in this habitat. Every four to six years, the trees produce an abundant crop.

The presence of this rich food source attracts many species of wildlife but none so intimately involved with pinyon as the Pinyon Jay. These all-blue jays are highly social—everything they do is done in flocks. When the pine seeds are mature in the fall, the jays begin harvesting them, judging each seed by its color—fully formed, dark brown seeds are kept; hollow yellow seeds are discarded. Pinyon Jays have an expandable esophagus, allowing them to store up to forty large seeds in their throats at one time, ten times the capacity of the closely related Western Scrub-Jay. They cache these seeds in clusters in thick leaf-and-needle litter on the ground in open areas.

After a successful fall and early winter of caching seeds, Pinyon Jays begin to breed, in many areas as early as February. One population of Pinyon Jays in New Mexico even breeds in the fall. Young jays generally remain with their natal flock. When the Pinyon Pine seed crop fails, flocks coalesce into groups of several hundred birds that roam the western United States looking for an alternative food source.

Utah Junipers have a cedarlike foliage and fibrous bark, and even from the window of a fast-moving car you can take in their distinctive aroma, likened by some to that of cat urine. They produce an ample crop of powder-blue berries. The Townsend's Solitaire is perhaps the bird most closely tied to juniper. These slim gray thrushes descend from their mountain breeding grounds and set up winter territories among the junipers, advertising the territories by singing long, warbling songs and defending them against all other birds. I'm often taken aback when I hear their songs—which I associate with warm summer evenings in the Ponderosa Pine forests around my home—on cold, sunny winter days in the foothills of the southern Rockies.

Other birds are attracted to the pygmy forests of pinyon and juniper, not so much for the promise of seeds and berries, but for the structure of the forest itself and the insect life on the trees and bushes. Perhaps not surprisingly, these birds tend to be gray to match the drab foliage of the shrubs associated with this habitat. Gray Flycatchers perch on junipers and large sagebrush, sallying down to the ground to pick up grasshoppers and other insects. Gray Vireos sing short songs through the heat of the day from the trees. Black-throated Gray Warblers, which are oak specialists in mountains along the Pacific coast, are associated with Pinyon Pine and junipers in the southern Rockies. Juniper Titmice, all-gray chickadees with a jaunty crest, probe the foliage for insects, while a lisping flock of Bushtits plays leapfrog through the trees.

Utah Juniper berries are a favorite food of birds, particularly the Townsend's Solitaire.

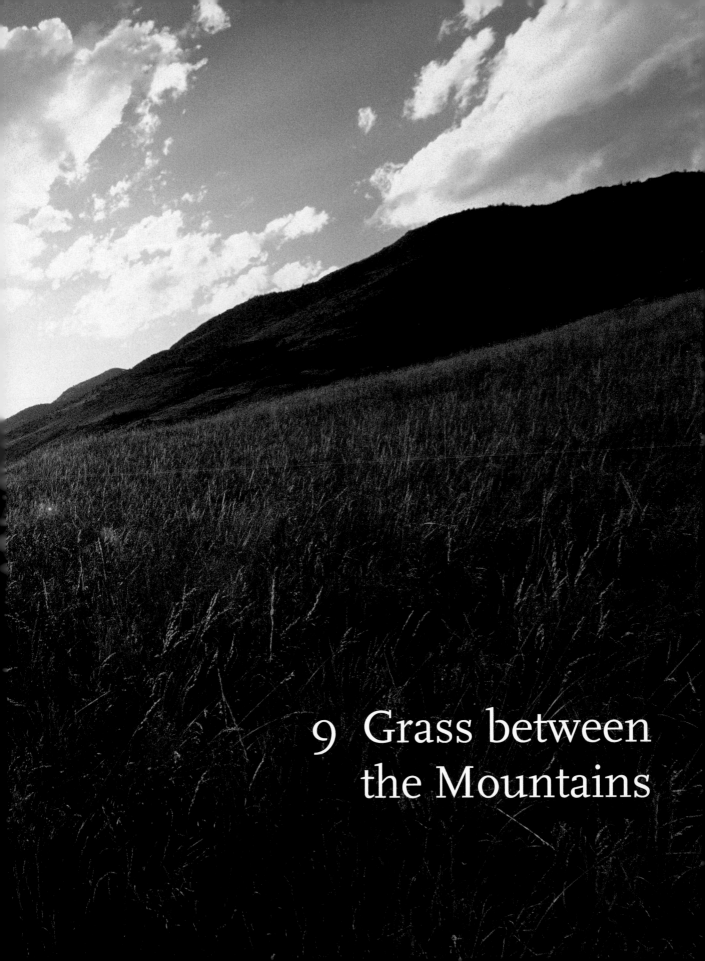

9 Grass between
the Mountains

I believe a leaf of grass is no less than the journey-work of the stars.

—Walt Whitman, *Leaves of Grass*

Grass between the Mountains

CHAPTER 9

GRASSLANDS AND MOUNTAINS GO TOGETHER like bread and butter—it is hard to find one without the other. Almost every mountain range in the world has its grassy partner—the Andes and Patagonia, the Himalayas and the central Asian steppes, the Rockies and the Great Plains. For grasslands are born of mountains. The high ranges block moist airflows, creating dry environments on their lee sides, where there is not enough moisture for trees to grow. These environments exist within the mountains as well—sinuous golden valleys tucked in behind high peaks. Grasslands are an integral part of the Rocky Mountains, from the southern Rocky Mountain Trench to Jackson Hole and the sagebrush hills of the Gunnison Valley. To many people, this is the habitat of the wild West, stagecoaches and cattle drives against a backdrop of snowy mountains; to naturalists, it means pronghorns and prickly pears, bluebirds and bunchgrass.

These grasslands are often called high deserts—they do have cacti and rattlesnakes, after all—but most ecological definitions of deserts exclude areas with perennial grasses. Technically, these are steppes—cool, continental environments too dry for trees. Although grasslands can look the same from a distance, they contain a tremendous diversity of species and associated plant communities as a result of differing soil chemistry, soil texture, and moisture. You can learn a lot about local conditions by knowing a few of the common grasses and shrubs.

Along the eastern edge of the Rocky Mountains in Colorado, there is a strip of tall-grass prairie where the grasslands meet the Ponderosa Pine forests of the mountains. These tall-grass species thrive in a narrow zone where summer thunderstorms grow out of the prairie sky, dumping their rain on the foothills as they rise against the mountains. But elsewhere in the Rockies, the predominant grasses are bunchgrasses.

BUNCHGRASSES

Grasses can survive in these inhospitable regions because they have small, ephemeral structures aboveground and large, fibrous root systems below. Approximately 75 percent of the biomass in a grassland is belowground, and most of the herbivores are there, too—bacteria, fungi, nematodes, mites, and other small creatures that live in the grass root system.

Because the bulk of their mass is underground, grasses can also survive fires and grazing. Historically, fire intervals for grasslands ranged from two to twenty-five years. When the land is tinder dry, lightning strikes spark wildfires that burn patches of grassland. Indigenous people also set fires for thousands of years for many reasons—to maintain grazing habitat for wildlife, to improve conditions for food plants, and to drive herding animals during hunts. These grasslands evolved with a large and diverse community of grazing animals, including camels, horses, pronghorns, Elk, and Bighorn Sheep, and so grazing is another important force. When a clump of bunchgrass is grazed, hormones secreted by the leaves naturally drop in concentration, signaling buds in the root crown to begin growing new shoots. The clipped blades themselves can grow from their bases as well. As long as fires are not

A fringe of tall-grass prairie grows along the eastern edge of the Front Range in Colorado.

Bluebunch Wheatgrass is used as an indicator of good range condition—it tends to decrease in abundance under heavy grazing.

too frequent and grazing is not too intense, bunchgrass can survive both assaults.

Bunchgrasses also tolerate drought well because their leaves contain a great deal of dry support tissue. Thus, they do not wilt, as orchard grass would, but just become dormant. The bunchgrasses of the Rocky Mountains sleep through the summer drought as a bear sleeps through winter; they actively grow only during late fall and again as soon as the snow melts in late winter and spring. These are known as cool-season grasses, since they function most efficiently at moderate temperatures and moderate light concentrations.

In contrast, warm-season grasses tend to form carpets of sod as opposed to growing in discrete clumps as bunchgrasses do. They also photosynthesize most efficiently at high temperatures and under intense light, so they flourish in regions such as the Great Plains, where summer rainfall is more dependable. This is perhaps why Bison did not occur on the intermontane grasslands, since they require grasses that continue to grow through the summer.

Bluebunch Wheatgrass—the state grass of Montana—is one of the most important grasses in the Rocky Mountains. It is easily recognized by its long flowering stalk, with the florets arranged along the stalk like tiny beads on a string. This species is favored by cattle and so tends to decrease in stature and abundance under grazing pressure. A healthy stand of Bluebunch Wheatgrass is used as an indicator of good range condition.

Various species of fescue are also common components of bunchgrass communities, generally growing at slightly higher altitudes, where conditions are cooler and more moist than in Bluebunch Wheatgrass zones. Fescues form tight bunches as well, but their leaves tend to be even finer and more tightly rolled than those of Bluebunch Wheatgrass, and their florets form open, loosely branched clusters. Another bunchgrass, Red Threeawn, often dominates sites with sandy soils, especially if they have been heavily grazed. The awns of its seed heads form a three-pointed star reminiscent of the Mercedes-Benz logo. Unlike most bunchgrasses, threeawns grow best in hot weather and prefer sites with regular summer rain showers.

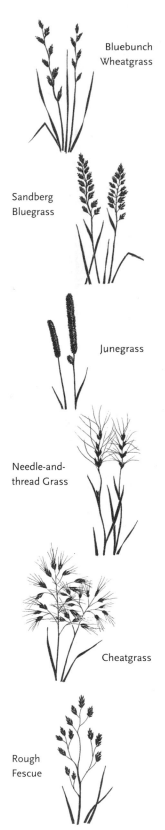

Bluebunch Wheatgrass

Sandberg Bluegrass

Junegrass

Needle-and-thread Grass

Cheatgrass

Rough Fescue

A living crust of the earth

True to their name, bunchgrasses grow in discrete bunches, and the ground between them appears relatively free of life until you look closely. Connecting the grass clumps and covering the soil of undisturbed grasslands is a fragile organic layer of lichens, mosses, liverworts, and cyanobacteria—collectively called cryptogams. Despite its relative obscurity, this cryptogamic crust is a critical part of bunchgrass ecosystems. It stabilizes the soil, restricts establishment of weedy species, and helps retain soil moisture. In addition, the cyanobacteria fertilize the soil by converting atmospheric nitrogen into nitrates.

The cryptogamic crust is also a beautiful little ecosystem to watch close up. Unfortunately, it can be difficult to find these days; much of it has been trampled and shattered by horses and cattle. The crust is especially fragile on dry, sandy soils, where it takes a long time to recover its structure and function. The opening of the soil surface and the subsequent invasion of alien weedy plants may have just as great an effect on grassland communities as the grass grazing does.

Spring blooms

Mountain grasslands are quiet through the winter. The plants are dormant under a shallow blanket of snow, and there are few signs of life—perhaps a lone Northern Shrike perched on a shrub, waiting for a Montane Vole

When Lewis and Clark crossed the Rockies in September 1805, they were starving, compelled to begin eating their horses as they followed a stream they named Hungry Creek. They chanced upon a trusting band of Nez Perce, who took them in and fed them bulbs of Blue Camas. They purchased more of these lifesaving roots and continued on their journey. On their return the following spring, they camped at Weippe Prairie, Idaho, and remarked:

> Our camp is agreeably situated in a point of timbered land on the eastern borders of an extensive leavel and butifull prairie. The quawmash [camas] is now in blume at a Short distance it resembles a lake of fine clear water, so complete is this deseption that on first Sight I could have sworn it was water.

Blue Camas grows in seasonally wet meadows that are quite different from the surrounding bunchgrass hills. Sedges and several species of grass, including Tufted Hairgrass, carpet the ground, and Western Blue Flag and buttercups join the camas in a spring wildflower spectacle. These meadows are among the most endangered habitats in the Rockies; most of them have disappeared under the plow or have been overrun by invasive species such as Reed Canarygrass.

Previous pages: Sagebrush Buttercups brighten inter-mountain grasslands shortly after snowmelt.

to surface. But as soon as the snow melts in March, life explodes onto the surface. Sagebrush Buttercups brighten the landscape as the bunchgrasses quickly green up. A few weeks later, Yellowbells and shootingstars add more color to the scene. In late April and May, the flower bloom begins in earnest; Arrowleaf Balsamroot spread brilliant yellow sunflowers across whole hillsides. Bright pink Bitterroot flowers appear out of nowhere, and in moister areas, the cream-colored blooms of Meadow Death-camas carpet the green meadows. By June the hills are splashed with the blue, yellow, and red of Silky Lupines, Brown-eyed Susans (blanket-flower), and Scarlet Gilias. Mariposa lilies, or sego lilies as some species are called, are often the only flowers left blooming by early July. These lilies store water and nutrients in their large bulbs and use them to create their exquisite flowers in the early weeks of the summer drought.

All these plants are trying to grow and bloom before the summer drought sets in. They must produce leaves, flowers, and seeds and then store enough nutrients underground to survive until next spring. It is amazing how such a flamboyant plant as balsamroot, with its broad leaves and huge spring flowers, can wither to a few brittle stalks and flakes of gray leaf litter on the August soil.

Bitterroot is even more dramatic. It arises as a rosette of succulent, cylindrical green leaves as soon as the snow melts. The leaves produce sugars that are stored as starch in the thick root through March and April; then the leaves wither away as the flowers develop. By the time the spectacular blooms open in late May, they seem to be springing *de novo* from the soil—there is no sign of the leaves at all. And by late summer the entire plant seems to disappear altogether, although the root lies underground, waiting once more for spring.

Insects

Keep an eye on the ground in front of you when walking through a dry grassland. You will step on fewer cacti and see a myriad of interesting insects and spiders. Female velvet ants—actually furry, wingless wasps—run along the ground searching for the nesting burrows of solitary bees to parasitize. Robber flies buzz through the air, and brilliantly metallic green tiger beetles wait on the sand below, both watching intently with excellent vision for the insect that will be their next meal. And watching the insects is so easy for us in this open country.

Reptiles

These hot, dry grasslands are also heaven for reptiles. They can bask in the early spring sun to get their bodies up to optimum temperature, ensuring a long active season compared with the season in the colder forests above. Although we call reptiles "cold-blooded," their blood is usually as warm as ours while they are active. "Warm-blooded" animals—birds and mammals—regulate their body temperature through physiological processes, whereas reptiles regulate body temperature through behavior. Throughout the spring, summer, and fall, they choose resting sites depending on whether they need to warm up or cool down. In spring they are often found on south-facing slopes, where the sun quickly heats them. As temperatures increase above their preferred body temperature in July, they often move down into shaded valleys, where deep grass and water offer cooling potential.

Easily the most famous of all Rocky Mountain snakes, the Western Rattlesnake is a shy, retiring animal that relies more often on its camouflage for protection than its warning rattle and sharp fangs. When you do hear that *chchchchch!* buzz in the dry grass, it does stop you in your tracks, though. While you scan the area around your feet for the snake, it is probably slipping quietly under a nearby rock. The bite of a Western Rattlesnake is dangerous but rarely fatal.

Rattlesnakes overwinter in communal dens in deep rock crevices on sunny, warm slopes. It never falls below freezing in these hibernacula, and the snakes manage to stay a few degrees warmer than air temperature by huddling together. They emerge from the dens in early spring—late March or April—although about one-third of the snakes in the den do not survive the winter. The snakes spend the summer away from the den but do not stray more than about 1.5 kilometers (1 mile).

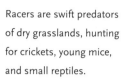

Racers are swift predators of dry grasslands, hunting for crickets, young mice, and small reptiles.

In the Rockies, rattlesnakes eat mainly small rodents but also shrews and small birds. On the edge of the Great Basin and Colorado Plateau they may also eat a significant amount of lizards. Mating takes place in late spring or summer on the foraging range, but females store sperm and the eggs are not fertilized until after the snakes emerge the following spring. This delay allows the embryos to grow inside their mothers throughout the summer, when the females can bask in the warm sun to encourage their babies' development. Unlike the rest of the rattlesnake population, pregnant females remain around the den site all summer. Each mother gives birth to about five to ten live young in the fall. The mothers immediately go into hibernation, while the young remain at the surface for about two weeks, until they shed their skin for the first time.

Incredibly, the mothers do not eat during this entire period—they fast for about one and a half years, from the time they enter hibernation after mating, through the summer of their pregnancy, and through another entire winter. This pattern means that females can only give birth every second year at best, and at higher latitudes and altitudes, every third year is probably more usual. Females are very emaciated after giving birth and must double their weight before mating again.

Female rattlesnakes must be at least 55 centimeters (22 inches) long from snout to vent before they become sexually mature; in the Rocky Mountains it takes four to eight years for females to reach that size. Male rattlesnakes must be about the same size or even larger before they can mate, but they reach that size in two or three years. This long period to reach maturity and

If you are very observant, you may see a small round lizard dart through the bunchgrass. This is the Short-horned Lizard, the smallest of a unique genus that specializes in hunting ants throughout the southwestern quarter of North America. Horned lizards have a squat appearance reminiscent of a toad, which gives rise to their scientific name *Phrynosoma*—literally, "toad body"—and their colloquial moniker, "horny toad." Their body shape may result from the need for a large stomach—ants are not especially nutritious so the toads have to eat a lot every day to survive—or from their high fecundity. One female can give birth to as many as sixteen young at one time.

Horned lizards spend much of their time sitting motionless next to ant trails—especially those of harvester ants—gobbling up the insects as they march past. Of all members in the genus, Short-horned Lizards are found at the highest latitudes and altitudes—they occur north to southern Canada. They are also one of the few species to give birth to live young, a common adaptation of reptiles of cool climate. About a quarter of their diet is of insects other than ants, perhaps an indication that ant supplies are less reliable in this environment.

Ants are full of nasty chemicals, especially formic acid, and not many animals eat them. Some horned lizards take advantage of this in a bizarre way. If a dog (or a fox) picks one up in its mouth, the lizard shoots a stream of blood out of its eye sockets into the predator's mouth. The lizard blood, replete with ant chemicals, must taste vile to the dog, for it immediately drops the lizard and tries desperately to rid its mouth of the blood. Once a dog has been blood-blasted, it never picks up another horned lizard. Interestingly, horned lizards rarely squirt blood when picked up by humans, and when other potential predators such as large snakes or birds approach them, they simply run away.

Left: Short-horned Lizard

the period of two or three years between female reproduction events results in an extremely low reproductive rate—an unusual trait in small animals. Rattlesnakes are therefore vulnerable to environmental disturbances, and small populations are especially susceptible to extirpation. So take care when walking in rattlesnake country, and don't harm the snakes unless you are in real danger. Be especially careful around possible den sites—not only for your own safety but for the well-being of the rattlesnakes.

Gopher Snakes—often called Bull Snakes—look similar to rattlesnakes and often cohabit with them in winter dens. The blotches on their backs are more rectangular than those of rattlesnakes, and they lack the rattle at the end of the tail. Gopher Snakes take advantage of this similarity to their venomous cousins in a defensive display that includes hissing loudly, striking with open mouth, and vibrating the tail rapidly, a movement that often sounds like a rattle if the tail is in contact with dry leaves. Gopher Snakes lay their eggs in early summer in underground cavities on south-facing slopes, either in rock slides or abandoned mammal burrows. They often share the nest with other Gopher Snakes or even other species such as Racers.

Mammals

The most conspicuous mammals in the grasslands are the ground squirrels. Their upright stance at the burrow entrance, always on the lookout for predators, and loud alarm whistles make them easy to find. There are a number of species throughout the Rocky Mountains. The Columbian Ground Squirrel is primarily a mountain meadow species in the northern Rockies but lives in semiarid grasslands as well. Its prairie equivalent, the Richardson's Ground Squirrel, is found wherever the Great Plains meander into the mountains. Columbian Ground Squirrels have been moving east in Montana, displacing the smaller Richardson's. The Wyoming Ground Squirrel is so similar to the Richardson's that it was once considered simply a subspecies of the latter, but recently discovered genetic differences have elevated it to full species status. It has two Rocky Mountain populations, one in Montana and Idaho and another in Wyoming and Colorado. The Uinta Ground Squirrel, identified by its blackish tail, may be found in dry grasslands but is also found in mountain meadows; it is especially conspicuous in Yellowstone National Park. The Idaho Ground Squirrel, found on the western edge of the Rockies in west central Idaho, is one of the most endangered mammals in North America. Its population has declined precipitously in recent decades, apparently because forests are encroaching on its mountain meadow habitat.

Columbian Ground Squirrels are found in grassy meadows from valley bottoms to mountain peaks.

Ground squirrels are deep hibernators. Most of them go underground in midsummer, when the grasslands begin to dry out and green vegetation becomes harder to find. They remain belowground until late March or April, when the males emerge and set up hierarchical territories. The females emerge about two weeks later and mate about four days after that. After the very short breeding season, the males leave the females' territories; the young are born about a month later.

Ground squirrels attract the attention of many grassland predators, including Golden Eagles, Ferruginous Hawks, Prairie Falcons, Badgers, and Coyotes. Badgers almost always set up their home burrows close to a ground

BISON

I first encountered Bison in the mid-1960s when my family visited the "Buffalo Paddock" in Banff National Park. I was disappointed to see the great beasts, emblematic of vast, open prairies, wandering a fenced meadow, a farmlike setting in the mountains.

Bison are animals of the Great Plains but are now largely confined to a few grassy valleys in the Rocky Mountains and scattered herds elsewhere in northern Canada and Alaska. Their range in the mountains was always restricted to valleys on the eastern slopes, where summer rains were sufficient to support grasses that grew throughout the season.

Bison were undoubtedly hunted by indigenous peoples from the moment humans arrived in western North America. The Bison's habit of forming large, migratory herds may have allowed them to escape the mass extinctions of large mammals at the end of the Ice Age; the herds were so large and mobile that local tribes may not have been able to significantly affect the overall populations, despite effective techniques such as forcing herds off cliffs, and despite the introduction of the horse by the Spanish. The rifle and the railway put an end to the Bison on the prairies, however. Large-scale commercial hunts for bison hides began in 1870, and by 1882 the big animals were essentially gone.

By 1900, only 23 Bison remained in Yellowstone, the only extant herd in the United States that was not entirely formed by restocking of captive animals. The Yellowstone herd was augmented by captive-bred stock and intensively managed in a ranchlike operation until 1968, when the population was allowed to fluctuate naturally. There are now about 4,000 Bison in Yellowstone. About 800 Bison roam freely in Grand Teton National Park, but they concentrate unnaturally in winter at feeding stations for Elk. The only other significant free-ranging herd in the Rocky Mountains is at Pink Mountain in northern British Columbia, where a small number of Bison escaped from a ranch in 1971 and now number about 900 animals. In 1908, 36 Bison were released into the National Bison Range in western Montana; that herd, free ranging but in a fenced area, is now maintained at about 400 animals.

So the great herds of plains Bison are gone, and these Rocky Mountain remnants are not permitted to make the migratory treks their ancestors made. Many Yellowstone Bison carry brucellosis, a disease brought to North America by cattle. Montana ranches are brucellosis free, and to maintain that status any Bison leaving Yellowstone National Park for the open spaces of Montana are immediately killed. In the winter of 1996–97, over a thousand Bison met their end that way. There are tentative plans to reintroduce Bison into Waterton Lakes National Park and Banff National Park, but these populations will undoubtedly be fenced in like most of their cousins elsewhere in the Rockies.

Badgers use their powerful claws to dig out ground squirrels, their favorite prey.

squirrel colony and can eat up to three ground squirrels a day. The Badgers hunt the rodents by digging into their burrows and catching them underground. If the ground squirrels make a run for it out a rear entrance, they risk being caught by a Coyote, since these two predators occasionally work in tandem, the Badger digging in the front, the Coyote waiting at the back. Coyotes working in this manner have a 30 percent better chance of getting ground squirrel for dinner.

Birds

Western Meadowlarks are the epitome of a grassland bird. Their strong legs, long toes, and sharp claws are built for a life on the ground. They are cryptically colored above to blend in with the dried grass stalks that cover their ground nest but brightly colored below—their bright yellow breasts are decorated with a jet-black necklace, and their tails are broadly edged in white. And the males sing loudly and beautifully, often from high in the air, where the finery of their breasts, bellies, and tails can be clearly seen by prospective mates.

Meadowlarks are related to the New World blackbirds and orioles, not to larks. The only lark native to North America is the Horned Lark, which is

Pronghorns are a uniquely North American mammal, the only member of the family Antilocapridae. The family name translates to "goat-antelope," but pronghorns are neither goat nor antelope and are probably most closely related to deer. Like cows, sheep, and goats, they have horns with a bony core and sheath of keratin, the same material that forms fingernails. Unlike other horned animals, however, Pronghorns shed the keratin sheath every year, much as deer do with their bony antlers. Pronghorns evolved about 20 million years ago, branching into several species before the Pleistocene extinctions whittled the family down to the single species present today.

Pronghorns are the speedsters of the grasslands, apparently able to reach speeds of 100 kilometers per hour (60 miles per hour) for short distances and able to run at more than 60 kilometers per hour (40 miles per hour) for long distances. They are able to do this because of remarkable physiological adaptations—they have a very large windpipe to bring air to the lungs, a heart three times larger than that of a goat of similar size, and a high concentration of red blood cells. When healthy, they can outdistance any predator in open country, an ability likely evolved in the face of predation from the American Cheetah, now extinct. The main predator of modern Pronghorns is the Coyote.

Like Bison, Pronghorns once numbered in the tens of millions in western North America. That number dwindled to perhaps 35,000 in 1920 but has since rebounded to about 1 million animals. Pronghorns are no longer found on 75 percent of their historical range; the highest populations are in Wyoming and Montana in the short-grass prairies along the eastern edge of the Rocky Mountains. Herds found within the Rockies, such as those in Yellowstone and Grand Teton national parks, are at the climatic limits of their range, and many succumb to drought and harsh winters.

The population that summers in Grand Teton—about three hundred animals—migrates each fall along the Gros Ventre and Green rivers to wintering grounds in south-central Wyoming. The 240-kilometer (150-mile) trip is the longest migration taken by a large terrestrial mammal population in the contiguous forty-eight states. That route is being progressively cut up by fences and new housing, which prompts concern among wildlife managers for the continued survival of the Grand Teton herd. Even the nonmigratory population in Yellowstone has declined dramatically, down to only about two hundred animals from six hundred in 1991.

found in areas of sparse grass throughout these mountain grasslands. Like the meadowlark, it is drab brown above, with a black necklace, a black-and-white tail, and a penchant for singing while flying high above its territory. The most common grassland sparrow is the Vesper Sparrow; it does not sing in flight and is more or less a drab stripy brown all over, but it does share white outer tail feathers with the lark and meadowlark.

SAGEBRUSH STEPPES

In many Rocky Mountain valleys, the grasslands are covered in a silver sea of sagebrush. This is the true West to me—the meadowlark's song and the smell of sage after a warm summer rain. The patterns that underlie the

Overleaf: Pronghorns live in small herds most of the year. Although they live exclusively in grasslands, they eat relatively little grass, grazing instead on soft forbs.

distribution of sagebrush and other shrubs in the intermontane grasslands are not always obvious, often obscured by the paths of previous fires and a history of climatic change. However, sagebrush does seem to occur on sites where most of the precipitation falls in winter.

There are several species of sagebrush in the Rockies. Big Sagebrush is the classic, widespread species; the other species are found in sites with more particular soil and moisture characteristics. Silver Sagebrush is found on more moist or sandy soils, whereas Black Sagebrush is restricted to dry, wind-blown ridgetops where little snow accumulates and to shallower soils where moisture is not retained. On some drier sites, Big Sagebrush occurs in strips where snowdrifts bring just enough moisture to allow it to survive. On wetter sites, the pattern is reversed, since these snowdrift sites in the lee of small ridges are too moist.

Sagebrush has several adaptations for life in an arid climate. Like most of the shrubs in this environment it has a long taproot and gray leaves covered in tiny hairs that reduce evaporation. Sagebrush produces two types of leaves in spring: ephemeral leaves that are dropped at the start of the midsummer drought, and overwintering leaves that remain on the plant for a full year. The strong smell of sagebrush comes from high concentrations of terpenes secreted in the leaves to deter browsing. Sagebrush often increases in density after heavy grazing has reduced competition from grasses. For some time many ecologists believed that sagebrush had only become common in the last century, after widespread cattle grazing, but old photos show large, healthy stands of sagebrush before cattle arrived. Sagebrush may do well with grazing, but it is not fire tolerant and disappears on sites with short fire intervals.

Common Rabbitbrush looks similar to sagebrush but has narrow, linear

WOOD TICKS

If you are walking through sagebrush country in spring—March through June—watch for Wood Ticks questing from the tips of sage twigs. The eight-legged creatures hold on with their back three pairs of legs while stretching out their long front legs, waiting for a big mammal to walk by. Although ticks are found in open forests as well, they do not jump from trees onto the heads of unsuspecting hosts. Rather, they like to climb up our bodies to find warm spots like the nape of the neck, armpits, and other similar body sites.

leaves and a spectacular yellow cluster of small flowers in late summer and early fall. It also lacks the pungent aroma of sagebrush, instead imparting only a subtle currylike smell to the air. This species grows especially well on disturbed soils and often dominates roadsides and abandoned agricultural land. Antelope-brush or Bitter-brush is another component of these shrub steppes, usually occurring on sandy soils below Ponderosa Pine forests. Its long, gangly branches and yellow spring blossoms make it easy to identify. Antelope-brush is an important winter browse plant for Elk and deer; in summer it is favored by Lark Sparrows, which sing glorious songs from the branches and forage on the bare soil below.

A long list of animal species is restricted to sagebrush ecosystems, most colored in various shades of drab to match the gray of the shrubs. Sage Sparrows sing tinkling songs in early spring, joined by the longer, warbling songs of Sage Thrashers. Brewer's Sparrows, perhaps the plainest-looking of their entire family, sing glorious canarylike songs from atop sagebrush.

But the strangest sounds come in the predawn darkness of an early-spring morning—strange hooting and popping sounds. As the day dawns, the source is revealed: a group of displaying male sage-grouse. These large birds—almost the size of a small turkey—gather each spring to strut on traditional dancing grounds, fanning their tails, erecting head plumes, and inflating big yellow air sacs on their chests. Females fly in from all over to look them over. Recent studies have shown that there are two species of sage-grouse in the Rockies— the Greater Sage-Grouse throughout the central Rockies, and the Gunnison Sage-Grouse in the Gunnison Valley of south-central Colorado and extreme eastern Utah. The Gunnison Sage-Grouse is only two-thirds the size of the Greater and has thicker head plumes and different display calls.

Overleaf: Many valleys throughout the southern and central Rockies are cloaked with bunchgrass and sagebrush. The hills of the Gunnison Valley of Colorado, shown here, are home to the Gunnison Sage-Grouse, a bird found nowhere else in the world.

After the tick finds an ideal spot, it inserts its mouthparts into the skin and begins ingesting blood. Within a few days, the ticks are the size of a raisin and drop to the ground. There the females lay a few thousand eggs and die. The eggs hatch into larval ticks that have only six legs; these find a small rodent host such as a mouse to get their first blood meal. After that they molt into nymphs, which resemble small adults. Nymphs get a blood meal from a larger rodent— usually a ground squirrel or chipmunk—then molt into the adult tick that quests for larger mammals such as humans, cattle, or deer. If adult ticks are unsuccessful in their quest in one year, they will live again to try next year. Laboratory evidence suggests that they could theoretically survive about forty years in the wild if they were unsuccessful in obtaining a blood meal and mating.

Wood Ticks are associated with several serious medical conditions. Most famous but least common is Rocky Mountain spotted fever, which was discovered in the Bitterroot Valley of Montana. This potentially fatal disease is caused by an intracellular bacterium, *Rickettsia rickettsii*.

Wood Ticks also transmit the virus responsible for Colorado tick fever, a disease that initially produces similar symptoms to those of spotted fever but is not nearly as serious.

Perhaps most interesting is tick paralysis, a condition caused by a toxin introduced in the tick's saliva as part of the anaesthetic needed to keep you unaware of the bite. Some ticks produce enough of this toxin to cause increasing paralysis, which can lead to death if the tick is not discovered. After the tick is removed, recovery is rapid and complete.

So have a good friend check you over after a hike through the spring sagebrush; if you find a tick embedded in your skin, simply take a pair of tweezers, grasp the tick as close to your skin as possible, and pull slowly and steadily back. No twisting is necessary. Do not try to coax it out with alcohol, gasoline, a lit cigarette, or any combination of the former.

Sage-grouse always nest under the shade of a sagebrush, both to stay cool and to hide the nest from predators. Part of the attraction of shrub-steppe habitats for all wildlife is the cover that the shrubs provide, whether for a young Pronghorn hiding from a nosy Coyote or an adult jackrabbit resting in the midday heat.

ALKALI FLATS

In hot, arid basins, where water evaporates quickly, soils are highly alkaline and special plant communities develop. The Great Divide Basin of Wyoming is the classic example of this situation in the Rocky Mountains and has many alkali flats, but there are many other smaller alkali flats scattered throughout the mountains. Saltbushes and Greasewood are common shrubs in this environment; Alkali Sacaton and Saltgrass dominate the grass community. Most plants cannot grow in these salty soils, but saltbush and Saltgrass have special glands on their leaves that secrete excess salt. Some of the plants that grow in seasonally flooded plains, such as Greasewood and Glasswort, gather water in spring and store it in succulent leaves. Where these alkali flats receive enough moisture to form lakes, they represent the favorite habitat of such striking shorebirds as the American Avocet and Black-necked Stilt.

LIFE ON THE ROCKS

You are never far from rocks in the Rocky Mountains, and the cliffs and talus slopes at lower elevations have a community all to themselves. Nuttall's Cottontails scamper through the grass at the base of talus slopes, ready to dash between the rocks for safety. Reptiles scurry and slither around and under the rocks at the base of cliffs, using the natural heat-absorbing properties of the rocks to maintain their body temperatures and even incubate their eggs. The Western Skink is one lizard closely tied to rocks. Like all skinks, it has smooth, shiny scales; its clear striping also helps identify it. Young skinks are very obvious—they have sky-blue tails that are obviously designed to distract predators. If a young skink is threatened by a Coyote, it immediately drops its tail on the ground and runs, leaving the Coyote staring at a wriggling blue worm that looks like something straight out of a catalog for psychedelic fishing lures. Once the skink matures, it should know to keep away from predators and the tail fades to a dull gray, but it can still be dropped if necessary.

A closely knit community of birds is also associated with rocks and cliffs. Canyon Wrens send cascading songs of descending whistles echoing off the sheer cliffs while they search deep crevices for spiders and insects. Their drabber relative the Rock Wren hops around the smaller rocks at the bases of cliffs. And if you look up, you could see groups of White-throated Swifts rocketing by.

Swifts are swallowlike birds that are more closely related to humming-birds, sharing wing and leg form with that seemingly disparate family. Swifts are truly built for speed. Most birds' wings have an extensive area of flight feathers for lift and only an outer section of primaries that provide forward speed, but in swifts the inner portion is shortened so much that almost all of the wing is made up of primary feathers. Their legs and feet are so small that their family is called Apodidae, Latin for "without feet." They can only cling to rock surfaces inside the crevices in which they nest. White-throated Swifts spend their days coursing through the blue mountain skies with their big mouths open, scooping up insects. Their mating rituals are spectacular; a male and female chase each other high in the air, chattering loudly, then unite in an embrace that sends them cartwheeling toward the ground. They break off and fly away just when you think they will hit the rocks below.

Cliff ledges also provide nesting sites for many larger birds, including Prairie Falcons, Golden Eagles, and Common Ravens. Even pigeons, intro-duced from Europe and normally associated with manmade cliffs such as skyscrapers, have returned to their original habitat in many parts of the Rockies, nesting on cliff ledges as they did before their urban period. In fact, their official name is Rock Pigeon.

The Decline of Grasslands

Of all the ecosystems in North America, grasslands stand at the top of the list of endangered spaces. The grasslands of the Great Plains have been affected most, almost all turned into monocultures of wheat and other crops, but the intermontane grasslands have not fared well either. It is estimated that 50 to 70 percent of low-elevation mountain grasslands has been lost. And what is left has largely been degraded by more than a century of heavy grazing and a more recent onslaught of invasive weeds. These changes affect the wildlife tied to grass as well—70 percent of bird species associated with grasslands in North America show population declines over the past three decades.

If you step out into today's grasslands, you may have a hard time finding native grasses. Some rangelands are a monoculture of Cheatgrass, acci-dentally introduced from Eurasia and now almost impossible to manage. Cheatgrass is an annual species that does extremely well in disturbed soils, such as overgrazed areas and recent burns. It germinates in the fall and grows quickly after snowmelt, putting out a huge crop of sharply pointed seeds. Cattle graze it early in spring, but once the seeds have formed, they leave it alone and turn to what native species they can find. Cheatgrass dries quickly in midsummer, creating an explosive fuel for ground fires. It has increased the frequency of fires over much of the American West to the extent

that native species cannot survive where it occurs. Sagebrush and wheatgrass, already affected by other range practices, retreat farther into the hills.

Spotted and Diffuse Knapweed have also invaded from Eurasia. These relatives of the artichoke produce masses of prickly seed heads that are unpalatable to cattle and almost all wildlife. Recent attempts at biological control, which include imported flies that eat only knapweed seeds and a beetle whose larvae devour the long taproots, show signs of promise. Similar strategies are also making headway in the battle against another invasive weed, Dalmatian Toadflax.

Another foreign species is planted intentionally by ranchers to provide a quick fix for barren, overgrazed lands. Crested Wheatgrass, a European relative of Bluebunch Wheatgrass, grows well as a dryland grass, and vast areas of the intermontane West have been harrowed and seeded with this species. This practice has turned a diverse, dynamic ecosystem into another monocul-

The Burrowing Owl is in serious decline in almost all of its North American range. It is losing grassland habitat to urbanization and intensive agriculture and is being killed by pesticides and collisions with vehicles.

ture with little life in it except the grass and scattered cattle. Many ranchers are taking a more long-term approach, reducing grazing pressure so that damaged grasslands can return to health, but this approach takes time. Even if cattle are totally excluded from rangeland, it can take twenty to forty years for the native grasses to fully recover. When they do, however, they provide more than twice the annual grass production of an overgrazed rangeland.

One of the biggest threats to grassland is fire suppression. Although these environments are born from mountain rain shadows, they are maintained at their edges by fires that keep young trees and shrubs from gaining a foothold in the dry valleys. Forests have reclaimed a third of the grasslands in the Rocky Mountains of British Columbia in the past thirty years, and a similar scenario is playing out over the entire range. Habitat managers are now using prescribed burns to reverse the trend wherever possible.

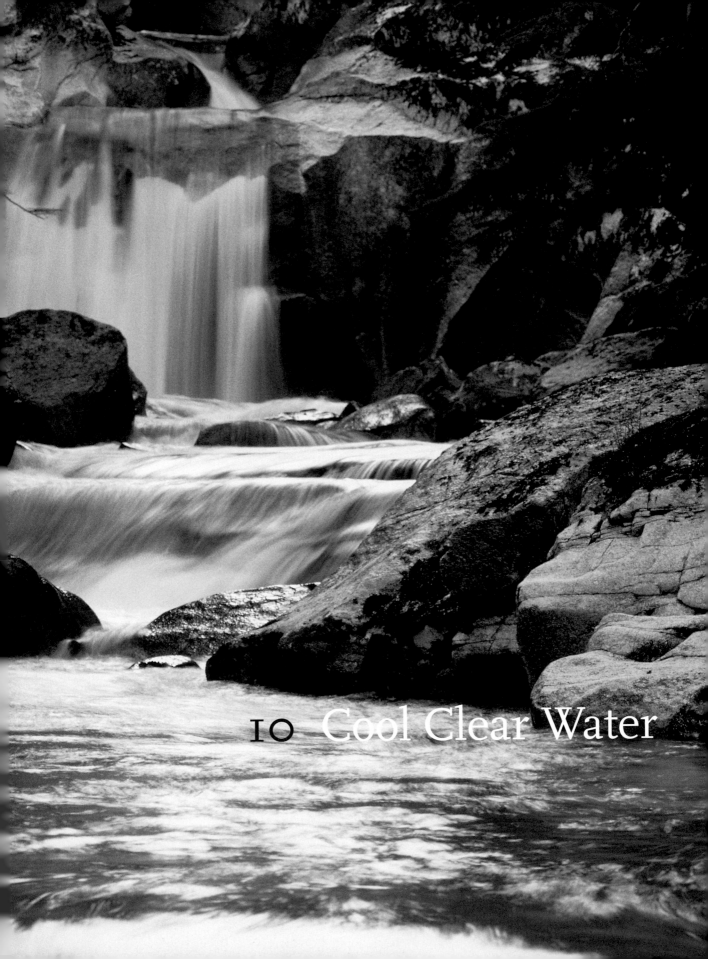

10 Cool Clear Water

Cool Clear Water

CHAPTER 10

ONE SUMMER I LIVED IN a log cabin in the British Columbia Rockies only a stone's throw from the Fraser River. Not the mighty Fraser of the south but a young Fraser, swirling green and white against canyon walls. A small bridge across the canyon linked our cabin to the outside world, and I would often pause on it to watch the restless current, thinking about the journey this river would take from these mountains to the distant Pacific. Not far downstream, huge Chinook Salmon spawned and died in gravel shallows, bringing riches from the sea to the redcedars of the Robson Valley.

Water is the one compound that binds all life together, a role made plain in the mountains, where waters from melting snowpacks cascade downstream to nourish arid valleys below and summer thunderstorms cool shimmering alkali flats. Rivers and lakes are not only a critical link in the circulatory system of mountain life but also worlds unto themselves. Creeks, ponds, marshes, and bogs add a natural diversity to the landscape unmatched by any other features.

RIVERS AND STREAMS

Throughout the Rockies, water is in a hurry to get to the sea, relentlessly moving downhill. From tiny brooks trickling out of alpine snowbanks to major rivers such as the Fraser, Columbia, Missouri, and Colorado, there is great variety in the waters flowing through the mountains.

Invertebrates

Mountain water begins its journey to the sea in small rivulets draining mountain snowpacks or alpine glaciers. Clear and cold, these creeks support little plant life except a slippery film of diatoms on the rocks and a few clumps of filamentous green algae clinging with special holdfast cells to the stones. This is no place for plankton; any unattached animal or plant is quickly swept

Stonefly larva

Mayfly larva

Caddisfly larva

224

downstream, and unless it can swim against the current, it will never return home.

One of the biggest problems for tiny stream creatures is to stay in one place. Some avoid the current altogether; mayfly and stonefly larvae with long and narrow or flattened bodies squeeze among or under stones and gravel. Some mayfly larvae lie flat on the tops of exposed rocks, exploiting the relatively calm boundary layer—about 2 to 3 millimeters (a tenth of an inch) thick—that buffers the upper rock surface from the rushing current.

Other stream insects display streamlining to perfection. Baetid mayfly larvae, among the most abundant animals in rocky, fast-flowing streams, revel in the current, standing high with abdomens free in the water. Their three long tail-like cerci swing from side to side, acting as vanes to keep the head turned into the current and making a larva's stance very stable. Many mayfly and stonefly larvae sport these long, stabilizing tails. Caddisfly cases are often long and tapering for the same reason. Other mayflies have ventral surfaces shaped like suction cups to stick themselves to rocks.

Many stream invertebrates lay adhesive eggs. Most stream-dwelling caddisfly larvae use adhesive to construct tubular homes out of sand grains

The slow currents of winding rivers provide water and nutrients for the rich ecosystems of Rocky Mountain valleys: Snake River, Grant Teton National Park, Wyoming.

Streamside Moss

or small stones. This added weight helps keep them in place; sharp claws to grip any toehold complete the package. Larval black flies independently invented Velcro—their salivary glands make sticky strands of silk that are smeared on the rock, and masses of tiny hooks on the larva's rear end grasp the tangled mat. The larva also anchors a silk strand to the rock so that it has a lifeline if dislodged.

The diversity of life in streams is very low near their icy sources but increases rapidly as the streams flow downhill, especially after they enter forests, where fallen leaves and other plant debris add nutrients to the flow. There, aquatic mosses such as Streamside Moss grow on the wet rocks, providing both food and refuge for invertebrates.

Amphibians

In the cool streams that flow through the wet forests of western Montana, Idaho, and southeastern British Columbia live two unlikely denizens of fast-flowing water—the Rocky Mountain Tailed Frog and the Idaho Giant Salamander. The frog's "tail" is found only on males and is essentially a penis used for internal fertilization. External fertilization would be inefficient in the tumbling streams these frogs live in, as most of the sperm would be swept away before reaching the eggs. The larvae, like many other stream algae eaters, have a big suction cup on their bellies so that they can stick to the boulders. They grow slowly in the cold water, taking three to five years to reach maturity.

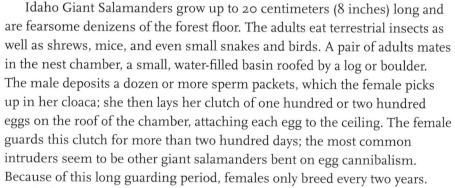

Tailed Frog larva

Idaho Giant Salamanders grow up to 20 centimeters (8 inches) long and are fearsome denizens of the forest floor. The adults eat terrestrial insects as well as shrews, mice, and even small snakes and birds. A pair of adults mates in the nest chamber, a small, water-filled basin roofed by a log or boulder. The male deposits a dozen or more sperm packets, which the female picks up in her cloaca; she then lays her clutch of one hundred or two hundred eggs on the roof of the chamber, attaching each egg to the ceiling. The female guards this clutch for more than two hundred days; the most common intruders seem to be other giant salamanders bent on egg cannibalism. Because of this long guarding period, females only breed every two years.

The larvae live in cool mountain streams, feeding largely on insect larvae, though larval tailed frogs may be an important part of the diet of older salamander larvae. At two years of age, most larvae metamorphose into adults, though some populations become sexually mature while retaining their aquatic lifestyle.

Another interesting salamander is found along cool creeks in this area but does not live in the streams themselves, sticking instead to the spray zone beside waterfalls and rapids. This is the Coeur d'Alene Salamander, the only lungless salamander found in the Rocky Mountains. Lungless salamanders breathe through their skin and so are restricted to moist environments. They lay a small grapelike cluster of large eggs in a damp spot, such as under a mossy rock. The female guards the eggs until they hatch—into fully formed terrestrial salamanders. The tadpole stage of the salamander occurs inside the egg—hence the need for the large eggs.

Birds

If you look closely as you travel along almost any creek or small river in the Rocky Mountains you can see an American Dipper, a gray tennis ball of a bird nervously doing knee bends on the polished rocks. Named for their frequent plunges into the cold water, dippers use their short wings to maneuver underwater along the stony bottom, looking under small rocks for insect larvae and fish eggs. Facing upstream, they angle their wings underwater so that the current keeps them on the bottom, where they grab onto rocks with their feet. Their constant knee bending is a habit peculiar to birds living near running water. Spotted Sandpipers, waterthrushes, wagtails, and pipits all bob up and down or wag their tails, perhaps imitating the movement of branches caught in the current.

The spherical shape of a dipper—very short tailed and almost neckless—is an adaptation to reduce the surface area available for heat loss in

American Dippers are remarkable songbirds that forage underwater in Rocky Mountain streams all year round in search of aquatic insects and larval fish.

frigid water. A dipper will stay on a productive stretch of creek all winter as long as there are one or two holes in the ice to provide access to the food below. Dippers are especially common in winter along streams that have salmon or trout spawning runs in the fall, lured by the abundance of fish eggs as well as all the invertebrates attracted to the bounty.

Not many species of waterfowl make their homes in rushing mountain streams, but the Harlequin Duck seems to relish the white water, the handsome male decked out in elegant slate-gray boldly patterned in white and chestnut, the female almost invisible in dark brown, spotted on the face with white. Harlequins spend most of the year surfing in that other wave-washed environment, the rocky Pacific coast. Pairs fly into the mountains in late April and May, taking up summer residence on rushing rivers and streams. The females lay their eggs in down-lined nests hidden among the overhanging roots of the riverbanks or in hollow trees; shortly thereafter the males wing their way back to the coast to molt amid the Bull Kelp forests along the shore. The female Harlequin Duck raises the young on her own but abandons them in mid-August to return to the coast herself. The young are left to find their own way to the sea—the few that survive usually appear there in early September.

Fish

When most of us think of creek fish, we think of trout and char—Rainbow Trout, Cutthroat Trout, and Bull Trout. These sleek predators hide in the shadowy eddies below boulders, snapping up any insect that loses its grip on its rock and leaping for the slow-moving adult mayflies and caddisflies that dance over green pools. Bull Trout are the top of the food chain in the streams; the adults eat almost exclusively fish. They require clean cold water to survive, and of all the salmon and trout, they are the most sensitive to habitat degradation.

Bull Trout spawn in autumn once the water temperature has gone below 9°C (48°F). Some adults live their entire lives in their natal streams, others move downstream to larger rivers, and still another form lives in large lakes. In the fall, all three forms return to their natal stream to spawn; those living in Flathead Lake, Montana, travel more than 160 kilometers (100 miles) to the spawning grounds. Bull Trout have been eliminated from more than half of the streams they historically occupied in the United States and are listed as a threatened species there. Overfishing—some of it intentionally done in previous decades to reduce their predation on other trout—and a decline in habitat quality due to logging and road building have had a similar effect in Canada.

Three species of Pacific salmon—Chinook, Coho, and Sockeye—migrate up the Fraser and Columbia rivers to spawn in Rocky Mountain streams. Their lives are part of a great cycle—the migration of fry or smolts from freshwater streams to the ocean; the grand travels of silvery adults through the North Pacific; the arduous migration upstream to their natal stream reach; the battles and lovemaking of gaudily colored, distorted bodies on the spawning grounds; and the inevitable swift decay and death of the battered fish among the eggs of the generation to follow. These spawning runs were once much larger, but hydroelectric dams, habitat degradation, and overfishing have all contributed to significant reductions in numbers and even extinction of many stocks, especially in the Columbia and Snake river systems.

Chinook Salmon are the largest of the Pacific salmon; they usually grow to 13 kilograms (29 pounds) and occasionally to over 50 kilograms (110 pounds). The fry spend little time in their natal river but swim directly to the Pacific Ocean, where they spend more time in coastal waters than other species.

They are usually the salmon found farthest up any large river system; they spawn in the Fraser River below Mount Robson and in the Snake River more than 1 300 kilometers (800 miles) from the Pacific.

At 2.5 to 4 kilograms (5.5 to 9 pounds), Coho Salmon are small cousins of the Chinook. They spawn in headwater streams that are smaller than those reached by other salmon species, leaping waterfalls up to 2 meters (6.5 feet) in height. Young Coho usually spend a year in their natal river before moving into salt water, then return to spawn at three years of age. Rocky Mountain populations were restricted to the upper reaches of the Snake River system but were effectively extinct by the 1980s, destroyed by the construction of a dozen large dams on the Columbia and Snake rivers in the twentieth century.

Unlike other salmon, the Sockeye Salmon has inserted a lake phase into its life cycle—fry usually spend one or two years feeding and growing in a lake near the spawning stream. Sockeyes then spend two or three years in the ocean, returning to their natal streams at age four or five. In the lakes, the fry are plankton feeders in open waters. Because there is nowhere to hide in the waters they feed in, juvenile Sockeyes usually spend the daylight hours deep in the lake, coming up to feed in warmer, plankton-rich waters at dusk and dawn. Since lakes have a larger rearing area than streams, Sockeyes are more abundant than stream-developing species such as Coho and Chinook salmon.

To find their nursery lake, young Sockeyes are programmed to swim in a certain direction and with a certain current. For example, some are "hard-wired" to swim north and upstream, others east and downstream. Because of this genetically determined behavior, it has proven extremely difficult to re-establish Sockeye runs that have been eliminated by overfishing or some other disaster. One such population is the Snake River run, reduced to a single lake—Redfish Lake in central Idaho. In 1991 this population was listed as endangered; in 1992 only one adult, a male nicknamed "Lonesome Larry," returned to spawn at Redfish Lake. Unable to find a mate, he was captured and his sperm frozen to be used in captive-rearing efforts. There have since been years when no fish at all return to Redfish Lake; only a handful come back in others.

The lake-rearing habit of Sockeye Salmon has independently given rise to a number of populations that remain in the lake and never make the dangerous trip to the ocean and back. These fish are called Kokanee. Most natural stocks of Kokanee evolved at the close of the Pleistocene, when meltwaters dammed by glaciers created large lakes. These glacial lakes flooded river reaches that contained barriers normally impassable to fish, such as Bonnington and Kootenai falls on the Kootenay River. When the ice dams forming these large lakes disappeared, the salmon could go down to the sea over the falls but could not return. Only the small portion of fish that matured in the lakes was able to spawn in the traditional creeks, forming a landlocked

THE PACIFIC SALMON OF THE ROCKIES

Chinook

Coho

Sockeye

Overleaf: Sockeye Salmon spawning in the Adams River, British Columbia

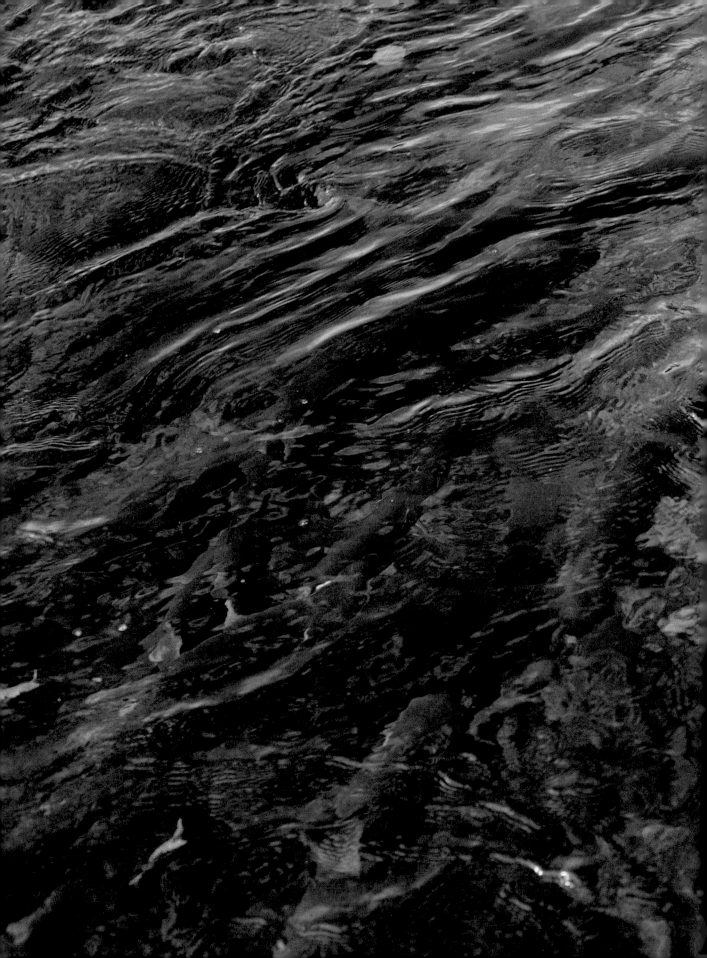

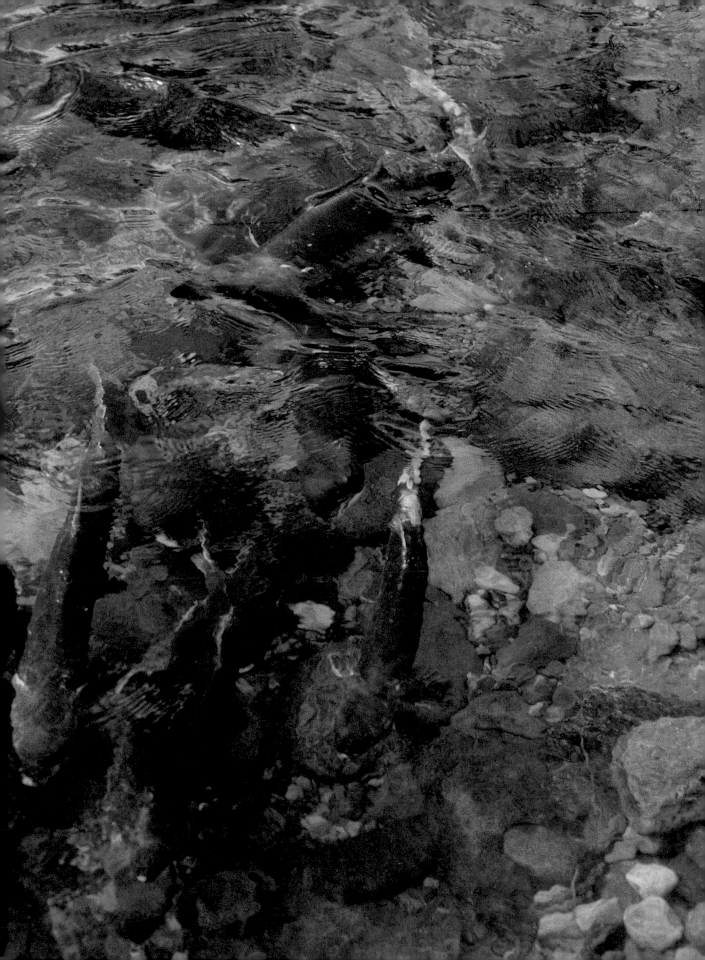

Flathead Lake, Montana, the largest natural lake in the Rockies, has a reputation for cool clear water and an unsullied environment. But a close look at its underwater ecology reveals a tangled web of misguided fish management. There are ten native fish species in Flathead Lake, and one of these, the Cutthroat Trout, is considered one of the finest game fish on the continent. Early fishermen wanted even more types of fish, however, and in 1905 they introduced Lake Trout into Flathead Lake, followed by Kokanee in 1909. For decades things seemed to go fine and the Kokanee thrived, swimming up the Flathead River to spawn in Glacier National Park. This late-fall spawning run attracted Bald Eagles from all over western North America as well as bears and other wildlife from within the park.

Then, from 1968 to 1975, biologists introduced Opossum Shrimp—a species native to central Canada—to three lakes in the upper Flathead drainage, having heard that plankton-feeding fish such as the Kokanee thrived on this species. The shrimp did very well, and many floated downstream into Flathead Lake, where their population boomed. The Kokanee and Lake Trout feasted on the shrimp. In 1981, in Glacier National Park, 100,000 spawning Kokanee were counted in one day as well as 639 Bald Eagles. It seemed as if the introductions had produced a wonderful food web that benefited shrimp, fish, eagles, and a host of other species, including the tourists who came to watch the eagles.

But by 1990, the Kokanee population in Flathead Lake had completely disappeared. It seems that the young Kokanee depend on very small plankton—primarily the water-flea *Daphnia*—when they first enter the lake at one year of age. Unfortunately, the burgeoning shrimp population proved to be far better at eating water-fleas than the young Kokanee, and the young fish starved. Throughout the 1990s, Kokanee were reintroduced into Flathead Lake, and a new problem surfaced. The relatively small numbers of Kokanee were being gobbled up by the Lake Trout. Fish managers now organize fish derbies each year to promote the catch of Lake Trout in an attempt to reduce the population to a level that can be tolerated by the Kokanee. When you ponder the effects of these three introductions on the ecological systems in Flathead Lake, it pays to remember that there are now fifteen species of introduced fish in the lake, all competing directly and indirectly with the ten native species there.

Above: Bald Eagle

population. Kokanee have also been introduced into many lakes and reservoirs throughout the Rockies.

The White Sturgeon is a giant of a fish that inhabits the Columbia River and its tributaries; adults can weigh over 600 kilograms (1,300 pounds). These fish spawn during the spring freshet, when water levels are highest. When the Libby Dam was constructed on the Kootenay River in 1975, the annual pattern of water flow in the river was reversed. The flow was restricted in spring and early summer to fill the reservoir behind the dam, then released in fall and winter. The sturgeon simply stopped spawning, and no young fish have been produced since the dam was built. There are still White Sturgeon in the Kootenay, but they are growing old. In the late 1990s, engineers began releasing water from the Libby Dam in June to re-establish the natural flow pattern, and recent studies have recovered a few fertile sturgeon eggs from the river. White Sturgeons also live in the upper Fraser River in the Rocky Mountain Trench; they grow very slowly there but seem to be reproducing, as young fish are regularly caught.

LAKES

There are relatively few lakes in the Rocky Mountains, where most water is trapped in steep, narrow valleys, rushing downhill. Flathead Lake, Montana, at the southern end of the Rocky Mountain Trench, is the largest natural lake in the Rockies, with an area of 496 square kilometers (192 square miles). A number of deep fjord lakes, filling valleys gouged out by glaciers during the Pleistocene, are found in the valleys of the Columbia and Cariboo mountains in British Columbia; Kootenay, Shuswap, and Quesnel are the larger examples. Quesnel Lake is the deepest fjord lake in the world, with a maximum depth of 530 meters (1,739 feet). Another large Rocky Mountain lake is in a class by itself—Yellowstone Lake (354 square kilometers / 136 square miles) floods part of the caldera of an enormous volcano.

White Sturgeon

But the biggest water body by far in the Rockies is a reservoir on the Peace River. Backed up by a dam on the east side of the Rocky Mountains, Williston Lake fills the 113-kilometer (70-mile) Peace River canyon through the Rockies as well as 230 kilometers (143 miles) of the Rocky Mountain Trench and is almost four times the size of Flathead Lake. There are large reservoirs on all the main-stem rivers in the Rockies except for the Fraser, which has so far escaped the engineers, mostly because of its still-healthy salmon runs.

One of the main ways ecologists classify lakes is by how rich in nutrients they are. Some lakes receive water that has flowed over and through glacial till, limestone, shale, and other easily dissolved nutrient sources. These lakes have high concentrations of nitrates, phosphates, and other compounds necessary for life, and are typically surrounded by thick marshes and covered with flocks of grebes, ducks, and geese. Such lakes are called eutrophic—meaning rich in nutrients. The low rainfall and high evaporation rates experienced by some lakes at lower elevations and latitudes in the Rockies also contribute to eutrophication, since minerals can become concentrated in basins where summers are hot and dry. Because they contain abundant, respiring life, eutrophic lakes tend to be relatively low in oxygen in their deep waters.

Eutrophic lakes are not as common in the mountains as they are in the prairie pothole country on the Great Plains or in some of the warm basins west of the Rockies. But some significant marshlands play important roles in Rocky Mountain valleys—the Columbia Wetlands in the Rocky Mountain Trench of British Columbia, Red Rock Lakes in southwestern Montana, and Grays Lake in southeastern Idaho are prime examples. And scattered throughout the Rocky Mountains are grassy "holes" and "parks" that mix flat land and abundant water to create rich marshes, fens, and other wetlands.

Overleaf: Columbia Lake in the Rocky Mountain Trench of British Columbia is the head-waters of the Columbia River.

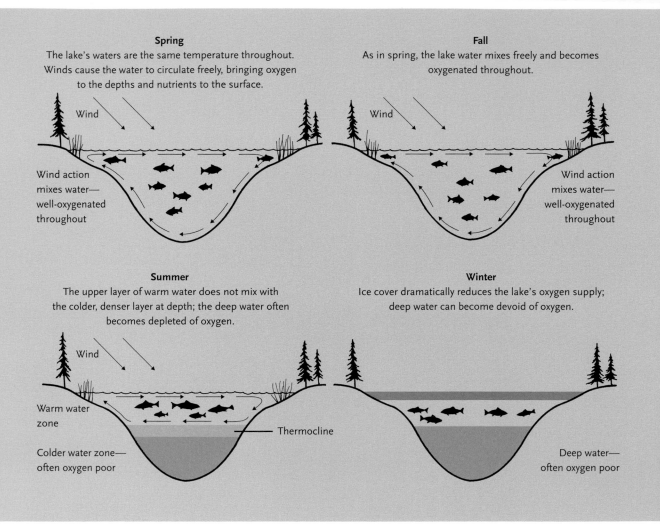

Spring
The lake's waters are the same temperature throughout. Winds cause the water to circulate freely, bringing oxygen to the depths and nutrients to the surface.

Wind

Wind action mixes water—well-oxygenated throughout

Fall
As in spring, the lake water mixes freely and becomes oxygenated throughout.

Wind

Wind action mixes water—well-oxygenated throughout

Summer
The upper layer of warm water does not mix with the colder, denser layer at depth; the deep water often becomes depleted of oxygen.

Wind

Warm water zone

Colder water zone—often oxygen poor

Thermocline

Winter
Ice cover dramatically reduces the lake's oxygen supply; deep water can become devoid of oxygen.

Deep water—often oxygen poor

FIGURE 10.1 A ROCKY MOUNTAIN LAKE THROUGH THE SEASONS

Many lakes in the Rocky Mountains are virtually free of dissolved nutrients and are called oligotrophic (having few nutrients). These lakes have clear waters that are rich in oxygen but sparse in life. Some of these lakes receive waters over granitic bedrock, others are too cold to support much life, and some are simply so big that their large volume reduces concentrations of nutrients from their shallow, productive shorelines.

Lakes through the Seasons

It is obvious to anyone who has swum in a mountain lake in July and skiied across its snow-covered surface in January that lakes change through the seasons. But some of the important changes are not obvious from the surface.

After the ice has melted in spring, the water in a lake is usually one temperature from top to bottom—about 4°C (39°F). Since all the water is at the same temperature and density, it intermixes freely. Spring breezes bring deep water up to the surface and send surface water down to the depths. But the structure of the lake changes significantly as warmer days heat the upper surface of the lake, making it warmer and less dense than the cold water below. As the surface water becomes warmer, the contrast in temperatures and densities between the two layers becomes so great that they do not mix at all. There is an invisible barrier between them—the thermocline—usually between 5 and 15 meters (16 to 50 feet) below the surface.

The surface waters have warmth, light, and abundant oxygen dissolved from the air above and thus support plentiful life. This is where the algae bloom, the zooplankton graze, and most fish come for dinner. The deep waters, in contrast, are cold and dark, cut off from the supply of oxygen on the surface. It is too dark for photosynthesis, so the basis of the food chain in the depths is the decomposition of organic material raining down from the sunlit waters above. This decomposition soon robs the water of what little oxygen it had.

As summer turns to autumn, the surface waters gradually cool. When they reach 4°c again, the two layers match each other in density and the bottom water can mix with the surface water. The lake "turns over," and its water becomes recharged with oxygen from top to bottom. This is an important process for life within the lake, especially if the lake freezes over in winter. Ice once again cuts off the oxygen supply to the water, and without large volumes of oxygen-charged water, the lake will become oxygen depleted before the spring thaw. Some lakes that are protected from autumn winds simply don't mix enough to recharge their oxygen and cannot support fish or other aquatic life through the winter.

The Littoral Zone

In eutrophic lakes and the protected, muddy bays of oligotrophic lakes, there is a rich zone along the shore where light and warmth mix to create a tremendous variety of life. This zone covers the entire wetland in marshes and shallow ponds. Two of the common emergent plants along such shorelines are Cattails and Hardstem Bulrushes. Cattails have long, flat leaves and flowering heads that look like fuzzy wieners. Bulrushes have cylindrical, pith-filled leaves and a small spray of brownish flowers.

Sedges dominate many mountain marshes. These look like big, coarse grasses, but if you try to roll the base of a sedge stem, you will find that it is solid and triangular, not round and hollow like a grass stem. In deeper water, you might see floating aquatic plants such as beautiful Yellow Waterlilies and pink-flowered Water Smartweed. These plants and other similar marsh vegetation provide food and important cover for many animals.

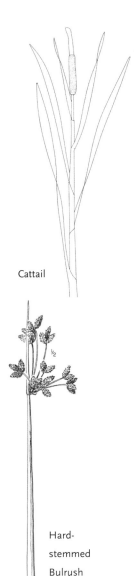

Cattail

Hard-
stemmed
Bulrush

Frogs and turtles

As every child knows, the marsh is where the frogs are. The common marsh frog of the Rockies south to the Yellowstone area is the Columbia Spotted Frog. This species, like most true frogs in the genus *Rana,* is rarely found more than a few hops away from a pond. The calls of this frog are very quiet, and you have to be very attentive to hear them. Another northern species is the Wood Frog. It is generally found at higher elevations than the Columbia Spotted Frog and has the amazing ability to freeze solid in winter, thawing the next spring to croak again. It shares this talent with the Western Chorus Frog, a small tree frog found mainly east of the Great Divide. Tree frogs have sticky pads at the ends of their toes that allow them to climb shrubs and trees; these pads are tiny in chorus frogs but more noticeable in their west side cousins, Pacific Tree Frogs. Male Pacific Tree Frogs give loud *ribit* calls as they gather around small wetlands in early spring and can create a deafening chorus at larger ponds.

Painted Turtles lead idyllic summer lives in Rocky Mountain marshes from southern British Columbia to central Wyoming, basking on logs in the sun or hanging motionless in the cool water with only their heads exposed. In midsummer the females lay eggs in nests dug about 5 centimeters (2 inches) deep into south-facing banks of gravel and sand. The young hatch in early fall

DISAPPEARING FROGS

All over the world, frogs and toads are disappearing, and even the relatively pristine marshes of the Rockies have not escaped this mysterious decline. The Northern Leopard Frog is gone from much of its northwestern range—it is now known in only one site in British Columbia and in two sites west of the Great Divide in Montana, and it has disappeared from the Idaho Panhandle. Columbia Spotted Frogs are declining almost everywhere. Boreal Toads, with only fifty small populations in the southern Rockies, are listed as endangered in Colorado and New Mexico. Wyoming Toads, found only in the Laramie Basin, were down to four males and one female in the wild at last count. What is happening?

As with most ecological problems, the decline of frog populations is likely due to a combination of factors. Amphibians are very sensitive to chemical pollutants because of their permeable skin. Some pesticides, such as the herbicide atrazine, occur essentially everywhere in the environment in very small concentrations; even at these low levels, atrazine causes severe developmental problems in frogs. Both Wyoming Toads and the Boreal Toads of Colorado have been found with massive infections of the bacteria *Aeromonas hydrophila.* This causes hemorrhaging, swelling the legs and bringing blood to the surface, giving rise to the common name of the condition—red leg disease. This disease apparently starts with a collapse of the toad's immune system. But the disease that seems to be having the biggest impact on Rocky Mountain toads is a chytrid fungus native to Africa that has recently spread around the world, perhaps through the trade in pet toads.

Frogs and toads do not like crossing large roads and are not especially successful when they try. As a result, small populations are isolated and can become extinct through random climatic events if they are not revived by immigration. In some cases, the problem is other frogs. Bullfrogs, native to eastern North America, have been introduced into several valleys west of the Great Divide. In the Bitterroot Valley, they have been cited as a likely cause for the demise of local Northern Leopard Frog populations and the declining numbers of Columbia Spotted Frogs. Eating everything that moves, the large Bullfrogs quickly lower the natural diversity of western wetlands.

Boreal Toad

and, instead of joining the adults in the pond, do nothing. The tiny turtles remain underground all winter, freezing solid with the soil around them.

Freezing normally kills organisms, since ice crystals rupture every cell membrane as they grow. Young Painted Turtles have two lines of defense against the ice crystals. First, a lot of water moves out of their cells into blood vessels and other body cavities, and then special proteins are distributed throughout these spaces. These proteins promote the crystallization of ice but in a very regulated manner, so the crystals don't get big enough to do damage. Second, the turtles' cells become filled with antifreeze compounds such as the sugar glucose. So their body fluids freeze quickly, but the fluids inside cells do not, at least not down to temperatures of −10°C (14°F) or so. Interestingly, the turtles cannot repeat this freezing performance; as adults they must bury themselves deep in the mud of marshes below the frost line.

Water insects

Perhaps more than in any other environment, insects play a key role in the watery realm of marshes. No pond is complete without the shining wings of dragonflies or the skimming wakes of water striders.

Overleaf: Painted Turtles sun themselves in a mountain pond.

Water boatmen

Giant Water Bug

Opposite page: Predacious diving beetles are top predators in mountain marshes that lack fish.

Many of the aquatic insects are true bugs, members of the order Hemiptera. True bugs have tubular, sucking mouthparts that on land are generally used for feeding on plant juices. The aquatic bugs, however, are fierce predators in many interesting ways. They do share one tactic though—they always kill and consume their prey by stabbing it with their mouthparts, injecting the prey with digestive enzymes, then sucking the nutritious soup out of the dead body.

Because they live on the pond surface, water striders are probably the most familiar bugs to the casual insect watcher. The slender insects spread out their weight on long thin legs, and their feet have pads of waxed hairs so that they can skate freely over the surface of the water. The water's surface tension not only provides them with their skating rink but gives them food as well; these predators specialize in prey that has become inadvertently captured in the surface film. Some water striders also use the water surface to send messages to each other, tapping out wavelets in a Morse code only water striders understand.

Backswimmers are the mirror image of water striders in locomotion and feeding strategy—they hang upside down from the surface of the water, rowing from place to place with long, oarlike hind legs and nabbing their prey from below. Backswimmers and other aquatic bugs breathe air that they bring down from the surface as a thin film around their bodies and under their wings. Water boatmen are similar to backswimmers but swim right side up. They are generally smaller than backswimmers, with relatively smaller legs, and hunt in the water column, catching small crustaceans and other plankton in their spiny front legs. Water boatmen are especially common in saline lakes, where they often form the bulk of the insect biomass.

The largest aquatic insect in the Rocky Mountains is the Giant Water Bug, about the size of a small frog with front legs that end in a sharp hook for capturing insects, tadpoles, and small fish. It is often called the toe biter for obvious reasons. On warm summer evenings, these bugs—and other pond insects as well—take to the air, flying on strong wings to find new ponds.

There are also many types of aquatic beetles, ranging in size from tiny to surprisingly large. All are smooth, streamlined, well-waxed insects superbly adapted to life underwater. They have long, hairy hind legs that row simultaneously for efficient swimming, and they carry air down from the surface under their wings.

Dragonflies are familiar to all pond watchers, their dashing flights and bright colors making them conspicuous and interesting subjects for serious observation. Their underwater lives are less well known to most people. The larvae are active predators within the pond, catching their prey with an incredible, hinged lower "lip" that shoots out with lightning speed. There are two

main types of dragonflies—the larger "true" dragonflies and the more delicate damselflies. Larval damselflies have three long, leaflike tails that are the insect's gills. Dragonfly larvae are more robust and lack the long tails—they get oxygen from the water by sucking it into their rectums, where the gas exchange takes place. They use their rectums for propulsion as well—quickly expelling the water and shooting through the pond water like small missiles.

The other abundant group of lake insects is the caddisflies, or as fly-fishers call them, sedges. These brownish insects look like their closest relatives, the moths, but have tiny hairs on their wings instead of scales. After a big emergence, there can be thousands skittering over the surface of the water like tiny hydroplanes, the trout jumping in a frenzy trying to catch them. Larval caddisflies look like caterpillars but are almost always seen within their cylindrical "houses" built of plant material or sand grains on the lake bottom.

Caddisfly

Life on the Bottom

The bottom ooze in a lake is the opposite of the littoral zone—dark, cold, and relatively lifeless. All the animals in the dark depths of the lake are scavengers, living on the rain of detritus from the life-filled, sunlit zone above. If you can grab a handful of the black mud and bring it to the surface, you will see bright red bloodworms wriggling in the muck. These are larval midges, which come in a variety of sizes and colors, but the big red ones stand out against the black mud. As the name bloodworm suggests, the red comes from hemoglobin, the same protein that carries oxygen in our blood. The insects use hemoglobin for the same reason—to hold on to all the oxygen they can in this largely anaerobic environment. When the larvae emerge as adult midges, they congregate to form towering, whining clouds over shrubs and people on the shore. They are not biting flies though, just a swarm of bachelors waiting for females to join the party.

Birds

Bird lovers love marshy lakes, where the diversity of bird life can be astonishing and the dawn chorus a cacophony of quacks, whinnies, and strange songs. The king of the marsh almost everywhere is the Red-winged Blackbird, the audacious males flaring out bright scarlet epaulettes while singing out their loud *konk-a-reeee* songs. This is truly the sound of spring in a Rocky Mountain wetland, for the males often return to the marshes and begin setting up territories as early as February—the real estate is that valuable. In many low-elevation marshes, they are later joined by the even more stunning Yellow-headed Blackbirds, which move the smaller Red-wingeds out of the richest parts of the marsh. The marshes are usually so food filled that males can control enough territory to support several females and their subsequent

MOOSE

The monarch of Rocky Mountain marshes is the Moose. The largest deer in the world, adult Moose weigh about 500 kilograms (1,100 pounds). Found throughout the coniferous forests of the Northern Hemisphere, Moose are called elk in Europe, a name mistakenly transferred to another large deer in North America. The word *moose* comes from the Algonkian language and means "twig-eater."

The long legs of Moose can carry them through deep snow and into the deep water of a marshy lake. In summer they eat water plants and will even dive for succulent roots, staying underwater for as long as thirty seconds. As the ponds freeze in winter, they turn to browsing shrubs and trees such as willows and aspen. They often move into older forests in winter, where the snow is less deep. Yellowstone moose move upslope into fir forests in winter and browse the fir twigs. If the snow becomes more than a meter (3 feet) deep, Moose can become confined to "yards"— small areas where they have trampled the snow down.

Moose are generally solitary animals for most of the year. During the fall, female Moose give low, bellowing calls that attract the males. If more than one male arrives, they often spar with their huge antlers before the female chooses which one she will mate with.

Moose populations increased through the 1900s in the mountains of western North America. Before 1970 they were very rare in Colorado, but a combination of natural immigration from Wyoming and a transplant program that brought Moose in from other states has produced a healthy population in that state.

Populations have recently declined markedly in the Yellowstone and Banff areas. Increasing Wolf populations are likely one factor in these declines, but in Yellowstone the availability of good wintering habitat may also be important.

Moose are susceptible to a number of parasites, notably the Giant Liver Fluke. This parasite is normally found in White-tailed Deer and Elk, which are usually not seriously affected by it. The fluke has recently been found in many Moose, which become weak and severely debilitated by the large worms. The immature stages of the fluke multiply in aquatic snails, then form resting stages that attach to pond vegetation. When a Moose eats one of these cysts, the fluke moves from the stomach to the liver and begins to grow. In deer and Elk, the flukes mature quickly in the liver and produce larvae that are excreted in the feces, but in Moose the flukes never mature and produce severe liver damage, often killing the Moose.

families—Yellow-headed Blackbird males can have up to six females in a harem, and some Red-winged males have as many as fifteen.

The Barrow's Goldeneye is one of the typical ducks of Rocky Mountain lakes. The males have purple-black heads with a white crescent moon between the bill and eyes; the females are more subtly colored but have a bright orange bill in spring. Most Barrow's Goldeneyes spend the winter eating mussels

A Sora, a marsh-dwelling member of the rail family, walks through the reeds on its long toes.

along the Pacific coast, then in spring move to mountain lakes, where they feed on freshwater shrimp and aquatic insects. They nest in tree cavities near the lake—the ducklings jump out of the hole shortly after hatching, bouncing on the ground like little balls of fluff before scampering down to the shore.

The largest waterfowl in the Rockies, and indeed one of the largest birds there, is the Trumpeter Swan. This magnificent bird was thought to be on the brink of extinction in the 1930s, when the Rocky Mountain population was down to less than two hundred birds. These swans wintered in a small area around Yellowstone, including the Red Rock Lakes of southwestern Montana; about seventy stayed to breed, but most flew north to nest in the northern Rockies and adjacent plains. Conservation efforts began in earnest and the numbers began to grow. A new, much larger population was discovered nesting in Alaska and wintering on the British Columbia coast, and its numbers flourished over the decades as well.

A female Barrow's Goldeneye leaves its nest cavity; these are the common diving ducks on small Rocky Mountain lakes.

There are now about twenty thousand Trumpeter Swans known in the world, about three thousand of them in the Rocky Mountain population. Winter habitat for swans is critical in the Rockies—they need the open water of slow-moving rivers and marshes, where there is abundant plant growth. The swans feed in the shallows, reaching underwater into the mud for starchy water plant roots.

One of the nesting sites for Trumpeter Swans in the Yellowstone area is Grays Lake, Idaho. This large complex of marshes is home to other marsh birds, including ducks, geese, gulls, and ibis, but it is best known for its

Overleaf: Trumpeter Swans are among the largest birds in North America, with a weight of about 12 kilograms (26 pounds).

Sandhill Cranes nest in remote marshlands.

Opposite page: The Cloudberrry is a creeping relative of the raspberry found in northern bogs around the world.

cranes. The Sandhill Crane is a tall wading bird that was once common across North America, but like its larger cousin the Whooping Crane, its numbers are now much reduced. About two hundred pairs of Sandhill Cranes nest at Grays Lake, one of the largest concentrations in the world.

Beginning in 1975, a novel attempt was made to create a new nesting flock of Whooping Cranes by bringing eggs in from their breeding grounds in north-central Canada and fostering them to Sandhill Crane nests at Grays Lake. The eggs hatched successfully, and the young cranes followed their foster parents south to wintering grounds in New Mexico. Unfortunately, the young Whooping Cranes never bred successfully, and the project was abandoned in 1997.

With a wingspan of 2.75 meters (9 feet), the American White Pelican is one of the largest birds in the Rockies. These huge birds nest in colonies scattered through western North America; perhaps the best-known nesting site in the Rocky Mountains is at Yellowstone Lake. Unlike their seagoing relatives, the Brown Pelicans, which dive from a great height to catch fish beneath the water, American White Pelicans fish on the surface in shallow water, scooping small schooling fish into their large bills, straining out the water, and swallowing the catch. They often fish in groups, forming a semicircle around a big school of fish and slowly moving inward.

American White Pelicans have an interesting breeding strategy, shared by cranes and a number of other large birds; they lay two eggs but almost always raise only one chick. The second egg is laid a day or two after the first and hatches at the same interval; its sole function seems to be an insurance policy in case the first egg does not hatch. If the first egg does hatch, the older chick usually kills its younger sibling; in only about one in a hundred nests do both birds survive.

The pelicans at Yellowstone Lake were heavily persecuted in the early 1900s because of their habit of eating Cutthroat Trout; elsewhere these peli-

cans eat mainly suckers and other nongame fish that are common in shallow, warm waters. The Yellowstone pelicans are now fully protected, of course; the number of young raised fluctuates widely but averages more than 300 per year, a healthy increase over the 100 produced annually a century ago.

BOGS AND FENS

Bogs and fens are wetlands where the substrate is made up primarily of organic material in the form of mats of sedges or moss in varying states of decay. These organic mats, also known as peat, can develop over open water along old lakeshores, forming "quaking bogs," which can result in unpleasant soakings for the unwary bog walker.

Bogs are dominated by peat mosses, which hold water like a sponge and over the years raise the wetland above the surrounding water table. Bogs often develop in nutrient-poor, acidic areas, but because peat mosses actively secrete acid, bogs become even more acidic than their surroundings and often have a pH of less than 4, in contrast with the neutral pH of 7. Because the vegetation within them does not easily decay, and because they are blocked from nutrient-bearing groundwater by peat—the only water they receive comes from rain or snow—bogs are also poor in nutrients. Because bogs usually develop in cool, moist environments, they are commonly found only in the northern Rockies and become a dominant feature at the north end of the range where the mountain forests merge with the taiga.

Labrador Tea

Bogs may be stressful places to live, but they are still full of life, all the more interesting because of the adaptations the plants have developed to survive in such a low-nutrient environment. The common shrubs, including Labrador Tea, Bog-rosemary, and Western Bog-Laurel, are mostly from the heath family; other heaths, such as Bog Blueberries, Bog Cranberries, and Cloudberries, trail along the mossy ground. These plants can use ammonia as a nitrogen source rather than scarce nitrates. Several bog plants have become carnivores to obtain nitrates through animal protein. Sundews capture insects on leaf hairs tipped with a sticky fluid. Butterworts have beautiful purple flowers, but their flat, yellowish-green leaves are much more interesting, trapping bugs on their surface slime.

Bog-rosemary

In contrast to bogs, fens form where there is ready access to groundwater, often where a creek or river spreads out over flat land, turning it into a rich

Western Bog-Laurel

meadow of sedges, grasses, and mosses. The mosses in fens—Sickle Moss and Giant Water Moss are examples—are different from those in bogs because the water is much less acidic; the pH is usually greater than 5. Fens are common features of high-elevation wetlands and are also found in the parks and holes of the southern Rockies—South Park, Colorado, and Jackson Hole, Wyoming, are examples.

Vivid Dancers are damselflies found only in spring-fed streams that remain ice-free all winter.

HOT SPRINGS

Hot springs attract visitors with their promise of a hot soak after a long day of skiing or hiking, but they also have a very interesting assemblage of plant and animal species that take advantage of these warm oases in the cold mountains. The mecca of hot springs in the Rockies is Yellowstone National Park, with its bewildering number and diversity of hot-water features, but there are warm spots scattered the length of the Rocky Mountains.

Although the bubbling, boiling hot springs at Yellowstone seem unlikely places to find flourishing life, there are microbes in the water and soil that have shaken the foundations of biology. In the late 1960s, scientists discovered a species of bacteria they called *Thermus aquaticus* near a boiling spring in Yellowstone. It requires temperatures of over 37°C (99°F) to live and can survive temperatures up to 80°C (176°F).

Other microbes around the hot springs looked like bacteria but on close examination proved to have cellular chemistry more similar to that of higher forms of life. The differences were great enough that biologists have placed them in a new kingdom: Archaea. These cells and the environments they live in are thought to provide clues to the origins of life, which may have occurred in steamy vats of organic chemicals around ancient volcanoes, much like modern-day Yellowstone. Lidy Hot Springs, deep below the ground in the Beaverhead Mountains of Idaho, has microbial systems rich in Archaea living at a temperature of 58°C (136°F), which may provide an even better picture of what life was like two billion years ago.

Many other hot springs have their own unique assemblages of aquatic species. The Banff Springs Snail is found only in five hot springs on Sulphur Mountain in Banff National Park. Ross's Bentgrass is found only around hot springs in Yellowstone National Park. In some cases, hot springs are home to plants and animals that are relicts of warmer times. At Fairmont Hot Springs in the Rocky Mountain Trench of British Columbia, there is a small population of Southern Maidenhair Fern, the only such plants in Canada. Flitting around the ferns at Fairmont are Vivid Dancers, deep blue damselflies found only in warm springs scattered through the mountains of western North America. And Liard Hot Springs, in the cold spruce taiga at the northern tip of the Rocky Mountains, has a population of Plains Forktail damselflies that are clearly out of their normal element—warm ponds on the prairies of southern Canada. Although some of these unique environments, such as Liard, have remained relatively pristine, many have been irrevocably altered, the hot water directed into swimming pools, the natural warm creeks turned into concrete drains.

RIPARIAN WOODLANDS

Winding like green ribbons along the creeks and rivers that flow out of the high ranges and lining the shores of mountain lakes are woodlands totally unlike the coniferous forests that cloak the mountainsides. The bird songs coming from these thickets on spring mornings—the rich, descending fluting of the Veery, the sneezy *fitz-bew!* of the Willow Flycatcher, the lazy call

Along creeks and wetlands in the grassy valleys of the American Rockies, you can often see a line of silver-leaved trees. These are Russian Olives—not really olives at all, but Eurasian relatives of the native Wolf-willow shrubs found along prairie streams. Since they are fast-growing and attractive, they were natural trees to plant around early homesteads. Their tiny yellow flowers bloom in June, releasing a gloriously sweet scent into the summer evenings. Small white berries, dry and pithy with a large seed, develop in the late summer and fall. These berries are very popular with birds in winter—American Robins, Western Bluebirds, Bohemian Waxwings, and Evening Grosbeaks find them irresistible.

And yet Russian Olive is considered a noxious weed by many ecologists. Its popularity with birds spreads the seeds far and wide, and their rapid growth allows them to outcompete native trees, even the fast-growing cottonwoods. They have nitrogen-fixing nodules in their roots, so they can germinate on nutrient-poor sands and silts. Beavers shun them, preferring the taste of willow, aspen, and cottonwood. As a result, riparian zones along many grassland creeks have changed from a narrow line of rich green to a broad swath of silver.

and response of the Red-eyed Vireo—are unknown in spruce and pine. Largely dominated by deciduous trees such as Black Cottonwood, Water Birch, Paper Birch, and willows, these river- and lakeside woodlands are called riparian woodlands by ecologists. They provide food, shelter, and water for most mountain animals, from Moose browsing willow twigs in winter and Raccoons sheltering in hollow cottonwoods to a myriad of insects chewing on tender leaves. Their ecological importance is totally out of proportion to the small area they cover on mountain maps, yet they have suffered more loss and degradation than any other forested habitat in the Rockies.

The king of the riparian woodlands is Black Cottonwood. This species grows quickly, forming a large trunk with deeply furrowed bark; it is the largest poplar in the world and the largest deciduous tree in the West. A small grove of cottonwoods along the Elk River in the Rocky Mountains of southeastern British Columbia lays claim to the oldest and largest cottonwoods in the world. Some of these trees are more than 50 meters (165 feet) high and 3 meters (10 feet) in diameter and are more than 400 years old.

Cottonwoods develop heart rot relatively early, providing excellent nesting opportunities for woodpeckers. Large trunks are often completely hollow and are used by colonies of Vaux's Swifts. These small birds glue twig nests to the inside of the hollow trunk with their sticky saliva; another swift, in Southeast Asia, makes its nest entirely from saliva—the source of bird's nest soup. The eastern counterpart of the Vaux's Swift, the Chimney Swift, has abandoned

hollow trees as nest sites and now uses large chimneys instead. Vaux's Swifts are beginning to use this tactic more and more, perhaps because of the steady loss of hollow cottonwoods from the western landscape.

Many other birds rely on these riverside stands. Western Screech-Owls are almost entirely restricted to riparian woodlands in the Rocky Mountains. These small owls live in old woodpecker cavities, leaving at night to hunt mice, birds, frogs, fish, insects, slugs, worms, and almost anything else the proper size. Larger cavities are used by Common Mergansers, fish-eating ducks seen on most Rocky Mountain rivers.

In grasslands and mountain meadows, willows are often the primary woody plant in riparian habitats. Willows are important browse for Moose and Elk and have in fact declined dramatically in parts of the Rocky Mountains as these species have increased in the last 150 years.

The Human Hand

Human / Homme Homo sapiens *Common in townsites and other inhabited places, fairly common on highways, occasional on trails, seldom seen in untracked places . . . Easily identified: our only mammal that habitually walks on its hind legs . . .* H. sapiens *is omnivorous, consuming everything from raw fish and grains to foods that apparently have no nutritive value whatever . . . Humans have difficulty surviving in the wild, but they have been known to live well over 100 years in captivity.*

—BEN GADD, HANDBOOK OF THE CANADIAN ROCKIES

The Human Hand

EPILOGUE

THE ROCKY MOUNTAINS are a symbol of wilderness in North America, a remnant of the frontier between industrial society and a landscape less affected by humankind. But how real is this frontier? We often make the mistake of seeing ourselves as separate from nature and natural history. We talk of "natural habitats," meaning those outside cities, suburbs, and farms, forgetting that the natural world is the entire world and that we are an important and increasingly disruptive part of it. This epilogue takes a closer look at our own role in the ecosystems of the Rocky Mountains, where we have been, and where we are headed.

A SHORT PREHISTORY OF THE ROCKY MOUNTAINS

Humankind first appeared in the Rockies sometime during the Pleistocene Epoch. Exactly when will likely be debated for decades to come, but it was probably between fourteen thousand and fifty thousand years ago. These first people came from Asia, crossing the Bering land bridge through the steppes of northern Alaska and Yukon, hunting the game that abounded there. They saw mammoths, mastodons, camels, and giant ground sloths as well as species of horse, pronghorn, and bison that do not exist today.

Some of the earliest human artifacts found in North America are elegant, long spear points, called Clovis points, after the site in New Mexico where they were first discovered. These points were found in association with kill sites of mammoths and extinct bison and were clearly designed to hunt large mammals. But Clovis points were used in North America for only a very short time, from about 12,500 to 11,000 years ago. During that same period, thirty of the forty-one species of large mammals present in North America disappeared. Whether humans caused this mass extinction of large animals has been the subject of fierce debate, but the evidence is accumulating for the prosecution; it is likely that we as a species are guilty in the case of the

disappearing mega-
fauna. Only a handful of
large mammal species
survived; the survivors
share attributes such
as being migratory
(Caribou, Bison, and
Pronghorn), using rocky
escape terrain (Bighorn
Sheep and Mountain
Goats), and sheltering
in forest cover (most
of the deer family) that
may have helped them
escape extinction.

When Lewis and
Clark and other early European explorers traveled in and around the Rocky
Mountains two hundred years ago, they noticed that game was plentiful only
in no-man's-land regions between the territories of warring tribes. In contrast,
they saw few or no deer, bear, or other large mammals when traveling within
areas controlled by a single tribe. The only exception was the herds of migratory Bison that crossed the landscape irrespective of tribal ownership. This
phenomenon clearly illustrates the effect that the indigenous people's hunting practices had on game animal numbers.

More indirect evidence of the effect of hunting comes from changes in
the aspen and willow communities of the Rockies. Photographs taken in
the 1800s show healthy stands of willows in valley bottoms and flourishing aspen copses on the hillsides. Today the numbers of willows are greatly

The Spring Beauty provides
nutritious corms that are
harvested each spring by
Native peoples.

reduced, and in many areas, especially in national parks, aspen groves are dying a slow death, since no young aspens survive to replace the old. The willows and aspens are being eaten by Elk, deer, and Moose, whose numbers are almost surely far higher now than they have ever been in much of the Rocky Mountains. These population increases are due not only to a lack of hunting pressure in parks but also to the disappearance of predators such as Wolves from much of the Rockies.

Indigenous people also managed the ecosystems of the Rockies in more general ways. Although they did not practice agriculture as we know it— whereas tribes to the south and east certainly did—they cultivated root crops such as Blue Camas, Spring Beauty, and Bitterroot in their native grasslands. And to perpetuate these open habitats, they constantly burned the forests in a carefully planned manner, a practice that, over the millennia, clearly shaped the ecosystem and the plants and animals in it.

Although indigenous people certainly impacted the mountain environment in which they lived, the arrival of the industrial and agricultural world in the late 1800s changed it forever. The early transcontinental railways, built through South Pass in Wyoming in 1869 and through Kickinghorse Pass in the Canadian Rockies in 1885, brought thousands of settlers. But more than that, the railways opened up the Rockies to distant markets. The Bison that migrated through mountain valleys were slaughtered; in their place came vast herds of cattle. The railways brought in prospectors and shipped out gold, silver, copper, lead, and coal. Logging operations removed centuries-old Ponderosa Pines, Douglas-firs, Western Redcedars, and Western Hemlocks from the valleys, then began working upslope into the subalpine forests. And the trains brought tourists.

> *Many people have not yet realized that sooner or later growth must stop, nor have they wondered* how *it will stop, and what the Rockies—and the world—will look like when it does stop.*
>
> —Paul Ehrlich, foreword to *Rocky Mountain Futures*

The human population of the Rocky Mountains grew steadily through the twentieth century, drawn by opportunities in mining, forestry, agriculture, and tourism. The population growth has climbed significantly in the past two decades, increasing at a rate three times the national average in the United States. Large cities on the edge of the Rockies such as Calgary and Denver are booming, and many smaller towns in the heart of the mountains are exploding with new residents. Jackson, Wyoming, and Canmore, Alberta, both doubled in population in the 1990s. This boom differs from previous settlement booms in the Rockies in that the immigrants tend to be affluent people drawn by the quality of life in the mountains. Teton County, Wyoming, had a per capita income of $107,694 in 2004—the highest of any county in the United States.

The population boom applies not only to permanent residents but to tourists as well—the national parks are recording unprecedented numbers of visitors. Banff National Park leads the way with 4.7 million visits per year, followed by Rocky Mountain and Yellowstone National parks, each with just over 3 million visits. All these extra people and their activities put a strain on the ecosystems of the Rockies. This strain is greatest in the southern Rockies, which has the most people, but is extending north year by year.

THE ECOSYSTEMS

The greatest impact of humans on the Rocky Mountain ecosystem has been in the warm valleys, which is where we prefer to live, where we build our highways and railways, and where we can best grow our crops. Not coincidentally, this is where the greatest diversity of life occurs as well, so our activities have a heightened effect on the ecosystem.

Grasslands

The valley grasslands were perhaps the first habitat to be seriously affected by human activities. Herds of cattle quickly overgrazed the entire region, especially the intermontane grasslands west of the Great Divide. These habitats had never experienced heavy grazing before, since Bison had been restricted almost entirely to valleys east of the Divide. Pronghorn and Elk were native grazers in the western valleys, but Pronghorn generally eat forbs rather than grasses, and Elk browse shrubs and trees as well as eat grass. In the late 1800s, cattle remained on the lowland grasses all year long. As a result, the grasses had no rest period in which to maintain nutritive stores through their long dormant period, and many valleys were reduced to dirt and stubble. Grazing practices have improved since then, but serious damage has been done to most of the region's grasslands, especially with the introduction and spread of alien species such as Cheatgrass, Crested Wheatgrass, Diffuse and Spotted knapweeds, Leafy Spurge, and Dalmatian Toadflax.

> *The intermountain grasslands have experienced the greatest extent of environmental transformation of any ecosystem type in the Rocky Mountain region. Settlers deliberately replaced the dominant native plants with their own favorites, and in the process they brought along some serious Euro-trash, a plethora of undesirable weeds.*
>
> —Timothy R. Seasteadt, in *Rocky Mountain Futures*

Overleaf: Huge expanses of the intermontane West have been planted with Crested Wheatgrass, to the detriment of grassland biodiversity, as shown here where the Lost River Mountains meet the Snake River Plain.

Grasslands are easily converted to agricultural croplands, since little clearing is needed before the crops can be sown—all the landowner had to do was plow and add water. Much of the intermontane rangelands are now waving fields of wheat or green seas of alfalfa, and sagebrush ecosystems have been further reduced as ranchers burn or mechanically remove the sagebrush to increase grass production.

Forests

Most forestry activity occurs in the northern Rockies—British Columbia, Idaho, and Montana. Early logging in the Rocky Mountains selectively harvested large trees out of the valley forests of Douglas-fir, Ponderosa Pine, and Western White Pine for use as railway ties and mine timbers and for construction. Later logging was much more thorough, especially as it moved into Lodgepole Pine, Engelmann Spruce, and Subalpine Fir forests at higher elevations. Clear-cutting has been the standard practice in those forests, and most of the clear-cuts have been replanted with Lodgepole Pine. The annual volumes of logged trees increased over the last half of the twentieth century, but these volumes were made up of increasingly smaller trees. For example, in the American Rockies between 1952 and 1992, sawmill production increased slightly, from 1 310 to 1 356 million cubic meters, but the volume of large trees used declined, from 152 to 105 million cubic meters.

The most serious concern about forest harvesting in the modern age is that there is no intent to allow the forests to regrow to their former age and species structure. In a sense, the history of forestry in the West has been a period of mining followed by a future of agriculture—we have eliminated old-growth forests and are replacing them with plantations. And many of the plantations, until recently at least, are monocultures of Lodgepole Pine.

But logging is not the only human activity that has affected the forests. Fire suppression—both putting out active fires and halting the indigenous practice of regularly setting strategic fires—has also changed the face of western forests. The combination of logging and fire suppression has created thick young forests that are prone to disease and insect infestations and are suboptimal habitat at best for most wildlife species. We must learn to use forest harvesting and fire to mimic natural disturbances so that the forest ecosystems remain healthy and diverse.

Rivers and Lakes

No ecosystem has been affected by humans in the Rocky Mountains more than the rivers and lakes. This phenomenon seems to be a simple case of out of sight, out of mind. Since we cannot easily see what goes on under the water, we do not think enough about it and we usually do not know enough

about it either. This attitude affects our relationship to the denizens of lakes and rivers as well. In national parks we are exhorted not to pick flowers, net butterflies, or collect colorful stones, but we are encouraged to kill large fish. To improve our chances of catching a large fish, we have poisoned whole lakes to kill nongame fish, we have introduced foreign trout into watersheds with healthy populations of native trout, and we have dumped alien shrimp into mountain lakes, all without a second thought about how these actions might destroy the fisheries we are trying to enhance.

These actions have been rampant in the Rockies. Sixty-five percent of lakes in the American Rockies and 20 percent of lakes in national parks in the Canadian Rockies have been stocked with non-native trout, eliminating entire populations of native fish, frogs, salamanders, and crucial zooplankton species. Although national parks are generally no longer stocked, Lake

Blue River Reservoir, Garrison River, Colorado. Most of the rivers in the Rocky Mountains have been dammed to produce reservoirs for electric power generation and water storage, destroying vital riverside habitats and altering natural river flow patterns.

Trout were recently introduced illegally into Yellowstone Lake, despite the disastrous consequences of similar introductions into lakes and reservoirs throughout the Rockies. Lake Trout are now gobbling up Yellowstone Cutthroat Trout in the heartland of this subspecies.

And the non-native fish are bringing their diseases with them. Introduced Brown Trout brought whirling disease to North America in 1958; the disease had spread to the Rockies by 1987. This disease is caused by a protozoan parasite, which burrows into young fish, causing skeletal abnormalities and often producing bizarre behavior in the fish. Some infected fish constantly swim in circles. These fish are quickly caught by predators if they do not die of starvation. As the dead fish decompose, the parasites are released into the water, where they are ingested by tubifex worms on the muddy bottom. The parasites reproduce inside the worms and are released again into the water, where they find new fish to infect. Native Rainbow Trout seem to be particularly susceptible, and significant declines in population have occurred in the American Rockies.

But the most far-reaching effects on aquatic habitats have come through the damming and diversion of rivers for hydroelectric projects, irrigation schemes, and domestic water use. Almost every river in the Rocky Mountains has been changed from a ribbon of clean water, ebbing and flowing with the seasons, to a series of steep-walled reservoirs rimmed by muddy shorelines, its flow regulated by electricity and water needs. Rich riparian woodlands, used by perhaps three-quarters of all wildlife species in the mountains, have been eliminated completely under the reservoirs and significantly altered downstream of the dams. These woodlands flourish on the narrow floodplains of the rivers but wither away when floods no longer come.

The dams have had a tremendous impact on larger fish, especially salmon that migrate to and from the ocean. Most dams are fitted with ladders to allow the fish to climb the barrier into the reservoir behind, so spawning is theoretically possible. But the long reservoirs of warm, low-oxygen water take their toll on the fish during both downstream and upstream migrations, and many young fish are lost in the turbines while trying to reach the sea.

The effects of reservoirs are not limited to dams on large rivers. There are more than seven thousand small dams scattered through the American Rockies and many in Canada as well. Each of these dams changes the seasonal pattern of water flow down its creek, creating a large cumulative effect on the downstream ecosystems. Most dams also flood mountain wetlands that once cleaned and filtered the water and provided habitat for wildlife.

Finally, diversion of water for domestic and agricultural use is a concern, especially in the drier southern ranges. Diversion projects have already removed large amounts of water from drainages in the greater Denver area.

And 78 percent of all water use in the American West is for crops. That use is inherently different from domestic use; since it goes into plants, much of the water is lost to the atmosphere through evapotranspiration, whereas water used for domestic purposes is returned to the watershed, hopefully after treatment.

The Atmosphere

We like to think of mountain air as being refreshingly cool and clean, but it may not be a surprise to learn that this is not entirely so. Because the mountains force air currents up to altitudes where they are cooled, pollutants that have been carried in the air for long distances fall onto the mountains in rain or snow. As a result, air pollutants are concentrated in mountain snowpacks. Studies in Alberta have found that polychlorinated biphenyls (PCBS) and organochlorine pesticides occur in Rocky Mountain snowpacks at concentrations one hundred times those at lower elevations.

Near urban centers such as Denver and Salt Lake City and around coal-fired power plants in Wyoming, large amounts of nitrates are carried to the mountains on air currents and deposited into watersheds. Mountain lakes in these areas are essentially being fertilized, causing algal blooms and ultimately acidification.

The Rockies have been mined for their mineral wealth ever since the trains arrived in the late 1800s. Massive open-pit coal mines have removed whole mountains in British Columbia and Wyoming, and mines in the Columbia and Cariboo mountains and the American Rockies have taken out metals such as gold, silver, lead, and zinc. Although the underground mines themselves do not have a huge effect on the environment, the local smelting operations certainly do. The classic case in this region is the huge smelter on the Columbia River at Trail, British Columbia.

The smelting industry at Trail began in 1896 but expanded dramatically between 1925 and 1927, when two large smokestacks were built and production doubled to make it the largest lead-zinc smelter in the world. One of the biggest problems with the smelter was the high level of sulfur emissions—9,000 tons per month. Release of sulfur into the air creates sulfur dioxide, and high concentrations of that chemical can severely damage plants over a wide area. The Columbia Valley quickly lost almost all of its forests between Castlegar and the United States border, and in 1928 the Government of the United States complained to Canada that emissions from the Trail smelter had damaged forests and agricultural crops in Washington State. The long legal procedures following these allegations resulted in damages paid by Canada to the United States and the construction of a large fertilizer plant that removed the sulfur from the emissions by the late 1930s. The decisions made by the International Joint Commission and its special tribunal remain one of the most important legal precedents cited in international laws regarding cross-border pollution. Fifty years later, the Trail Smelter case formed the basis of one of the principles cited in the Rio declaration of 1992, and the legal battles continue over heavy-metal pollutants flowing downstream in the Columbia River.

CLIMATE CHANGE

Anyone who is not yet convinced that global warming is real should visit the Rocky Mountains. Melting glaciers, mountain meadows filling with trees, drought-stricken forests consumed by flames—all point to a warming world. In Colorado, Yellow-bellied Marmots emerge from hibernation three weeks earlier than they did twenty-five years ago, and robins arrive on mountain breeding grounds two weeks ahead of time.

Predicting climate change into the future is difficult and local differences may be significant, but some general trends emerge from recent models. Winter precipitation is expected to increase in the mountains, but more of this precipitation will fall as rain instead of snow. Summers will be longer, hotter, and drier, exacerbating recent drought conditions.

The effects on the environment will be gradual but significant. Forest fires will occur more often and burn with more intensity, gradually moving the lower tree line up mountain slopes, replacing Ponderosa Pine and Douglas-fir forests with grasslands. At the upper tree line changes will be subtle; subalpine meadows will gradually fill with small spruce and fir. On krummholz mats, leader twigs that have been killed back each year for a century will successfully form vertical trunks.

Perhaps the most dramatic change will be in the glaciers and the rivers they produce. For more than a century, the glaciers of the Rockies have been in full retreat. Mary Vaux, a pioneer glaciologist, began visiting the Canadian Rockies in 1887. Her favorite glacier was the Illecillewaet at Rogers Pass in the Selkirk Mountains; in 1898 she reported that the glacier had melted upslope rapidly over the previous decade. Since then, similar reports have come in from all over the Rockies, and the melting rate has tripled in the past fifty years. The Columbia Icefield, at 325 square kilometers (125 square miles) the largest ice sheet in the Rockies, took thousands of years to reach its present size but has lost a third of its volume in the past century. Glacier National Park in Montana had 150 glaciers in 1850 but will likely have none within thirty-five years. Glacier National Park, British Columbia, has lost more than 25 cubic kilometers (6 cubic miles) of ice, including much of the mighty Illecillewaet Glacier. Will these parks have to be renamed Glaciated National Park?

If you think that this loss of ice simply means that tourists will have to walk or drive farther to see alpine glaciers, think again. The Columbia Icefield is the headwaters of the Columbia River. The Bow Glacier feeds the Bow River, which provides all of Calgary's water needs. The Fraser River, home of some of the largest salmon runs on the planet, arises in glacial cirques along the west slope of the British Columbia Rockies. A receding glacier is spending water capital built up over many centuries. We are using this capital right now to keep our lawns green, flush our toilets, and grow our crops. It will be gone within a lifetime.

THE FUTURE

To meet the challenges of the future in the Rocky Mountains, we must combine small-scale plans—what we do in our own homes and backyards— with large-scale plans that look at the entire range from New Mexico to the Yukon border. Many of the pressing issues that face the Rockies—such as water supply, climate change, fragmentation of habitats—operate at all scales. We can make big plans outlining what has to be done to tackle these issues, but we can do nothing without the participation of individuals and communities throughout the mountains.

Large-scale plans have been drawn up by such nonprofit agencies as the Nature Conservancy of Canada and Yellowstone-to-Yukon as well as through government-sponsored initiatives such as the Shining Mountains Project. The latter effort gathered ecosystem data from British Columbia, Alaska, Alberta, and Montana to provide a framework for other broad-scale initiatives such as Grizzly Bear conservation planning.

Many of these large-scale plans emphasize the concept of core areas and corridors. The Rocky Mountains have many protected areas that can act as core sites for wildlife populations—some of the oldest and largest national parks in the world as well as many sizable wilderness areas and provincial parks. These parks not only provide protected habitat for wildlife but also welcome millions of visitors annually. These visitors are essential to conservation efforts in the Rockies, since they will be the advocates for the landscapes and wildlife they cherish. Parks must maintain a delicate balance between visitors' needs and those of wildlife but must never become walled wilderness zones where people cannot enter.

Despite their relatively large size, most of these parks and wilderness areas are small compared with the landscape covered by some wildlife over a lifetime. Wolves, Lynx, and male Grizzly Bears typically disperse over great distances at certain times of their lives. It is essential that they be able to move between core areas at these times, since these movements maintain genetic diversity and offer rescue potential for populations that may be critically low.

Overleaf: The Robson Glacier in British Columbia, like almost all glaciers in the Rocky Mountains, has been steadily retreating for the past century.

The Ramparts rise above Tonquin Pass on the border between British Columbia and Alberta.

Hence the need for corridors—broad avenues of habitat that need not be protected to the same extent as in the cores but that should be maintained in healthy condition so that animals can move in safety along them. For instance, a series of corridors would allow animals to move from Yellowstone to the Bitterroots and into the Salmon-Selway ecosystem of Idaho, then north through the Missoula area to the Glacier–Waterton Lakes parks region of Montana and Alberta. From there another corridor would lead southeast along the Great Divide back to the Yellowstone ecosystem.

Development and maintenance of these corridors brings us to smaller-scale planning, and communities within the Rockies must provide input and be involved for the plans to succeed. These ecosystem plans must allow for the economic viability of communities while providing habitat for animals and plants. Long-term planning is always difficult, but it is the only way to achieve conservation goals that will last into the future.

What can you do? Be curious about the world around you. Keep daily notes about the birds you see, the flowers that are blooming, the weather. After a year or two, you will have a remarkable dataset that you and others can use to really understand the changes that are happening around you. Team up with your neighbors—join a naturalists or outdoors club so that you can learn from the expertise of others.

Plant native shrubs and flowers in your backyard to make it an oasis for regional wildlife. In drier areas, this will help conserve water as well, since native plants don't guzzle water like a green lawn does. Thick shrubbery will provide shelter for birds and small mammals; birdhouses will give cavity-nesting species a home if there are no snags available in local woodlands.

The Rocky Mountains present us with an opportunity, one of the last available in North America, to maintain an ecosystem that stretches across the continent from north to south. We must inform ourselves and our communities, and we must act quickly before further damage to the rivers, grasslands, and forests eliminates the options. The diversity of their structure and their species makes the Rockies the backbone of the continent in more ways than one. We need the clear water the mountains provide, we need to refresh ourselves in their cool air, we need their forests and valleys, and we need the humility and awe we feel while resting on a mountain peak in these Shining Mountains. The view spread out below gives us the feeling that the whole world is in our hands, and indeed it is.

...And none but the sun and incurious clouds have lingered
Around the marks of that day on the ledge of the Finger,
That day, the last of my youth, on the last of our mountains.

—EARLE BIRNEY, *DAVID*

APPENDIX: MAP OF THE ROCKY MOUNTAINS

○ Major city
National park/reserve
Provincial park (in Canada)
National forest (in U.S.)
Major highway

BRITISH
COLUMBIA

ALBERTA

SASKATCHEWAN

Edmonton

Jasper

Glacier
Revelstoke
Yoho
Kootenay
Banff

Kamloops

Calgary

Vancouver
Castlegar
Cranbrook
Waterton Lakes

Victoria

Seattle
Spokane
Glacier
Great Falls
NORTH
DAKOTA

WASHINGTON
Missoula
MONTANA

Helena
Billings

Portland
Butte
Bighorn
Canyon
SOUTH
DAKOTA

OREGON
IDAHO
Sheridan

Eugene
Yellowstone

Boise
Idaho
Falls
Grand Teton
WYOMING

NEBRASKA

Casper

Rawlins
Cheyenne

Salt Lake City
Dinosaur
Rocky
Mountain
Denver

Colorado Springs
KANS

NEVADA
UTAH
COLORADO
Pueblo

Great Sand
Dunes

San Francisco

CALIFORNIA
Las Vegas
Bandelier
Santa Fe

ARIZONA
Albuquerque
TEXA

Flagstaff
NEW MEXICO

Los Angeles

0   200 miles
0   200 kilometres

276   The Rockies: A Natural History

For Further Reading

REGIONAL NATURAL HISTORIES

Bengeyfield, P. 1996. *Mountains and mesas: The northern Rockies and the Colorado Plateau.* Flagstaff, AZ: Northland Publishing.

Cannings, R. J., and S. G. Cannings. 2004. *British Columbia: A natural history.* Rev. ed. Vancouver, BC: Greystone Books.

Emerick, J. C. 1995. *Rocky Mountain National Park natural history handbook.* Niwot, CO: Roberts Rinehart Publishers.

Gadd, B. 1995. *Handbook of the Canadian Rockies.* Jasper, AB: Corax Press.

Goward, T., and C. Hickson. 1995. *Nature Wells Gray.* Edmonton, AB: Lone Pine Publishing.

Hahn, B. 2000. *Kootenay National Park.* Calgary, AB: Rocky Mountain Books.

Jones, S. R., and R. C. Cushman. 1998. *Colorado nature almanac.* Boulder, CO: Pruett Publishing.

Knight, D. H. 1994. *Mountains and plains: The ecology of Wyoming landscapes.* New Haven, CT: Yale Univ. Press.

Mathews, D. 2003. *Rocky Mountain natural history: Grand Teton to Jasper.* Portland, OR: Raven Editions.

Mutel, C. F., and J. C. Emerick. 1992. *From grassland to glacier: The natural history of Colorado and the surrounding region.* 2d ed. Boulder, CO: Johnson Books.

Rockwell, D. 2002. *Exploring Glacier National Park.* Guilford, CT: Falcon / Globe Pequot Press.

Wuerthner, G. 1992. *Yellowstone: A visitor's companion.* Harrisburg, PA: Stackpole Books.

GEOLOGY

Alt, D. D., and D. W. Hyndman. 1986. *Roadside geology of Montana.* Missoula, MT: Mountain Press.

———. 1989. *Roadside geology of Idaho.* Missoula, MT: Mountain Press.

————. 1995. *Northwest exposures: A geologic story of the Northwest.* Missoula, MT: Mountain Press.

Ferguson, S. A. 1992. *Glaciers of North America: A field guide.* Golden, CO: Fulcrum Publishing.

Gadd, B., and C. Yorath. 1995. *Of rocks, mountains, and Jasper: A visitor's guide to the geology of Jasper National Park.* Toronto: Univ. of Toronto Press.

Kronich, H. 1980. *Roadside geology of Colorado.* Missoula, MT: Mountain Press.

————. 1987. *Roadside geology of New Mexico.* Missoula, MT: Mountain Press.

————. 1990. *Roadside geology of Utah.* Missoula, MT: Mountain Press.

Lageson, D. R., and D. R. Spearing. 1988. *Roadside geology of Wyoming.* Missoula, MT: Mountain Press.

McPhee, J. 1986. *Rising from the plains.* New York: Farrar, Straus & Giroux.

Yorath, C. J. 1997. *How old is that mountain? A visitor's guide to the geology of Banff and Yoho national parks.* Victoria, BC: Orca Book Publishers.

ECOLOGY AND ENVIRONMENT

Arno, S., and R. P. Hammerly. 1977. *Northwest trees.* Seattle: The Mountaineers.

————. 1984. *Timberline: Mountain and Arctic forest frontiers.* Seattle: The Mountaineers.

Baron, J. S., ed. 2002. *Rocky Mountain futures: An ecological perspective.* Washington, DC: Island Press.

Zwinger, A. H. 1970. *Beyond the aspen grove.* Boulder, CO: Johnson Books.

Zwinger, A. H., and B. E. Willard. 1996. *Land above the trees: A guide to American alpine tundra.* Boulder, CO: Johnson Books.

WEB SITES

American national parks. http://www.nps.gov/parks.html.

Canadian national parks. http://www.pc.gc.ca.

Golden Eagle monitoring in the Alberta Rockies. http://www.eaglewatch.ca.

A guide to common plants, animals, birds, and landforms of the Canadian Rockies. http://www.mountainnature.com.

A guide to the reptiles and amphibians of Colorado. http://www.coloherp.org/geo/comindex.php.

Montana wildlife identification and information. http://fwp.state.mt.us/wildthings.

Yellowstone to Yukon Conservation Initiative. http://www.y2y.net.

Index

Boldface indicates a photograph, table, figure, or illustration. Species are listed by their common names unless the Latin name is used in the text.

Swifts, 218–19; Black (*Cypseloides niger*), 99, **99**; Chimney (*Chaetura pelagica*), 256–57; Vaux's (*Chaetura vauxi*), 256–57; White-throated (*Aeronautes saxatilis*), 218–19

Tall-grass prairie, 196, **197**
Talus, 5, 218
Tamarack (*Larix laricina*), 143
Tanager, Western (*Piranga ludoviciana*), 174–75
Tarns, **50**, 56, **64–65**
Temperature: in the alpine, 88; chinooks, 77; cricket thermometer, 182; hot springs, 253–54; inversions, 81, 113; in lakes, seasonal changes, 236–37; regional variation, 70–71, **80**
Terracettes, 89
Teton Mountains, 9, 42–43, **42–43**
Thermocline, **236**, 237
Thermus aquaticus (hot spring bacterium), 254
Thimbleberry (*Rubus parviflorus*), **160–61**
Thrasher, Sage (*Oreoscoptes montanus*), 215
Threeawn, Red (*Aristida longiseta*), 199
Thrushes, 119
Thrust faults and sheets, 5, 34–35, **35**, 38–39
Tick, Rocky Mountain Wood (*Dermacentor andersoni*), 214–15, **214**
Timberline, 85, **85**, **86–87**.
 See also Krummholz line; Tree lines
Titmouse, Juniper (*Baeolophus ridgwayi*), 192
Toad, Boreal (*Bufo boreas*), 238, **239**
Toadflax, Dalmation (*Linaria dalmatica*), 220, 263
Tonquin Pass, **275–76**
Trail smelter case, 269–70
Tree lines, 85, **85**; climate change impacts, 270; in ecoregions, 15–17; in late Pleistocene, 63; in Little Ice Age, 61, 63; montane forests, 170; Rockies vs. Okanagan, 13; and tall-grass prairie, 196; temperature and latitude, 70–71, 88; and valley inversions, 113
Triple divides, 12
Trout: in bear diet, 134; Brown (*Salmo trutta*), 268; Bull (*Salvelinus confluentus*), 228; conservation issues, 228, 267–68; Cutthroat (*Salmo clarki*), 228, 250–51, 268; Lake (*Salvelinus namaycush*),

267–68; Rainbow (*Oncorhynchus mykiss*), 228, 268
Tundra, alpine. *See* Alpine environments; Nunataks
Turkey, Wild (*Meleagris gallopavo*), 189
Turtle, Painted (*Chrysemys picta*), 238–39, **240–41**

Uinta Mountains, **4**

Vaux, Mary, 270
Veery (*Catharus fuscenscens*), 254
Vermilion Pass, **72–73**
Vireo, Gray (*Vireo griseus*), 192
Volcanic processes, **25**; hot spots, 45; hot springs, 253–54; plutonic rocks, 23; in Rockies orogeny, 9, 34, 38, **38**, 39
Voles, 104, 129, 199; Heather (*Phenacomys intermedius*), 104

Wagtails (*Motacilla* spp.), 227
Wapiti. *See* Elk (Wapiti, *Cervus elaphus*)
Warblers: Black-throated Gray (*Dendroica nigrescens*), 192; Townsend's (*Dendroica townsendi*), **174**, 175
Wasatch and Uinta Montane Forests ecoregion, **14**, 16
Wasatch Range, **4**, 5
Wasps (velvet ants), 203
Water boatmen, 242, **242**
Waterlily, Yellow (*Nuphar polysepalum*), 237
Water striders, 242
Waterthrushes (*Seiurus* spp.), 227
Waxwing, Bohemian (*Bombycilla garrulus*), 256
Weather. *See* Climate
Weeds. *See* Introduced and invasive species
Wells Gray Provincial Park, 16, 39, **40–41**
West Elk Mountains, **38**, 39
Wet interior forests, 154–67; vs. coastal rain forests, 154–55; old-growth, 163–66; shrubs and understory, 158–63; soil organisms, 166–67; tree biodiversity, 155–58
Wetlands: birds, 244–45; bogs and fens, 251–52; dams and, 268; lakes and, 233, 237–44; muskeg, 143–44
Wheatgrass: Bluebunch (*Elymus spicatus*), **198**, 199, **199**; Crested (*Agropyron cristatum*), 220–21, 263, **264–65**
Wilcox Pass, **86–87**
Wildlife trees, 141, 156, 158, 163, 256–57

Williston Lake, 233
Willows (*Salix* spp.), 257, 261–62
Wind River, 39
Wind River Range, **4**, 9, 12, 16
Wolves, 126; Dire (*Canis dirus*), 62; Gray (Timber Wolf, *Canis lupus*), 141, 143, **143**, 262, 271, 274
Woodpeckers, 141, 146, 158, 256; American Three-toed (*Picoides dorsalis*), 124, **125**; Lewis's (*Melanerpes lewis*), 111, 179; Pileated (*Dryocopus pileatus*), 167
Woodrats (*Neotoma* spp.), 67, **67**
Woody debris, 163, 166–67
Wrens: Canyon (*Catherpes mexicanus*), 218; Rock (*Salpinctes obsoletus*), 218
Wyoming Basin Shrub Steppe ecoregion, 9, **14**, 16
Wyoming Range, **4**

Yellowbell (*Fritillaria pudica*), 202
Yellowstone Lake, 233, 250–51, 268
Yellowstone National Park, 16, **276**; Bison herd, 208; fire, 1988, 132; geysers and hot springs, 45, 253–54; human impacts, 263; Pronghorns, 211; volcanic hot spot, 45; wolf reintroductions, 143
Yellowstone Plateau, 9, 12, 39
Yellowstone River, **4**, 45
Yew, Pacific (*Taxus brevifolia*), 156, **156**

Photo and Illustration Credits

Patricia Drukker-Brammall in W. B. Schofield, *Some Common Mosses of British Columbia*
(Victoria: Royal British Columbia Museum, 1992): p. 226
Robert Cannings: p. 236
G.B. Straley and R.P. Harrison, *An Illustrated Flora of the University Endowment Lands*,
University of British Columbia Technical Bulletin No. 12 (Vancouver: The Botanical
Garden, University of British Columbia, 1987): p. 237

Permission to use quoted material from *David* by Earle Birney on pp. 22, 84, and 274 given
by the Earle Birney Estate, c/o Madam Justice Wailan Low.

Other David Suzuki Foundation/Greystone Books

Prairie by Candace Savage

Tree by David Suzuki and Wayne Grady

The Sacred Balance: A Visual Celebration of Our Place in Nature by David Suzuki and Amanda McConnell with Maria DeCambra

From Naked Ape to Superspecies by David Suzuki and Holly Dressel

The David Suzuki Reader by David Suzuki

When the Wild Comes Leaping Up by David Suzuki, ed.

Good News for a Change by David Suzuki and Holly Dressel

The Last Great Sea by Terry Glavin

Northern Wild by David R. Boyd, ed.

Greenhouse by Gale E. Christianson

Vanishing Halo by Daniel Gawthrop

The Sacred Balance: Rediscovering Our Place in Nature by David Suzuki and Amanda McConnell

Dead Reckoning by Terry Glavin

Delgamuukw by Stan Persky

DAVID SUZUKI FOUNDATION CHILDREN'S TITLES

Salmon Forest by David Suzuki and Sarah Ellis; illustrated by Sheena Lott

You Are the Earth by David Suzuki and Kathy Vanderlinden

Eco-Fun by David Suzuki and Kathy Vanderlinden

The David Suzuki Foundation

The David Suzuki Foundation works through science and education to protect the diversity of nature and our quality of life, now and for the future.

With a goal of achieving sustainability within a generation, the Foundation collaborates with scientists, business and industry, academia, government and non-governmental organizations. We seek the best research to provide innovative solutions that will help build a clean, competitive economy that does not threaten the natural services that support all life.

The Foundation is a federally registered independent charity, which is supported with the help of over 50,000 individual donors across Canada and around the world.

We invite you to become a member. For more information on how you can support our work, please contact us:

The David Suzuki Foundation
219–2211 West 4th Avenue
Vancouver, BC
Canada v6k 4s2
www.davidsuzuki.org
contact@davidsuzuki.org
Tel: 604-732-4228
Fax: 604-732-0752

Checks can be made payable to The David Suzuki Foundation. All donations are tax-deductible.

Canadian charitable registration: (BN) 12775 6716 RR0001
U.S. charitable registration: #94-3204049